Foreign Direct Investment in Central and Eastern Europe

Foreign Direct Investment in Central and Eastern Europe

Multinationals in Transition

Saul Estrin
Kirsty Hughes
Sarah Todd

London and Washington

PINTER
A Cassell imprint
Wellington House, 125 Strand, London WC2R 0BB, England
PO Box 605, Herndon, Virginia 20172, USA

First published 1997

British Library Cataloguing in Publication Data

A catalogue record for this book is available from the British Library.
ISBN 1–85567–481–5

Library of Congress Cataloging-in-Publication Data

Estrin, Saul.
Foreign direct investment in Central and Eastern Europe: multinationals in transition/Saul Estrin, Kirsty Hughes, Sarah Todd.
p. cm.
Includes bibliographical references (p.) and index.
ISBN 1–85567–481–5 (hardcover)
1. Investments, Foreign–Europe, Eastern–Case studies. 2. International business enterprises–Europe, Eastern. 3. Post-communism–Economic aspects–Europe, Eastern. I. Hughes, Kirsty. II. Todd, Sarah, 1969– . III. Royal Institute of International Affairs. IV. Title.
HG5430.7.A3E88 1997
332.6'73'0943–dc21 97–608
CIP

Typeset by BookEns Ltd, Royston, Herts.
Printed and bound in Great Britain by Biddles Ltd, Guildford and King's Lynn.

Contents

Acknowledgments

This book reports the results of a one and a half year study carried out at London Business School and, initially, at the Policy Studies Institute and, subsequently, at the Royal Institute of International Affairs. We are grateful to the Economic and Social Research Council for financial support that enabled the project to take place (ESRC grant number R000235357). We have had discussions and assistance from a large number of people and organizations during this project. We are particularly grateful to the ten US, UK and German firms that agreed to act as case studies for this project and to their staff both in headquarters and subsidiaries for the time they took in discussing their activities with us. We are also grateful to a large number of different business, government and international organizations – chambers of commerce, embassies, government ministries, business organizations – both in western and eastern Europe, for discussing their experience of foreign direct investment. Additionally, we would like to thank numerous officials within the OECD and the European Commission, notably Rolf Alter and John Sheahy. Presentations of various aspects of this study were made at a number of seminars – at the London Business School, and the Institute for German Studies, Birmingham – and at a one-day conference at the Royal Institute of International Affairs. We are grateful to all the participants for their comments. While it is not possible to thank all the people who have helped us by name, we would like, in particular, to thank Judit Antal, Zoltan Antal, Heather Grabbe, Soma Horvath and Klaus Meyer. Finally, our especial thanks go to Stella Horsin for her work in preparing the manuscript for publication. Despite this formidable list of acknowledgments, any remaining errors or misinterpretations are our own.

Saul Estrin
Kirsty Hughes
Sarah Todd

Note

Totals in tables may not always add up, owing to rounding up or down.

1

Introduction

In this book, we provide a detailed analysis of foreign direct investment (FDI) in the reforming post-communist economies of central and eastern Europe (CEE). There already exist substantial literatures on FDI, and on economic transition from plan to market. Our aim in this study is to bring these two areas together: to analyse how the motivation for, and experience of, foreign investment from the West are affected by the fact that the host countries are in a process of post-communist transition, and to assess the impact on the particular costs and benefits of such investments for the transition process. To achieve this, we develop a conceptual framework for the analysis of FDI to the region, and present a detailed picture of the nature and scope of these investments.

In order to analyse in depth the impact of the investments from the perspective of Western multinational firms and of the recipient firms or industries, and of the broader process of economic transformation, we adopt a case study approach. This allows examination of the FDI from a number of angles: the viewpoints of the investing firm, the recipient firm or sector, the host government, suppliers, retailers and capital market observers. At the centre of the book, therefore, is a group of 10 case studies of foreign investments in central and eastern Europe, based on a series of in-depth interviews with both the Western headquarters and the eastern European subsidiary.

The book addresses a number of key themes. One important question is how much FDI there has actually been to central and eastern Europe, and whether the flows have been disappointing. In the early stages of the transition in central and eastern Europe, much emphasis was placed on the potential role of FDI in encouraging and supporting successful transition. This initial emphasis was followed by disappointment at what were perceived to be relatively low inflows of FDI into the transition economies. We argue that, in fact, FDI is playing an important role in transition in some countries. FDI flows are rather high and appear to be positively linked to progress in transition. In general, FDI into transition economies appears to be a positive experience for the investing company. For the transition economies, FDI provides an effective vehicle for transfer of knowledge in the widest sense and for quick restructuring, although it appears that wider spillovers may be weak or in some cases even negative.

A second theme concerns who is investing, and why. We find Germany and the United States to be the leading foreign investors into the region, though their activities have rather different patterns. UK and particularly Japanese investment has been very modest, especially in comparison with global investment levels of these countries. We seek to explain the differing levels of foreign investment flows from the UK, Germany and the United States in terms of motivation for investments and transaction costs of operations.

A third theme in the study is the relationship between motives for foreign investment by the Western multinational, which we classify according to markets, market share and costs, and performance of the investments from the perspective of the Western firm, the eastern European subsidiary and the host transition economy. We find that most Western investments into the region have been very or at least moderately successful from the perspective of the multinational involved (though there are obviously selection biases in a case study project of this sort). The investments also had very important positive consequences for the host country's firms in terms of productivity, technology transfer, and the upgrading of managerial and labour force skills. However, spillover effects from the investments appear so far to have been more modest, and there are dangers that some externalities may be negative, e.g. in terms of domestic supply chains and domestic market structures.

The remainder of the book is organized as follows. Chapter 2 sets out the analytical framework for investigating the relationship between FDI and transition, drawing on the two previously distinct literatures covering these areas. The chapter identifies the main anticipated motivations for FDI – markets, market share and costs – and discusses how the specific characteristics of transition may impact on more general motivations. It goes on to assess the different routes through which FDI may impact on transition, distinguishing between the likely impacts on the individual subsidiary, and the wider sectoral and economy impacts.

Chapter 3 analyses the available data on both FDI and trade flows into the transition economies. Obtaining reliable information in this area is difficult, particularly for FDI, as different data sources do not always agree. Nonetheless, by comparing across different sources it is possible to compile a comprehensive overview of the levels, trends and distribution of FDI into central and eastern Europe. The data show that FDI flows have increased substantially as the transition has developed, and the leading CEE countries, in terms of levels of FDI attracted, are comparable both to EU member states and to leading developing countries.

A detailed analysis of the determinants and effects of FDI in transition economies is not possible at this stage on the basis of the existing macro data. The study, therefore, goes on in Part II to present 10 case studies of Western firms investing into central and eastern Europe. Chapter 4 sets out the methodological approach used to select and to undertake the case studies. The cases are of multinationals from the United States, UK and Germany investing into the Czech Republic, Hungary and Poland. They cover four main sector groupings. The individual cases are presented in Chapters 5 to 14.

Part III is devoted to a comparative analysis of the cases. Chapter 15 argues that while multinationals' experience of investing in central and eastern Europe has been largely positive, their experience has varied in ways which appear related both to mode of entry and to sector and product characteristics. Chapter 16 sets out the final conclusions to the overall study, emphasizing that FDI is important and has been larger than many critics have recognized. The fact that FDI flows have been larger into the countries more advanced in their transitions suggests that FDI inflows may increase into other transition economies as they develop. Policy implications of the study are also developed.

Part I

2

Foreign Direct Investment in Transition: an Overview of the Issues

Introduction

In this chapter, we provide an overview of the issues raised by foreign direct investment (FDI) by Western companies into the transforming economies of central and eastern Europe (CEE). We address three fundamental questions. The first is why Western firms might choose to extend their production capacities into this region, rather than, for example, seeking to export domestically manufactured products or to supply from an investment in another region, and how the specific characteristics of transition may impact on their motivations and decision-making. The second concerns the impact of the FDI at the enterprise level, which can be evaluated from both the perspective of the investing firm and that of the subsidiary in central and eastern Europe. The final issue concerns the broader impact of foreign investment on the recipient country as a whole – the external benefits and costs of FDI. These last two issues will be addressed from the perspective of the particular problems raised by the transition process, including severe deficiencies in capital, technology and managerial skills.

There is already a very large literature on FDI (see, for example, Caves, 1982; Dunning, 1980 for summaries), and on the transition process (see Blanchard *et al.*, 1990; World Bank, 1996). Our focus here is on their intersection, rather than an attempt to provide a full summary. The key questions are the influence of transition problems on the nature and determinants of FDI and the effects of such investment on the transformation process itself.

The chapter contains four further sections. In the first, we set the context for the empirical and case study material at the heart of our analysis of FDI, by considering broad trends in the process of transition in Poland, Hungary and the Czech Republic. The question of why firms undertake FDI in general, and to the transitional economies in particular, is the subject of the third section, which also discusses how firms make decisions about FDI and the policy elements in the host countries conducive to such decisions. The potential impact of FDI is discussed in the fourth section, which considers the question from the perspective of the macro-economy, of firms and sectors, and with respect to the broader effects on the economy as a whole. Conclusions are drawn from the existing evidence in the fifth section.

Foreign direct investment and the transition

Economic transition began in 1989 in most of central Europe, as a consequence of the collapse of communist political hegemony in the region.[1] In the previous decades, economic progress in the socialist bloc had been at best lacklustre, and development levels were generally well below those pertaining in most of western Europe (see Barr, 1995). The economic situation prior to reform is summarized for the countries of our study in Table 2.1. The first three economies to reform – Czechoslovakia, Hungary and Poland (later the Visegrad four after the disintegration of Czechoslovakia) – were rather different in certain key respects. Poland and Hungary had significant international debts, and Poland had severe repressed inflation. However, all were relatively open, and thus exposed to a major trade shock when the communist trading block – the CMEA – disintegrated in 1991 (see de Melo *et al.*, 1995). The Polish market is by far the largest in the group. The Czech Republic, Hungary and Poland have attracted the bulk of the FDI to the region so far (as discussed further in Chapter 3).

To understand the reform process, we need first to characterize planning. We can stylize the supply side of the economy under planning as follows (for further references see, for example, Ellman, 1989; Gregory and Stuart, 1988). Output was disproportionately concentrated on industrial production, and within industry on heavy industry, intermediates and defence. Economies were closely integrated into the CMEA trading group, which was highly integrated and failed to reflect national comparative advantage (see, for example, Hare and Hughes, 1992). Surprisingly few consumer goods were made, and even fewer produced to a standard that might satisfy world markets. Firms were basically production units managed by engineers, with finance, marketing, international sales, investment and other research and development being organized through some other parts

Table 2.1 Preconditions for reform

	Population 1989 (million)	Development level 1990	Share of industry in gross domestic product 1990 (per cent)	Natural resources
Czech Republic	10	High	59	Poor
Hungary	9	High	56	Poor
Poland	38	Middle	52	Moderate
Slovakia	5	Middle	59	Poor

High = > $6,000 at 1988 purchasing power parity (PPP).
Middle = $3,000–6,000 at 1988 PPP.

Source: Estrin (1995), de Melo *et al.* (1995).

of the central bureaucratic apparatus. More or less every firm was state owned, and to fit the convenience of planners, most were relatively large: the economy contained almost no small or even middle-sized enterprises. Banking, financial and service sectors were largely absent.

Within firms, incentives to maximize profits or control costs were weak. Rewards to managers were typically distributed on the basis of plan fulfilment, with targets oriented to output and growth. Indeed, 'good' managers were those best able to secure scarce inputs of raw materials, labour and capital to meet the exacting production targets year after year, without regard to product cost, quality or development. With slow growth and low investment in much of the region throughout the 1980s, capital equipment was also very dated by 1990, with technological backwardness deriving both from the deficient incentive and information systems generally (see, for example, Hayek, 1944) and from the Western strategy of restricting the transfer of militarily sensitive technology.

To shift production and consumption in the direction of Western market economies, the CEE countries therefore needed to restructure in numerous ways, notably from heavy to light industry, from industry and agriculture to finance and services, and from CMEA to world trade. To become like the West, large firms would have to shrink or break up and numerous small firms would have to be founded in almost all sectors. Within existing firms, new product lines and production methods had to be developed while simultaneously reducing input waste, notably in terms of energy, labour and the environment. Most importantly, firms would have to shift from being driven by supply to being driven by demand, increasing their sensitivity to consumers both domestically and internationally.

Table 2.2 Progress in institutional reform, 1989–95

	Laws and legal institutions[a]	Banking sector[b]	Role and management of government[c]
Czech Republic	4	4	3
Hungary	4	4	2
Poland	4	4	2
Slovakia	4	3	3

[a] Category means scope and quality of legislation.
1 = little progress in reforms;
2 = some progress on law reform, little in institutions;
3 = some progress in both;
4 = extensive progress in both.

[b] Measures quality of banking sector (e.g. independence, skills, credit allocation practices, banking supervision).
1 = little change;
2 = some initial progress;
3 = system functioning adequately;
4 = system functioning adequately with large group of better banks.

[c] Indicates market orientation of government and effectiveness of management.
1 = little change;
2 = significant change in attitude, little in management;
3 = major change in orientation, some change in management;
4 = major improvement in both.

Source: World Bank (1996).

The key components of economic transition are therefore macro-economic stabilization, liberalization of the domestic economy and trade, privatization and establishing market-oriented institutional legal structures. For the Visegrad countries, progress in some of these various dimensions between 1989 and 1995 is summarized in Tables 2.2 and 2.3. All have made considerable progress across a wide front. However, one can also note from Table 2.4 that the Visegrad countries have been going through an exceptionally deep recession, though inflation has now been brought under control to varying degrees and economic growth has now resumed.

Changes at the macro-economic level were intended in the various reform programmes to be stimulated by liberalization in the domestic and international economy and by privatization. In principle, the former provides the signals and the information from the marketplace about what consumers desire, while the latter gives managers the incentives to pursue profitable restructuring. In the Visegrad countries

Table 2.3 Progress in privatization: share of gross domestic product in private sector, 1990–95

	1990 (per cent)	1995 (per cent)
Czech Republic	5	70
Hungary	19	60
Poland	27	58
Slovakia	6	59

Source: World Bank (1996).

Table 2.4 Macro-economic performance in reform, 1989–95

Country	Lowest level of GDP attained/ GDP 1989 (per cent)	Growth in 1995 (per cent)	Average inflation (per cent)	
			1993/94	1995
Czech Republic	83	5	15	8
Hungary	80	3	21	21
Poland	82	5	33	23
Slovakia	76	3	19	10

GDP = gross domestic product.

Source: Estrin (1995).

at least, as we can see from Table 2.2, liberalization both in domestic markets and international markets has been very successful. But the rapid pace of reform has meant that privatization, the scale of which is noted in Table 2.3, has for the most part been based on management–employee buyouts or mass voucher privatization schemes (see Estrin, 1994). This has led to ownership rights in most countries being concentrated in the hands of 'insiders' – managers and workers – who may not be the best agents for change (see Earle and Estrin, 1995).

In general, the Western literature on corporate governance would suggest that outsider ownership, either through a capital market on Anglo-Saxon lines, or a Germanic system of concentrated bank ownership, would be preferable to majority insider ownership. This is especially true when major enterprise restructuring is required (see, for example, Boycko *et al.*, 1995), because insiders would not bring new funds and expertise. Moreover, with insider ownership there could be agency problems restricting the ability of the firm to borrow, as well as perverse incentives towards restructuring, e.g. with respect to employment. But stock markets are in their infancy in the transitional economies, and subject to serious problems of undervaluation and illiquidity,[2] while banking sector reform lags behind that of enterprises (see European Bank for Reconstruction and Development, 1995). The prospects for domestic non-insider forms of governance in transitional economies are therefore poor in the short term. This suggests that the involvement of foreign owners in the post-communist countries, as a source of outsider ownership, could be a particularly important feature of the transition process.[3]

Motivations for foreign direct investment into central and eastern Europe

The literature on FDI contains several frameworks for analysing its determinants. For example, Caves (1982) has stressed the role of intangible assets, while Dunning (1980) developed the 'eclectic' approach, which categorizes motives for FDI into the ownership, locational and internationalization advantages of trans-national production (the 'OLI paradigm'). More recently, Dunning and Rojec (1993) have proposed a four-fold typology of foreign investment with particular reference to transitional economies: resource seeking, market seeking, efficiency seeking and strategic asset seeking. The first two are expected primarily to motivate new FDI while the latter ones underlie subsequent investments.

Here, we argue for a three-fold categorization of motivations for FDI into central and eastern Europe – markets, strategic motives (principally market share) and costs. These motivations are not specific to FDI into transition economies, but transition is likely to impact in various ways on the opportunities, decisions and constraints involved with FDI and so on the particular motivations for FDI. We first summarize some of the literature to date on motivations for FDI in transition economies and the particular impact of transition on FDI. We then discuss the main motivations, which we here categorize into markets, market share and costs, and how they may be affected by the transition context. In later chapters, we provide a more detailed categorization of motives. We go on to consider other specific effects that the characteristics of transition may have on FDI.

Survey evidence

Most studies suggest that new markets are the main attraction for foreign investors in the region. Numerous papers and books contain survey evidence about the pulling power of new markets in central and eastern Europe for Western multinationals (see, for example, surveys by McMillan, 1993; National Economic Research Associates 1991; Gatling 1993; Wang, 1993; Hoesch and Lehmann, 1994; European Bank for Reconstruction and Development, 1994; Organization for Economic Cooperation and Development, 1995). However, the literature also isolates many cases of firms solely following a low-cost-motivated strategy. Factor cost incentives, and in particular lower labour costs, are found to be more important for small firms and firms from neighbouring countries such as Germany and Austria (Mollening *et al.*, 1994; Duvvuri *et al.*, 1995; Szanyi, 1995). German firms also appear to use outward processing contracts relatively more frequently, so as to exploit the differential with domestic costs of production (Naujoks and Schmidt, 1994).

Thus, surveys of Western firms suggest that market size and expected growth are the most important determinants of FDI into the region, along with political and economic stability. Another factor frequently noted in the early stages in Hungary and Russia has been learning about the local environment and market, to be prepared for later opportunities (see Marton, 1993). There is also evidence that suppliers of intermediate products followed their customers, notably in the automobile industry (see Holmes, 1993).

The main deterrents to investment noted in the literature are risk and uncertainty, the poor legal framework and weak infrastructure, and a lack of reliable information about the region (see, for example, Organization for Economic Cooperation and Development, 1995; European Bank for Reconstruction and Development, 1994). McMillan (1993) and Meyer (1995) also suggest that foreign investment is inhibited because investors cannot find suitable local partners and suppliers able to offer inputs and services at the required quality standard.

Motivations – markets

New market opportunities in central and eastern Europe thus provide one major motivation for FDI in the region. One recurring theme in the FDI literature is whether and when FDI and exports represent complementary or alternative means of entering or supplying a market. Frequently, the two are found to be complementary, as there may be various advantages to locating close to the market, and we find examples of this in our cases. Locating in the market may be beneficial in terms of suppliers, customers and/or government relations, resulting in the firm being seen as quasi-local and in it gaining local knowledge and close interaction with supplier and distribution networks. Exports may then be used to add flexibly to capacity as the market requires it. The choice and balance between FDI and exports will also depend on a number of other factors, including tariff and non-tariff barriers, transport costs, local input costs and scale economies. Multinationals also choose between direct investment and licensing where local firms have advantages in production and/or sales, although in transition economies we would expect licensing to be used less frequently, given local firms' need for Western know-how in terms of managerial as well as production expertise. Market opportunities exist not only in final goods; Western firms may also enter intermediate or capital goods sectors where their technology, quality or standards may give them competitive advantages.

CEE countries may represent a particularly attractive prospect for Western companies. This is both due to the absolute size of the region in terms of population and because consumption levels for many consumer products are low relative to per capita income. Most of these countries had been, for more than a generation, completely insulated from Western goods, especially from consumer goods with a strong brand image. Consumer demand in the Visegrad countries of our study may grow under the combined influences of rising income, new and wider ranges of products, and advertising. This pent-up demand could allow for very rapid market growth for some products, even in the context of sluggish macro-economic performance overall. Obvious examples are the markets for hamburgers, cola and pizza. However, these specific characteristics of transition economies also represent a challenge for Western multinationals and exporters in assessing the most effective combination of quality, variety and price, and in developing advertising strategies for these countries. Local knowledge and understanding may play a critical role in constructing the best strategy, and multinationals may find themselves competing both with each other and with domestic companies in their consumer strategies.

A second market-related motive derives from the fact that the reforming economies, especially the Visegrad ones, may be able to sustain high growth rates for some years in the future. This is because economic liberalization and integration within the EU will probably permit them to begin to catch up with the rest of Europe. The argument is strongest for countries like the Czech Republic, where living standards which were among the highest in Europe in the inter-war period have slipped below those of most EU members. Reintegration into Western trading blocs (with or without EU membership) and sound government polices could be sufficient for one to predict equalization of living standards, say within a generation. This, however, implies rapid growth rates over a long period of time, by European if not East Asian standards. Such arguments carry less conviction for more volatile and less developed parts of the region, but could hold for all the Visegrad countries. Expectations of market growth may therefore be an important reason for foreign investment.

Motivations – trade policy

An important factor motivating market-driven investment can be the trade policy regime. Countries or trading blocks which erect high tariff barriers or strict controls shift the balance of advantage for foreign firms from exporting to direct investment. Similarly, policies of neighbouring countries can be influential – countries can attract FDI if they can form a base for exporting to the surrounding countries because of favourable regional trade agreements.

These factors may be of some significance for the transitional economies, especially those which have already signed Association Agreements with the EU (the Visegrad four plus the three Baltic countries, Romania, Bulgaria and Slovenia). Multinational firms from outside the EU may be motivated to invest in these countries to gain such trading advantages as are already available and in the expectation of full EU membership in the future. Others may see the prospect of the Central European Free Trade Area evolving into a customs union offering significant benefits to investing in a particular member state. Moreover, especially in the early days of reform, when the future of the communist block in general and the former Soviet Union in particular was not yet determined, Western firms may have chosen to invest in central European economies because of their links to other members of CMEA. However, the opposite argument has also been put forward. Baldwin (1994b) argues that because the Europe Agreements are bilateral between the EU and each individual transition economy, they encourage a 'hub and spoke' effect, whereby firms may choose to locate in the EU and supply each CEE country from there rather than locate in a transition economy as a base for supplying other transitional economies. Thus, Baldwin argues that this may encourage FDI in the EU rather than in CEE, the latter markets being supplied with exports. We consider this argument further in Chapter 3.

Motivations – market share

FDI may also be motivated by strategic factors, especially since multinationals tend to be concentrated in sectors which are oligopolistic, and tend to compete on a regional or even global scale for market share. Multinational firms' decisions on investing in the transition economies are therefore not made independently of their competitors' activities and expectations about their competitors' likely behaviour and responses. With the prospect of major new markets being opened up, companies may be concerned to move into an economy early, to obtain first mover advantages with respect, for example, to the government, to customers, to suppliers or in the acquisition of existing domestic firms, sites etc. Firms may wish to enter first, to develop distribution networks, or to build brand loyalty through advertising so as to raise the sunk costs for other potential Western entrants. Companies may also move into particular countries or regions as part of a wider strategic game in which the investment in the transition economies may operate as some sort of threat or strategic commitment. Finally, firms may enter particular markets to exploit price discrimination, product differentiation or vertical integration opportunities. Other firms may follow leaders into a country or sector simply to ensure that they do not lose competitive advantage.

The transitional economies seem in a number of ways to be particularly suited for multinationals to seek first mover advantages, particularly in the building of brands and customer loyalty, because the relationship between firms and customers was so underdeveloped under central planning. Similarly, the rapid construction of market relations and infrastructure opens up fruitful first mover opportunities, e.g. in developing distribution systems and supply relationships, and in locating retail or distribution sites. However, especially in the early stages of transition, the risks and uncertainties surrounding these economies were high, and there was a general lack of knowledge as to how the processes of political and economic transition may operate.

There were, and to a varying degree remain, problems in the legal, institutional and physical infrastructure; see European Bank for Reconstruction and Development (1995) for some measures of these problems. Furthermore, there were and remain many general challenges in operating in these markets, including the development of appropriate strategies, such as for brand marketing as discussed above. In many ways, the region was overly bureaucratic, poorly organized and resistant to change at an administrative level. First movers may, therefore, find or have found that they face steep and costly learning curves which later entrants may not have had to face. The relative advantage of being first or second in a market may, therefore, depend on a different range of factors for the economies in transition.

Strategic advantages through acquisition?

The transition economies have offered a wide range of acquisition opportunities through their privatization programmes. In general, multinationals may acquire firms for a variety of reasons, including to gain access to technology, plant and equipment or market share. When we consider transitional economies, Western multinationals may acquire formerly state-owned firms through privatization programmes in order to buy market share, even though the actual value of pre-existing brands and market relationships may be low. Thus, firms might be motivated to invest in central and eastern Europe because market structures have been highly imperfect; monopoly or near-monopoly was not uncommon, and competition laws in some countries are as yet only weakly enforced.

By contrast, technology and capacity are unlikely to be major motivations for investment in the region in their own right. This is because of the generally antiquated nature of much capital in planned economies, though this may vary significantly across countries and sectors. Investment patterns under central planning were very uneven, with up-to-date equipment frequently being used in the same plant alongside obsolete capital. Incoming multinationals may attempt to take advantage of this mixture of vintages. Moreover, while the transition economies were not in most sectors at the forefront in technology and innovation, there are some important exceptions. In particular, there may have been research and development teams providing valuable scientific output which socialist managers were unable to translate into innovation. Examples include the chemicals sector in Hungary, or space technology in Russia. Decisions concerning acquisition versus greenfield investments, therefore, are likely to be influenced by transition-specific factors in both positive and negative ways. This is discussed further below.

Motivations – costs

Low costs, particularly low labour costs, represent another important motivation for FDI into central and eastern Europe. In general, economic theory would predict that firms will move their production between regions and countries to exploit relative factor cost differences, e.g. with respect to raw materials, energy or labour. The incentives will be particularly sharp in industries which are intensive users of the relevant cheaper input, e.g. goods with labour-intensive production methods such as textiles gradually shifting from relatively high labour cost regions like western Europe to lower-cost ones, such as in the Far East. However, the bulk of global FDI stocks are still located in the more industrialized economies, emphasizing the importance of market and strategic factors in FDI as discussed above.

Nonetheless, relative costs do form part of multinationals' motivations for FDI and this provides a further explanation for FDI in the transition economies. Although labour costs are not as low as in many developing countries, they are low by western European standards, with average Czech wages about one-tenth of German wages. Combined with lower transport and generally lower logistical costs due to location, the cost advantages of central and eastern Europe may be fairly attractive to a number of firms, especially those in labour-intensive sectors. Furthermore, the transition economies' labour forces are relatively highly skilled, or at least a high proportion of workers have been employed for many years in sectors such as chemicals, engineering, machine tools, vehicles and aerospace. Other inputs which might encourage inward investment are raw materials, notably oil, gas and precious metals, which are to be found predominantly in the former Soviet Union, and access to relatively cheap intermediate products such as iron, steel and non-ferrous metals. Energy costs have traditionally been low and supplies plentiful, though in the Visegrad countries prices have begun to move to Western levels. Environmental constraints have also in the past been much more lax, though standards are again now being raised.

While the transition economies, therefore, offer cost and labour skill advantages, there may also be disadvantages which relate to the specific characteristics of these economies. In particular, as discussed above, the experience of central planning did not encourage the development of managerial skills. Both managers and workers may be more used to working in hierarchies and lacking experience in crucial areas such as attention to quality, and, more generally, work ethics – individual responsibility, decision-making, time-keeping etc. – may not be equivalent to those in Western economies. Skills in managing company finances were also particularly underdeveloped, matching the broader deficiencies in capital markets. This may again affect the strategies that inward investors adopt in transferring and implementing their particular managerial practices, training strategies and organizational structures. As we will find in the cases, competitive success then partly depends on which companies develop the most appropriate and effective managerial and labour strategies.

Other effects of transition on foreign direct investment decisions

We have considered above how transition-specific factors may have an impact on the three main motivations we identify for FDI into central and eastern Europe. There are a number of other aspects of transition that may be particularly important in affecting the inward investment decision. We consider first three factors that may represent potential risks and so may deter investment – political stability, the policy environment, and institutional and infrastructure development. We then consider in more detail how transition may have an impact on the foreign investor's choice (already referred to above) between entry by greenfield investment and entry by joint venture or acquisition.

Political stability

Political stability is a general factor taken into account in FDI decisions globally. Clearly, firms may be prevented from undertaking apparently profitable investments by the threat of political instability, or a volatile or unpredictable political situation. Particularly unattractive will be threats of civil disorder, unrest or even civil war. Only marginally more attractive will be the threat of major government change, perhaps to parties unsympathetic to multinational firms and heralding a change in fiscal regime or even outright nationalization.

Assessing the likelihood of political stability in the transition economies was inevitably particularly difficult at the start of the transition process. The extent and reliability of political stability remains an important issue in many of the transitional economies, especially those of the former Soviet Union or in the Balkans. In the Visegrad countries, however, commitment to the reform process and to a market economy seems to be soundly based. However, actual political power is sometimes fragmented, and former communists have begun to win elections. It may be noted that there is a close interrelationship between commitment to reform and FDI. Countries which have been successful in attracting large amounts of foreign investment can use this as a signal of their commitment to reform, and as a precommitment to continued reform policies and vice versa; FDI is attracted by successful reforms.

Policy environment

A second issue for firms contemplating FDI into a particular country or region concerns the policy environment. Having discussed trade policy above, we will focus on two elements: macro-economic policy and policy towards investing firms.

Macro-economic policy

Slack macro-economic policy, high inflation and stabilization programmes are relatively common in emerging markets, and add significantly to exchange rate and other risks borne by Western investors. The problem is in part one of infrastructure – governments may find themselves in a position where expenditures for social policies or defence are high, but traditions of a low incidence of personal taxation make these hard to finance. This may lead to monetary emission and to an inflation tax. High inflation rates often also imply declining and uncertain exchange rates, which may be damaging for foreign investment, e.g. if debt or input supplies are denominated in foreign currencies. Exchange rate uncertainty in itself leads to higher costs in terms of hedging risks. Moreover, stabilization programmes to address the underlying imbalances may, in the short term, lead to capital losses associated with drastic currency devaluation.

Such problems were pertinent in the early years of reform in almost every transitional economy, with the possible exception of Hungary. This is because almost all entered the reform process with serious monetary imbalances (the monetary overhang) associated with poor macro-economic management in the final years of communism. Most countries then introduced macro-economic stabilization programmes between 1990 and 1992, though degrees of success were varied. However, stabilization was very successful in Poland and Czechoslovakia (see World Bank, 1996), and, as we noted in Table 2.4, all the Visegrad countries now have low inflation rates by the standards of the region (though, with the exception of the Czech Republic, high by the standards of Organization for Economic Cooperation and Development (OECD) countries).[4]

Inward investment policies

FDI can be influenced by the specific policy regime with respect to foreign investment, and in particular by preferential treatment offered to foreign firms. Multinational firms clearly respond to positive incentives, and react against restrictions and disincentives, especially when the economic environment is relatively stable. When it is not stable, as we have noted, commitment to reform becomes important, while the role of specific investment incentives is open to debate. For example, subsidies to inward investors can be important if they are large, but since the transition economies are usually not in a position to offer direct incentives they will tend to choose mechanisms such as tax incentives that represent foregone income rather than actual payments. However, as many investors may not make large profits in the early years of an investment – and may anyway be involved in various transfer pricing strategies – such incentives may not in fact be particularly important in motivating FDI into CEE. Government policy regimes towards FDI have varied across the transition economies and over time. In central and eastern Europe, Poland and the Czech Republic offer no special incentives, while Hungary used to offer significant tax and other incentives to foreign firms.

As in other countries, positive government action simply to provide information to foreign investors can be important. In the transition economies this may be particularly helpful. For most Western companies the idea of investing in central and eastern Europe is relatively new, and the mechanisms for gathering and assessing information may need to be developed from scratch. This may give firms which have traditional links with the area – e.g. for geographical, cultural or historical reasons – strong advantages which may motivate them to become first movers. In the early days at least, this factor may also bias potential investment towards sectors which had traditionally been active in the region, e.g. capital equipment, engineering and metallurgy. As information sources about the business environment and prospects multiply, these initial advantages to traditional sectors will probably diminish. However, at least initially, such advantages seem likely to work to the benefit of firms from Austria, Germany and, to a lesser extent, Italy. Many German firms may also benefit by approaching central and eastern Europe after recent experiences in the transitional economy of the former East Germany.

Multinationals may also be sensitive to other relevant elements of economic policy, including personal tax rates for their staff, and the nature and effectiveness of competition policy. In the Visegrad countries of our study, the latter is largely dictated by the Association Agreements with the EU, which lay out a framework for competition policy analogous to that pertaining in western Europe (see Estrin and Cave, 1993).

Institutional and infrastructure development

Another element which may deter firms concerns the institutional arrangements in the country in question and its infrastructure. At the most basic level, Western firms will be wary of committing themselves to countries where the rule of law is haphazard, because their property and income will be only poorly protected. Such countries may also have corrupt public administrations, which can reduce significantly the profitability of doing business, since the bureaucracy may seek to take rents for itself. Western firms will also shy away from countries where telecommunications are poor, transport expensive and inadequate, and utilities such as energy supplies unreliable. Many of these problems used to exist in communist countries, although, as is noted in Table 2.2, the legal and institutional deficiencies are beginning to be put right, especially in the Visegrad countries. But there remain serious deficiencies in legal structures and even more glaring problems in attempts to enforce the existing laws. Moreover, in much of the region, corruption and lawlessness are on the increase, albeit from low initial levels, notably with the rise of mafias in much of the former Soviet Union and the Balkans. However, profound weaknesses in the infrastructure are beginning to be corrected, notably in telecommunications within the Visegrad countries, but much remains to be done with respect to transport, energy and the environment.

The impact of transition on entry strategies

Foreign investors' choice of entry strategy – greenfield, joint venture, acquisition or a combination of these such as 'brownfield' entry, to be discussed below – is likely to be affected in a number of ways by transition. Firms could choose to enter a country using a greenfield site, which would entail developing organizational structures, building factories and distribution systems, and hiring workers *de novo*. Alternatively, they could acquire outright an existing firm as a subsidiary. Intermediate strategies include joint ventures, either by taking a part share in an existing firm or joining forces with a local enterprise to create *de novo* a jointly owned subsidiary. Developments are what we term 'brownfield' when they involve acquisition of a firm in the region for market share reasons, but entirely new production facilities are then developed within the firm. Transition-specific factors, however, may operate to increase the attractiveness of greenfield or brownfield acquisitions in some dimensions while decreasing them in others. Furthermore, the balance of advantage may change over time as privatization processes are completed and as transition develops.

Especially in the early stages of transition, the economic environment may be perceived as risky or volatile, with local knowledge being an important element in economic success. This would point firms in the direction of joint ventures, especially of a risk-sharing variety. Furthermore, the attempt to privatize large chunks of the national economy at a time when domestic savings are very low (see Estrin, 1994) opens up the prospect that assets will change hands at very low prices, creating 'bargains' that might tempt Western firms otherwise not contemplating investments in the region. Foreigners were in practice largely excluded from the 'voucher privatizations' in the Czech Republic and Poland because of a fear of large-scale foreign acquisitions, but they were still able to participate significantly in all privatizations by tender, notably in Hungary. Indeed, Estrin (1996) has argued that the privatization process itself is a major determinant of the scale of FDI; for example, early restrictions on foreign involvement in privatization in Poland and Czechoslovakia helped Hungary to establish a large initial lead.

Against this attraction, however, are the special problems associated with the acquisition of former state firms in transitional economies, the most serious of which probably relate to hidden unemployment and the environment. We noted previously that productivity levels in most firms are far below Western standards and that Western partners would probably seek immediate and major labour force reductions. However, the feasibility of this strategy in many situations is uncertain, not only because of the costs of redundancies but because employees in some countries, especially

Poland and the former Soviet Union, have extensive formal and informal rights. Moreover, in much of heavy industry, environmental standards are currently well below international requirements, and liability sometimes rests with the newly privatized companies. In the Czech Republic, for example, the state passes on with privatization all environment-related liability, even though in some situations the implied loss could outweigh the value of the firm. The necessary pace of attainment of environmental standards and the liability for previous deficiencies could be a major disincentive to foreign investment in some cases.

Furthermore, the heritage of planning will have left few firms with an appropriate mix of skills and inputs to offer a convincing package to a Western partner. In particular, as we have argued, many central and eastern European firms will lack either the financial muscle or the managerial skills to make appropriate partners for Western enterprises in joint ventures, particularly of a *de novo* form. For many firms, the putative costs of restructuring such firms might exceed the later benefits in terms of revenue and profits, especially in environmentally damaging sectors.

These considerations suggest that Western firms may either need subsidies to be persuaded to acquire socialist firms – as, in effect, often occurred in the former East Germany – or will seek to combine the advantages of greenfield developments and acquisition via the privatization process – 'brownfield' development. The main mode of entry in the early years of transition was the joint venture, but there has been a major shift to fully owned affiliates, and a trend towards greenfield sites (Svetlicic, 1994; Rojec and Jermakowicz, 1995; Meyer, 1995).

Overall, the specific characteristics of the transition economies are, therefore, likely to influence the entry strategies of multinationals in a number of ways. Over time, as the transitions progress, these specific influences will lessen and the set of factors influencing entry strategies will be more similar to those in other countries.

The impact of foreign direct investment in transitional economies

Having discussed motivations for FDI into the transition economies, in this section we put forward a framework for analysing the impact and outcomes of FDI into central and eastern Europe. The experiences and consequences of FDI can be considered from three angles – the macro-economy; for the multinational enterprises involved; and the effects on the transition economies, both directly on acquired firms and through joint ventures, and indirectly via spillovers. It is also important to analyse actions from both perspectives: those of the source and the host.

The macro-economic effects of foreign direct investment

At the broadest level, the reintegration of the transitional economies, with their large capital requirements and low domestic savings rates, may put upward pressure on world interest rates. This impact has so far been very modest because the total flows to the region have been relatively small, comprising less than 3 per cent of total FDI. However, the capital requirements of the region are large, and likely to increase over time, so the effects may be more pronounced in the future.

For the host countries, FDI can be an important source of hard currency, permitting the country to finance a balance of payments deficit or to maintain interest payments on international debt. Considerations of this sort were behind the Hungarians' focus on FDI in their privatization; it flowed from their objective of maintaining the payments on their international debt. In part, it may have been the low level of Czechoslovak international indebtedness that offered policy makers the luxury of an almost entirely domestically based voucher privatization scheme. In Poland's case, successful international debt negotiations probably reduced the pressure for the widespread involvement of foreign investment in what quickly became a highly politicized privatization process.

However, FDI is not entirely beneficial to the macro-economies of host countries in the transitional context. This is because stabilization and the anti-inflationary programmes associated with stabilization are usually based around strict monetary controls and managed exchange rates. This implies that capital inflows need to be sterilized, and the resulting interest payments can become a major drain on the national budget, especially in small countries with large investment inflows. This problem applies with even more force to foreign portfolio investment, which can be withdrawn at very short notice. FDI also has an impact on the trade balance – according to the literature, the impact seems to have been negative on average, because though foreign-owned firms export more than domestic ones, they also import a larger share of their inputs (see Hamar, 1995; Lakatos and Papanek, 1995). Direct effects on employment are also argued to be negative because the investment tends to contribute primarily to capital formation.

The impact of foreign direct investment on firms

From the perspective of the donor company, the impact of FDI will primarily be measured by its effect on corporate profitability. Investment will presumably only occur if expected real returns are positive, and the nature of those returns will depend upon the reason for the investment being made in the first place – for example, to reduce costs or to increase sales or sales growth. In addition, the subsidiary will affect to some extent the company's overall global structure and may also require some changes in standard practices with subsidiaries, owing to particular transition characteristics. Firms may find that behaviour and performance in the subsidiary do not follow their standard expectations. These expectations will cover areas as diverse as required managerial inputs, possibly including expatriates, technological transfer, labour training and wage levels, infrastructure and government business relations, as well as conventional financial indicators.

For Western firms involved in some variety of greenfield development – either alone or with an eastern European partner – a number of issues need to be resolved. The first question concerns the ownership structure, and how the investment is to be financed. The Western firm must also consider how the new subsidiary fits into the organizational structure in terms of decision-making and reporting, the appropriate level of technology for the new plant, and the role, if any, for research and development in the new site. On the labour side, levels of wages, skills and training have to be determined, and the possible role for expatriates evaluated. The company must establish both supply chains and marketing strategies, notably concerning branding, advertising and distribution markets. The relationship between local and international marketing efforts will also need to be established.

The same issues need to be researched in formerly state-owned firms partially or fully acquired by a Western partner. Here the planning heritage may also bring a number of special problems noted above, e.g. in technology, overmanning or waste. For example, the acquired firm may own extensive social assets – housing, holiday accommodation, creche or medical facilities – which the Western firm will not want to retain. The key role of expatriates in management may also be highlighted in such acquisitions. This is because the market for some managerial skills, notably in marketing and finance, is notoriously thin in transitional economies. However, cultural and linguistic differences may make it hard for expatriates to perform effectively in the transitional context, because of their lack of experience, e.g. in dealing with socialist bureaucracies, with poorly motivated workers and with the rather different business ethics carried over from the socialist era. Taken together, those factors may make the investment into transitional countries somewhat different from that originally expected or planned by the Western multinational, probably in a direction favouring greenfield over acquisition as an entry vehicle.

The impact of foreign direct investment on the transition process

This can be considered from the perspective of the direct impact on formerly state-owned firms as well as the indirect impact via spillovers on specific sectors and the economy as a whole. To assess the direct impact on firms, the inward investment must involve a joint venture or acquisition, though perhaps used as the basis for brownfield development. We first evaluate foreign ownership at the enterprise level before discussing some broader spillovers.

Firms in transition

Earle and Estrin (1995) propose four broad criteria for evaluating alternative ownership forms in terms of their ability to assist or hinder the transition process at the enterprise level. These are as follows.

Depoliticization

Firms under socialism can be viewed as focused to maximize output in pursuit of the plan and to maximize rent from the state. An important priority in transition is therefore to reorient company behaviour in the direction of profit maximization, to eradicate soft budget constraints, and to develop the institutional capacity to sustain legally enforceable voluntary contracts. Foreign ownership may be one significant mechanism for achieving this goal. As noted previously, foreign firms will probably only go into the country on the basis of clear legal frameworks and contracts. Indeed, the prospect of foreign ownership may help to ensure clarification of, for example, the ownership of land, which might not otherwise occur. Moreover, foreign owners will be primarily oriented to profit, and to satisfying the demands of foreign shareholders. As such, they may be distant from the temptation to exploit bureaucratic connections to seek rents, subsidies and special concessions, and poorly equipped to do so anyway because their managers will probably not belong to the relevant elites. On the other hand, it may be argued that multinationals have particular expertise in negotiating special agreements with governments, and recent Western experience shows that Western firms are not always averse to exploiting bureaucratic connections.

Restructuring the organization

An inappropriate development path has left most central and east European firms technologically backward and not competitive on international markets in terms of quality and factor productivity. There are three implications for restructuring the organization. In the first place, the lack of property rights and the associated absence of autonomy of decision-making at the enterprise level in socialist economies brings into question the very existence of firms as distinct entities, in the standard Western sense. A principal mechanism of the transition is therefore the reorganization of the existing group of productive units through vertical and horizontal disintegration and reintegration to form an industrial structure in which the boundaries of the firms are set to ensure that transaction costs within the new enterprises are at a minimum.

This will be particularly hard for the state or for insiders to achieve, because sectional interests will be threatened by unbundling. For example, employee-owners may be unwilling to break up a multiplant firm in which one plant is clearly profitable, but the others would have to close or downsize considerably in the absence of subsidy from the successful one. Being concerned primarily with the profitability of the multinational as a whole, outside owners in general and the foreign investors in particular would have less difficulty with such enterprise disintegration.

The establishment of property rights and market orientation will also need to be reflected in changes in the organizational form of firms. The structure of the organization itself will have to adapt in order to be able to respond to the changing demands of customers, to ensure adequate mechanisms for managerial control, and to provide appropriate information for rational decision-making. Necessary changes stressed in the literature will include the creation of functions and departments for sales, marketing, finance, human resources (in the Western sense), and product and technological development. Also significant might be the development of new internal organizational arrangements, e.g. a shift from a plant-based structure to profit centres. This is a specific area in which the multinational firm offers a wealth of experience and know-how, and in which transitional managers and owners are traditionally very weak.

Finally, there is the basic and fundamental need for capital, technology and management in order to transform the firm. This cannot be provided by the state, and even if insiders have the necessary skills and information, they face inherent agency problems dealing with capital markets because of their simultaneous control over costs and the allocation of surplus. These problems will be less serious for all outside owners, but in most situations especially for Western firms with diversified portfolios and access to international capital markets.

With respect to technology, it is also important to consider potentially negative impacts that FDI could have. This relates to the question of the level and nature of technology that is transferred and its impact on existing technological abilities, including research and development (R&D). However, the question of the counterfactual – as well as of actual behaviour – has to be considered. For example, although incoming multinationals may not use or may close R&D facilities, in many cases there are such gaps between the R&D departments and actual production and products that integrating R&D units into firms in the process of restructuring may not be feasible.

The literature contains an implicit consensus that the major impact of foreign investment in transitional economies is via the transfer of technology, broadly defined to include managerial, financial, organizational and marketing know-how (see McMillan, 1993; Kogut, 1994; Svetlicic, 1994). In some sectors, such as automobiles, the technology implemented may be of a world-leading standard. However, the diffusion of the technology beyond the foreign affiliate has so far been modest, and multinational owners have tended to reduce their R&D in locally acquired companies (see Papanek, 1995).

Restructuring employment and other inputs

Another category of restructuring consists in the reallocation of resources, in response to the associated changes in relative prices, e.g. in energy, to ensure that inputs are used efficiently and that suppliers satisfy the new patterns of final demand. This implies that the newly privatized firms should be responsive to market signals in terms of both the products they choose to supply and in their use of factor inputs. In firms for which the optimal level of output has fallen, the governance system must be able to effect large decreases in employment.

These are again areas in which foreign owners might reasonably be expected to dominate insiders, though the differences may not be so great in comparison with domestic outsider owners. East European managers were typically engineers, and well understood how to reduce non-labour-variable costs, to improve factor efficiency and to reorient the product mix. Indeed, empirical evidence from, for example, Belka *et al.* (1993) and Estrin *et al.* (1994) suggests that such restructuring was fairly common within a year or so of reform, even within state-owned firms. However, the evidence suggests that insiders are unwilling to reduce employment, even when overmanning is very high. One can assume that foreign owners would have fewer reservations in this area, though the social and political implications of foreigners creating widespread unemployment might be damaging. In practice, however, the multinationals might prefer only to go into situations in which employment reductions or cuts in social benefits have already been achieved by the previous owners.

The choices that multinationals make are also likely to be different from those of purely domestic firms, as their subsidiaries form part of their global strategy and, for example, they will avoid any unnecessary duplication, whereas a national firm will assess its strategy differently. Thus, whether a firm is a branch plant of a global firm or a selfstanding firm may have an impact on strategy and behaviour in a number of ways.

Broader political implications for transition

We have noted that significant portions of the capital stock inherited from the centrally managed systems may be of such poor quality that they merit little or no maintenance expenditure or replacement investment. In a frictionless world, much of this equipment should be shut down immediately, and workers retrained for new jobs. But layoffs and retraining introduce social externalities, and the costs of reallocating a substantial part of the workforce across industries, occupations and geographical regions are likely to be immense in the short term. We have suggested that multinationals, because of their clearer profit orientation and their more effective governance system, will be more easily able to ensure company restructuring than either insider or perhaps domestic outsider owners. However, an implication is that social problems will be accelerated by foreign ownership. Widespread FDI might set off political forces which could then affect the entire transition process. It is arguable that such a phenomenon has been experienced in Hungary.

In considering the impact of FDI on enterprise-level transition, it is also important to have clearly in mind alternative transition paths. For many firms, the alternative to FDI is continued state ownership, with no access to additional financial or managerial resources, and little to prevent the gradual looting of physical and human assets through 'spontaneous privatization'. Any form of external ownership looks very attractive in this context, and the comparison probably continues to look relatively favourable with reference to insider control of the firm which has emerged as a result of privatization in most of the region (see Earle and Estrin, 1995). However, all privatization methods can ensure some progress in the various criteria, and a balanced evaluation will depend on sectoral and regional characters, as well as broader political issues.

Spillovers

One can consider the broader external effects from multinational investment in terms of the markets in which those effects may be felt: product, capital, managerial and labour markets. The effects of multinationals on the broader economy may be positive or negative, depending on the particular manner in which the investment is undertaken.

In the case of product markets, the impact of FDI could be positive and/or negative. Multinationals may have positive effects on their own sectors through technological diffusion, or on the domestic supplier industries, e.g. by improving systems of product quality, delivery and stock control. They may also, however, damage local supplier industries, or at least the prospects for development and stimulation of local supply networks, by using their traditional suppliers in their global networks. Lakatos and Papanek (1995) suggest that multinational firms have emphasized the integration of acquired firms into their global networks, though there has also been some development of local supplier relations.

There are also serious questions about the impact of multinationals on host country market structures, highly imperfect in transitional economies. Foreign direct investors may be motivated to enter the region by the oligopolistic market structures currently pertaining, and by their presence create an important barrier to increased competition. Some studies have also reported the development of some anti-competitive practices by multinationals, e.g. regulatory protection for their locally produced goods, crowding out local competitors and establishing Western lobbying practices to obtain special advantages (see Svetlicic, 1994; Nachum, 1996).

Similarly, the role of foreign multinationals in the development of capital markets is not necessarily always beneficial. This is because ownership is external to the transitional economy, and the problem of governance does not fall to local capital market structures. If major segments of the economy pass into foreign hands, local markets will fail to develop the experience of evaluating performance and projects in key sectors. Similarly, multinational reliance on their home country banks or internal financing may hinder the development of the banking sector, e.g. relative to the same firm being placed in domestic outside ownership.

The impact on labour markets seems more likely to be positive, in that multinationals will in part be attracted by the relatively high labour skills of transitional economies, and the resulting training of their labour forces will help to upgrade the entire labour pool. The same applies even more sharply to the managerial market: the operation of multinational firms in a transitional economy provides managers with the experience of working within a Western organization, an experience that can be gradually disseminated throughout the economy.

While the impact of foreign direct ownership on CEE firms has typically been found to be beneficial, both for the firms themselves and in the context of the transition process (see, for example, Belka *et al.*, 1994), more detailed investigation of strategies and impact is needed. While the literature suggests likely positive benefits deriving from management, training and technology transfer, more investigation through case studies and surveys is needed. Furthermore, as suggested here, there may not only be problems with regard to emerging competitive market structures but other wider spillover effects may be both positive and negative.

Conclusions

In conclusion, it is apparent that an analysis of FDI in central and eastern Europe requires an understanding of general determinants and effects of FDI flows, of the behaviour of multinational companies, and of the nature of transition. In this study, we are concerned with how transition affects and changes motivations for FDI, and in how FDI affects transition. An answer to these questions requires both an analysis of the general pattern of FDI flows into the region and a more detailed analysis of the micro-economics of individual company decision-making, behaviour and performance.

Our approach in the subsequent chapters is first to analyse the available data on FDI flows and then to assess in detail 10 case studies of foreign investment, before providing a comparative evaluation in Chapter 15. This chapter has suggested that the key issues in FDI in central and eastern Europe concern the impact on the subsidiaries themselves, and on the broader transformation process. We predict that these outcomes will vary according to the character of the investing company, the motives for the investment as analysed above, the chosen mode of entry and the performance of the investments from the Western perspective.

Notes

1. Yugoslavia had, however, effectively abandoned central planning in 1952, followed by Hungary in 1968 and Poland in 1981 (see Ellman 1989). Hungary also followed a more gradual transition process, which probably commenced around 1988. Transition began in the former Soviet Union in 1991.
2. For example, Boycko *et al.* (1995) calculate that the entire manufacturing sector of the Russian economy was then valued at most at $10 billion.
3. Economic development is of course not dependent on FDI; Japan and more recently Korea and Taiwan made rapid economic progress with only limited foreign investments. But in the transitional economies, alternative governance forms are less well developed, and many firms are in urgent need of Western technical and managerial know-how.
4. A more critical view of macro-economic policies and their effectiveness in the Visegrad countries is contained in Portes (1994).

3

The Nature and Scope of Foreign Direct Investment in Central and Eastern Europe

Introduction

In this chapter, we assess the level and pattern of foreign direct investment (FDI) flows into central and eastern Europe (CEE). We also consider these data in the context of trade flows in and out of central and eastern Europe. It has been argued (World Bank, 1996; Baldwin, 1994b; Faini and Portes, 1995) that flows of FDI into the region have been relatively disappointing. Our analysis of the data indicates that flows are in fact now fairly high, in particular for the more advanced countries where transition is well established and in medium to large markets. The pattern of FDI flows is uneven by both source and host countries, and the chapter discusses a number of potential explanations for this. It focuses in particular on an explanation of the dominance of FDI flows by the United States and Germany.

Overall foreign direct investment flows

In order to analyse and assess the nature and impact of FDI flows into central and eastern Europe, it is necessary to place them in a global context. Table 3.1 sets out the global stocks of FDI of the five largest source countries – the United States, the UK, Japan, Germany and France. It also gives outflows between 1990 and 1994 for the five countries and for the world total. The five accounted for 65 per cent of the global stock of FDI in 1994 and 59 per cent of FDI outflows in 1994. The United States dominates with one-quarter of the stock, followed by the UK and Japan at just under 12 per cent and Germany and France at around 8 per cent. The pattern of the overall flows

Table 3.1 Outward stocks and flows of FDI from the five major source countries ($bn)

	Stock		Outflows		
	1994[a]	% of total	1990	1992	1994[a]
United States	610.0	25.6	27.1	38.9	45.6
UK	281.1	11.8	18.6	19.1	24.1
Japan	277.7	11.6	48.0	17.2	17.9
Germany	205.6	8.6	28.6	16.0	20.5
France	183.4	7.7	34.8	31.2	22.8
World total	2,378.0	100.0	243.1	190.6	222.2

[a] UN estimates.

Source: UN World Investment Report (1995), Geneva: United Nations.

demonstrates the decline in FDI levels in the early 1990s and some recovery by 1994. These variations in flows are probably connected in part to the recessions of the early 1990s; the US and UK recessions were earlier in the 1990s than those of Germany and France. This may explain the slower recovery in the flows of the latter two, although it does not explain low investment flows to 1994.

A priori, it may have been expected that all five of these leading FDI countries would be strongly represented in the capital inflows to the new post-communist markets of central and eastern Europe. In fact, as demonstrated below, the United States and Germany dominate, while France and the UK have at best a modest presence. Japan has so far minimal activity levels in the area. One explanation might relate to locational factors, with Japan focusing more on the market opportunities of Southeast Asia. However, whether location is sufficient to explain the UK's low presence in the region is open to question and we discuss below reasons for the higher levels – absolutely and proportionately – of German and US FDI.

Cumulative flows into transitional economies

Table 3.2 sets out the total cumulative flows of FDI to central and eastern Europe, including the former Soviet Union, comparing across major data sources. The data discussed in this chapter do not include portfolio investment flows, which in many cases are somewhat larger than FDI, but which are typically more volatile. This study, and

Table 3.2 Cumulative flows of FDI to CEE – comparison across data sources

	1989–94, $m Data sources		
Host countries	UN[a]	OECD	EBRD
Czech Republic	3,102[b]	3,028.7	2,981
Hungary	6,801	9,907.7	6,913
Poland	4,184	3,574.2	1,523
CEE 10[c]	16,870	19,922.6	13,909
Russian Federation	2,300	3,015.4	1,600
Total: CEE and CIS	20,755	26,092.4	17,709

[a] UN data are estimates for 1994.
[b] Own estimates made of FDI allocation to Czech Republic from Czechoslovakia, 1989–92.
[c] The 10 CEE Europe Agreement countries.

Sources: UN World Investment Report (1995), Geneva: United Nations. OECD unpublished estimates (1996), European Bank for Reconstruction and Development (1995).

the cases which follow, all focus exclusively on FDI. It also reports data for the largest four host countries – Hungary, the Czech Republic, Poland and Russia. Reliability of data on FDI has been problematic during the early years of the transition, and different international data sources conflict substantially with each other and with national data sources. However, Table 3.2 suggests that there is now beginning to be some convergence across data sources, especially between the Organization for Economic Cooperation and Development (OECD) and UN. In particular, while their earlier estimates of Polish FDI were lower – more similar to those of the European Bank for Reconstruction and Development (EBRD) – the UN and OECD estimates are now similar, higher and much closer to Polish national estimates. Furthermore, as shown in Table 3.3, reports of the most recent UN data also suggest a convergence in estimates of Hungarian FDI. Hungarian FDI increased substantially in 1995, in part due to utilities privatization. Overall, these data sources suggest FDI into the region from 1989 to 1994 of about $20 billion or more, and of about $27 billion by 1995.

Table 3.4 analyses the UN data in more detail. The three largest host recipients – Hungary, Poland and the Czech Republic – account for two-thirds of total FDI. The 10 CEE countries with Europe Agreements with the EU account for over 80 per cent of cumulative

Table 3.3 Cumulative flows of FDI to CEE, 1995 estimates

Host countries	1989–95, cumulative, $bn Data sources	
	UN[a] 1989–95	OECD 1989–1995/Q2
Czech Republic	5.6	3.4
Hungary	11.2	9.9
Poland	n/a	3.9
CEE 10	n/a	22.3
Russian Federation	5.5	3.3
Total: CEE and CIS	n/a	27.9

[a] 1994: UN estimates: 1995/Q2 = second quarter of 1995.

Sources: UN World Investment Report (1996), Geneva: United Nations, reported in *Financial Times*, 17 July 1996; OECD unpublished estimates (1996).

Table 3.4 FDI inflows to four largest recipients, CEE and the CIS, 1989–94[a] ($m)

	Cumulative flows	%	Per capita
Czech Republic	3,102	14.9	301.1
Hungary	6,801	32.7	660.2
Poland	4,184	20.1	108.9
CEE 10	16,870	81.2	159.9
Russian Federation	2,300	11.0	15.5
Other	1,585	7.6	n/a
Total	20,755	100.0	n/a

[a]1994: UN estimates.

Source: UN World Investment Report (1995), Geneva: United Nations.

flows. Ranked on a per capita basis, the dominant role of Hungary in attracting FDI is apparent, although Czech levels are also fairly high. In contrast, Russian FDI is surprisingly low. FDI outside the CEE 10 and Russia is very low.

Table 3.5 reports a comprehensive picture of FDI flows to central and eastern Europe and the CIS. The table indicates the lack of data as well as the low level of flows in the early years of the transition. The data for individual countries are also very sensitive to large individual investments in particular years. Hungary's success in maintaining continuing high levels of FDI inflows is apparent – a success which continued into 1995 and which is related to the sale of utilities in the

Table 3.5 Inflows of FDI to CEE and the CIS, 1989–94 ($m)

Host country	1989	1990	1991	1992	1993	1994[a]
Albania	–	–	-1	20	58	53
Bulgaria	–	4	56	42	55	300
Czech Republic	–	–	–	–	568	862
Former Czechoslovakia	257	207	600	1,103	–	–
Estonia	–	–	–	80	168	260
Hungary	–	–	1,462	1,479	2,350	1,510
Latvia	–	–	–	14	20	30
Lithuania	–	–	–	10	12	10
Poland	11	89	291	678	1,715	1,400
Romania	–	–	40	77	94	650
Slovakia	–	–	–	–	–	70
Slovenia	–	–	–	111	112	73
Former Yugoslavia	9	67	118	64	25	–
Russian Federation	–	–	–	700	700	900
Ukraine	–	–	–	200	200	200
Other CIS[b]	–	–	–	164	219	190
Total	277	367	2,566	4,742	6,296	6,508

[a] UN estimates.
[b] UN gives data for Belarus, Moldova, Kazakhstan, Uzbekistan.

Source: UN World Investment Report (1995), Geneva: United Nations.

telecommunications, power generation and energy sectors. Inflows into Poland picked up in 1993 and 1994, while Czech investment started to increase again in 1994 – and in 1995 – after a slowdown in 1993 which may be related to the Czechoslovakian split. Although these are the most important flows, a modest increase can also be seen in other countries, including Romania, Bulgaria and Estonia. FDI into Slovakia appears remarkably low according to the UN data, though OECD estimates put it at about $550 million by the end of 1994.

While Western analysts have asserted that FDI into central and eastern Europe has been low (World Bank, 1996) and potentially inhibited by the Europe Agreements (Baldwin, 1994b), we would argue that the data for CEE – though not the CIS – do not support this conclusion. FDI flows were low in the first years of the transition, particularly 1990, but this is not surprising, given the risks and uncertainties surrounding the transition countries at the start. Important issues here were the time needed to develop appropriate legal frameworks and market structures, and the varying speeds of implementing privatization. Even by 1992, FDI flows had increased substantially and grew more in 1993 and thereafter. Indeed, although starting from a very small base, FDI growth rates – whether using UN or OECD data – are much higher than trade growth rates, in 1990 and 1991 being well over 100 per cent (UN data showing a growth rate of almost 400 per cent in 1991), in 1993 being about 80 per cent and in 1994 about 40 per cent.

The concentration of FDI on specific countries may reflect both a 'demonstration' effect of initial FDI attracting subsequent FDI and the relative attractiveness of countries in more advanced stages of economic and political transition (including physical and legal infrastructure), together with medium to large market size. Location may be a further factor. If this is the case, it implies that countries such as Romania and Bulgaria could attract substantially more investment if their transitions progress along the lines of the more advanced countries.

The arguments that FDI flows have been disappointingly low also reflect both excessively high initial expectations and comparisons with flows to certain developing countries. However, if FDI flows into central and eastern Europe are compared with the EU cohesion countries (Greece, Ireland, Portugal and Spain), with the larger EU member states or with the largest FDI host developing countries, the picture still looks fairly positive. Table 3.6 shows FDI flows into the cohesion countries from 1989 to 1994 and FDI per capita. Flows vary substantially across the four cohesion countries, with Spain attracting high inflows, Portugal and Greece lower but still substantial levels, and Ireland low FDI levels. In 1994, both Hungarian and Polish inflows were greater than those into Greece, Ireland and Portugal. Czech inflows were substantially higher than Irish inflows and comparable to Greek and Portuguese inflows.

On a per capita basis, the comparison is different. Table 3.7 sets out per capita inflows in 1994 to the largest four EU member states, the four cohesion countries and the main CEE host countries. The per

Table 3.6 Inflows of FDI: the EU cohesion countries

	Cumulative inflows, 1989–94[a] ($m)	Annual inflow, 1994[a] ($m)	FDI per capita, 1989–94[a] ($)	FDI per capita, 1994[a] ($)
Greece	6,098	1,085	594.3	57.9
Ireland	568	96	161.3	27.2
Portugal	11,439	1,255	1,160.1	127.2
Spain	55,828	8,216	1,414.0	208.1

[a] 1994: UN estimates.

Source: UN World Investment Report (1996), Geneva: United Nations, and own calculations.

Table 3.7 FDI inflows per capita: a cross-country comparison, selected European countries, 1994[a]

	Per capita ($)
EU	
France	291.8
Spain	208.1
UK	178.7
Portugal	127.2
Italy	64.3
Greece	57.9
Germany	54.4
Ireland	27.2
EU 15	192.3
CEE	
Hungary	146.6
Czech Republic	83.6
Poland	36.4
CEE 10	48.9

[a] UN estimates of FDI and own calculations.

Source: UN World Investment Report (1995), Geneva: United Nations.

capita for CEE 10 as a whole cannot match that of the EU average but is nonetheless higher than those of various individual EU member states. Hungarian FDI per capita places it among the highest FDI recipient EU member states, along with Spain, France and the UK. The Czech Republic per capita flows are higher than those of Germany, Italy, Greece and Ireland, while Polish flows are relatively low, especially given Poland's large market and population.

Table 3.8 looks at the largest FDI host developing countries in 1994. The inflows per head to these countries are not particularly high, and Hungary, the Czech Republic and even Poland either compare or are substantially higher. On an absolute basis, these flows are mostly higher – though the level of Hungarian inflows in 1993 would compare with those into Thailand, Brazil and Indonesia, and the flows in 1995 (as seen from Tables 3.2 and 3.3) into Hungary (about $4 billion) and the Czech Republic (about $2.5 billion) would also compare with absolute flows into these countries. That the leading CEE recipient countries are coming close to or matching the level of FDI inflows into the largest FDI host developing countries within four or five years of transition is not appropriately described as disappointing. It may also offer some hope of potential for larger

Table 3.8 The largest FDI host developing countries: FDI inflows and inflows per head, 1994[a]

Host country	$m	Per capita ($)
China	33,800	28.3
Malaysia	4,500	228.4
Mexico	4,432	50.0
Indonesia	3,000	15.7
Thailand	2,700	46.5
Brazil	2,241	14.0
Argentina	1,250	35.0

[a] UN estimates.

Source: UN World Investment Report (1995), Geneva: United Nations, and own calculations.

FDI flows into other CEE countries. FDI may, therefore, have a larger role to play in ongoing transition than has been recognized, an issue explained at the micro-economic level in the remainder of this book.

The distribution of investment by host and source country

Locational issues may also play a role in explaining the distribution of FDI across the CEE countries. To investigate this further, we consider the source countries for investment into central and eastern Europe, focusing on investment into the largest three – Hungary, Poland and the Czech Republic. Obtaining accurate data to identify the nationality of investing companies is particularly problematic. Balance of payments data only indicate the immediate country from which the capital flow came. We, therefore, use available data from national sources in the host countries which aim to identify the nationality of investing countries. In the Hungarian case, data on this basis were only identified for joint ventures and acquisitions – excluding greenfield – and thus are indicative only. Table 3.9 sets out the data for Hungary to October 1995. The two dominant investors are Germany and the United States, followed by Austria. Germany and the United States account for almost half the total investment. The table also indicates a typical pattern – that US investments tend to be larger than German investments and so focused on a smaller number of companies. Many small German and Austrian firms have invested on a cross-border basis, although due to their size they do not tend to show up in such data sets. Nonetheless, they would increase the

Table 3.9 FDI in Hungary, cumulative to October 1995

Country (ranked by value of investment)	US$m (HUF billion)	% share	Number of companies
Germany	822.6 (82.26)	24.1	83
United States	793.5 (79.35)	23.2	30
Austria	457.8 (45.78)	13.4	111
UK	281.3 (28.13)	8.2	34
France	229.1 (22.91)	6.7	37
The Netherlands	180.5 (18.05)	5.3	13
Other	652.7 (65.27)	19.1	112
Total	3,417.5 (341.75)	100.0	420

Note: These are the data for the joint ventures and acquisitions only, and do not include the data for FDI by greenfield investment.
HUF = Hungarian forints.

Source: The Gazette of the Ministry of State Privatisation and Property Agency, 24 October 1995, I/17.

difference in the pattern of US relative to German and Austrian investment.

As the Hungarian data exclude greenfield FDI, we compare Table 3.9 with Table 3.10, which gives balance of payments data for Hungary to 1993. While, as explained above, the data are problematic in identifying source countries, it is interesting to note that it gives a similar picture of the top three investing countries, although it gives a higher figure for Austria. The UK's position is also much reduced on these data, presumably because UK firms invest via subsidiaries based elsewhere, e.g. in Austria or Germany. This issue arises in our cases.

Table 3.11 sets out FDI in Poland by nationality of investing country. The total inflow figure is cumulative to 1995 and so is higher than the UN and OECD figures given in Table 3.2 for 1994. On the basis of the UN data, it implies an inflow of about $1.8 billion in 1995, which would be fairly consistent with the UN flows for 1993 and 1994. The United States dominates investment into Poland, accounting for 30 per cent of the total, compared to 10 per cent for Germany. The Netherlands and UK follow with about 7 per cent, with a number

Table 3.10 Flows from the OECD to Hungary (the top investors) (US$m)

	To 1990	1991	1992	1993	Cumulative	%
Germany	176.0	250.7	546.8	554.0	1,528	28.8
Austria	420.7	376.8	291.2	245.8	1,335	25.2
United States	141.0	174.0	152.0	761.0	1,228	23.1
The Netherlands	–	81.8	154.7	123.8	360	6.8
Japan	35.0	181.0	4.0	72.0	292	5.5
Belgium/Luxembourg	26.1	60.4	10.0	132.2	229	4.3
UK	6.7	23.0	90.0	19.5	139	2.6
Italy	–	–	26.8	51.5	78	1.5
Other	21.2	16.0	24.9	56.0	118	2.2
Total	826.7	1,163.7	1,300.4	2,015.8	5,307	100.0

Source: OECD Statistics from *International Direct Investment Statistics Yearbook* 1995, Paris: OECD. Data collected from the National Central Banks, based on balance of payments.

of other countries between 4 and 6 per cent. The particular dominance of the United States may partially reflect US interest in the largest market in the region.

Table 3.12 sets out FDI in the Czech Republic by nationality of investing country to March 1996. Here the Polish picture is reversed, with Germany responsible for almost 30 per cent of FDI, and the United States, The Netherlands and Switzerland all around 14 per cent. France has a share of almost 9 per cent, while UK investment is lower than that of Austria and so included in the 'others' total. Data from earlier years also indicate that Italian FDI – although low – is also greater than UK FDI. While locational factors may partially explain German dominance in Czech FDI, this explanation is somewhat weakened by the Polish picture. The low UK FDI into the Czech Republic contrasts with its higher involvement in Hungary and Poland, even though in neither case is it comparable to the United States and Germany (though closest to Germany in the Polish case).

In order to obtain an approximate overview of the role of different source countries in FDI inflows into CEE, Table 3.13 estimates the distribution of FDI into Hungary, Poland and the Czech Republic, based on the national data presented in Tables 3.9, 3.11 and 3.12. This table should be interpreted as indicative of the structure of FDI rather than as a precise description. The United States and Germany together dominate investment flows, accounting for over 40 per cent of total FDI. The Netherlands is in third place with 9.3 per cent. Switzerland, France and Austria follow with about 7 per cent each, while the UK and Italy lag behind with 4.5 and 3 per cent respectively.

Table 3.11 FDI in Poland, cumulative[a] to September 1995, investments > US$1m

Country	$m	%
United States	1,830	30.8
Germany	641	10.8
The Netherlands	431	7.3
UK	419	7.1
Italy	390	6.6
France	335	5.6
Switzerland	292	4.9
Sweden	258	4.3
Austria	248	4.2
Others	1,089	18.4
Total	5,933	100.0

[a] Most investments are since 1991, but some are earlier.

Note: PAIZ statistics have been altered to distribute the company investments that they have classified as 'international'. Investments have been allocated according to ownership structure for Unilever, ABB, Kraft Jacob and Ciementies. Other companies and international financial institutions have been placed in the 'other' category.

Source: Polish State Investment Agency (PAIZ).

Table 3.12 FDI in the Czech Republic by source country, cumulative, 1990 to 31 March 1996

Source country	US$m	%
Germany	1,759.3	29.5
United States	848.9	14.3
Switzerland	830.2	13.9
The Netherlands	824.4	13.8
France	531.5	8.9
Austria	307.0	5.2
Others	853.4	14.4
Total	5,954.7	100.0

Source: Czech National Bank.

Table 3.13 Total FDI by source country in the Visegrad 3: Czech Republic, Hungary[a] and Poland

	Cumulative 1990–5[b]	
	$m	%
United States	3,472.4	22.6
Germany	3,222.9	21.0
The Netherlands	1,435.9	9.3
Switzerland[c]	1,122.2	7.3
France	1,095.6	7.1
Austria	1,012.8	6.6
UK[d]	700.3	4.5
Italy[e]	472.1	3.0
Other	2,771.0	18.1
Total	15,305.2	100.0

[a] Hungary, excluding greenfield.
[b] Czech data to March 1996; Hungary to October 1995; Poland to September 1995.
[c] No data available for Swiss investment in Hungary.
[d] No data available for UK investment in Czech Republic.
[e] No data available for Italian investment in Hungary; Czech data only to 1994.

Source: Tables 3.9, 3.11 and 3.12.

A comparison of the UK, Germany and the United States

This ranking of source countries for FDI into central and eastern Europe may be compared to the global ranking set out in Table 3.1. Whereas US investment in the region is comparable to its share of global FDI stocks, Germany's CEE stock is two and a half times larger. France also has a share of the CEE stock comparable to its global share, while the UK's share is only about one-third of its global share, and Japan has no significant FDI presence in central and eastern Europe. As suggested above, part of the explanation for low Japanese investment may be locational, including the advantages it can obtain from investing in low-cost regions of Southeast Asia. In the UK case, given its global FDI position, its low investment in central and eastern Europe is perhaps more surprising. However, a number of different factors may contribute to an explanation of its relatively low levels, in particular compared to Germany and the United States.

The high absolute level of German FDI in central and eastern Europe and relative to the UK may be due to various characteristics of the two countries. Geographical proximity is one part of this:

Germany's location in central Europe, sharing borders with two of the three main CEE FDI locations, means that German firms can benefit from both faster and cheaper transport links and from swifter, more effective communication and information links (especially where travel is involved). Furthermore, its geographical position also relates to its stronger pre-1989 links to central and eastern Europe in the economic, political and cultural domains. These relationships were in part, but not only, inherited with the absorption into West Germany of the former GDR. As we will see below, Germany has always traded somewhat more with the former COMECON than, for example, the UK or France. Language factors may also play some part here – German rather than English was a second language in much of central Europe at the start of transition, though this is changing rapidly now.

The literature suggests that neighbouring countries have been predominant in each country's privatization process (see Lane, 1994b) and in the early stages of transition. This is especially true for the role of Austria in Hungary, Germany in Hungary and the Czech Republic, Italy in Slovenia, Greece in Bulgaria and the Scandinavian countries in the Baltic states.

The cost differentials and benefits from low-cost labour available in central and eastern Europe may also have been more attractive to German firms. Concerns about German competitiveness in the early 1990s focused in particular on high German costs. Not only could German firms benefit from nearby low-cost locations, but the absolute cost differential for German to Czech wages, for example, is about 10 to 1, while for the UK it would be closer to 5 to 1. The incentives for cost-motivated FDI in CEE countries are, consequently, greater for German firms.

Other factors that may also contribute to an explanation of the different German and UK FDI levels include the timing of the recession, attitudes to risk, government policies and global patterns of FDI. The UK recession (1991–2) began before that in Germany (1992–3). Foreign investment flows have some tendency to be pro-cyclical, so just as the early opportunities for FDI in central and eastern Europe were opening up, UK firms were facing recession at home. Furthermore, once German firms were also facing recession, they were by then alert to the cost-saving benefits of investment in central and eastern Europe – indeed, in 1993, although total German FDI outflows showed almost zero growth, FDI in CEE countries and the CIS increased by close to one-third, reaching almost 9 per cent of total German FDI outflows. Thus, concerns about German cost competitiveness which were emphasized during their recession may have stimulated further interest in central and eastern Europe.

FDI in central and eastern Europe, especially in the early years of the transition, was particularly risky, as the unprecedented nature of the transition made prediction of future economic and political developments difficult. Nonetheless, these markets had considerable, though uncertain, potential. Germany may have had informational advantages in this early stage from its political and cultural links to the region, and because of its experiences in the former GDR. These experiences may have particularly influenced German firms which had practical experiences of restructuring companies in eastern Germany. It is also commonly argued that UK firms are more short term and risk-averse in their outlook than German firms because of differences in the nature of corporate governance, i.e. the UK reliance on stock markets and the absence of long-term strategic investors. This may also have affected attitudes to investment.

Government policies towards central and eastern Europe more generally may also have affected business attitudes. Germany has major and immediate political, economic and security interests in central and eastern Europe, given its location, whereas, although the UK government has also supported EU enlargement, it has been less active in encouraging the development of economic links with central and eastern Europe. There may also be cumulative interactions between different actors – German banks are much more active in the region than UK banks. This may be because they have followed German businesses into central and eastern Europe, while German business may be reassured about investing in CEE countries when it sees national banks in place, and the attitudes of both may be further influenced by overall government policy. On the other hand, UK firms, especially smaller ones, contemplating entry need to add the difficulty of building new relationships with foreign banks to the already formidable costs of entry to the region.

Finally, German and UK global patterns of FDI differ – substantially more German investment is concentrated in Europe than is UK investment, which is more global and, in particular, more concentrated on the United States. German and UK companies may, therefore, have differing global strategies and differing global experience and information sets which will affect the range of investment locations they consider.

In assessing the reasons for the differing levels of US and UK FDI in central and eastern Europe, some similar and some different arguments may be relevant. US global stocks of FDI are over twice those of the UK, and US multinationals are substantially larger than most UK ones and may have a wider global reach. Furthermore, about 50 per cent of US FDI stocks are in Europe, so it is not surprising to see US firms being alert to new market opportunities in the 'new Europe'. Ideological factors, such as playing a role in rebuilding capitalism on the ruins of communism, may also have been significant in some cases, especially for emigrés or their children. The US investments in central and eastern Europe, as discussed above, have been concentrated in a relatively small number of very large investments (including large infrastructure projects) – substantially larger, on average, than German investments. According to Lane, US investments tend to be by large firms, in large projects and with majority ownership (see Lane, 1995). US firms appear, therefore, to be moving relatively rapidly in investing where there are substantial market and infrastructure opportunities, especially where there are activities with large scale-economies in which US firms may be particularly competitive.

US firms may also be more prepared to take on the risks of the uncertain CEE environment, and the risk–return trade-off may be different for very large-scale investments. Some of the large US multinational enterprises (MNEs) also seem to be cash-rich, in this period, certainly more so than their UK counterparts in our cases, with this liquidity assisting fast entry where there are key opportunities. More generally, US MNEs may, overall, have higher levels of competitiveness than UK firms and different managerial know-how, technology, existing global market share and organizational structures. All these may impact on FDI positions.

There are, therefore, a number of explanations for the relatively low FDI from the UK into central and eastern Europe – a position which is matched, as shown below, in its trading links. These low levels may change in the near future, both as CEE markets expand and as they become less uncertain. However, it is an interesting question whether UK firms, and perhaps also Japanese ones, may be placed at a disadvantage by coming so late into these markets. More generally, the differing positions across the EU member states, and the dominant position of Germany, mean that European economic structures and economic geography are changing, and this may affect both relative competitiveness and relative dynamism of different regions of the European economy (Hughes, 1996).

The sectoral pattern

There are relatively few sectoral data available on FDI into central and eastern Europe. The literature suggests that sector allocation appears largely to have been to manufacturing in the early years, though

Table 3.14 Sector breakdown of FDI into Hungary, January–July 1995

Sector	US$m	% of total
Agriculture	2.62	2.7
Mining	1.46	1.5
Manufacturing	30.63	31.5
Food, beverages, tobacco	3.78	3.9
Textiles, clothes, leather	1.52	1.6
Wood, paper, publishing	1.74	1.8
Chemicals	14.19	14.6
Non-metal minerals	4.19	4.3
Metals	1.11	1.1
Machinery	3.74	3.9
Others	0.36	0.4
Electrical energy, gas, heat, water supply	0.05	0
Construction	21.30	21
Trade, vehicle and public goods repair	22.94	23.6
Accommodation, catering	1.56	1.6
Transportation, storage, post, telecommunications	0.95	1.0
Financial services	0.52	0.5
Real estate	14.45	14.8
Public administration	0	0
Education	0.1	0.1
Health and social care	0.03	0.03
Other	0.44	0.5
Total	97.05	100.00

Source: KSH, Havi Közlemények (monthly reports) 1995/8.

services have been becoming more important recently. Within manufacturing, food processing and consumer goods were most important, with vehicles also very significant (Svetlicic, 1994). Tables 3.14 to 3.16 set out some of the available data for Hungary, Poland and the Czech Republic. The data for Hungary should be treated with particular caution, as they only represent the first half of 1995, whereas the Polish and Czech data cover the period since 1990. A number of sectors stand out from these tables. Transport and communications are particularly important in the Czech Republic, while property and financial services show high inflows in Hungary and Poland respectively. The Czech Republic also has high inflows in consumer goods and tobacco, and Poland in electro-machinery, and all three have some emphasis on construction. Chemicals and food-processing have more varied importance across the three countries.

Table 3.15 FDI into Poland by sectors, cumulative from 1990 to second quarter of 1995

Sector	Equity and loans (US$m)	% of total FDI
Industry	3,198.3	59.4
Fuel and energy industry	119.9	2.2
Metallurgy industry	46.4	0.9
Electro-machinery industry	921.8	17.1
Chemical industry	273.2	5.1
Mineral industry	318.9	5.9
Wood and paper industry	402.6	7.5
Light industry	169.7	3.1
Food-processing industry	899.1	16.7
Other	46.7	0.9
Construction	463.4	8.5
Agriculture	8.0	0.1
Transportation	29.9	0.6
Telecommunications	240.4	4.5
Trade	342.3	6.4
Municipal economy	20.4	0.4
Finance	1,073.7	19.9
Insurance	13.1	0.2
Total	5,389.50	100.0

Source: Polish State Investment Agency, 1995.

Table 3.16 FDI into the Czech Republic by sectoral structure, cumulative from 1990 to 31 March 1996

Sector	$m	%
Transport and communications	1,377.6	23.1
Transport equipment	1,035.0	17.4
Consumer goods and tobacco	854.2	14.3
Construction	471.2	7.9
Chemicals	440.0	7.4
Food	416.1	7.0
Other	1,360.6	22.9
Total	5,954.7	100.0

Source: Czech National Bank.

This limited information on sectoral distribution of FDI does not particularly suggest the build-up of major new areas of comparative advantage and appears to emphasize more low-technology sectors. This sector distribution indicates different influences – the food-processing sector is generally seen as an area of comparative advantage for many of the CEE countries, while construction and communication investments may, rather, represent reconstruction and infrastructure development associated with transition, and transport investments are linked to the various automotive investments in the region.

Within the transitional economies, more than half of the projects are located in or around the capitals. Other important locations are close to western borders, gateway coastal regions, natural-resource-rich areas and, in Poland, the industrial southwest (Meyer, 1995). There appears to be only very modest intra-regional investment (Meyer, 1995).

Trade relations with central and eastern Europe

There has been substantially more analysis of trade flows and trade agreements with central and eastern Europe than of FDI (see, for example, Faini and Portes, 1995; Winters, 1995; Inota, 1994). These analyses have focused both on the pattern and impact of trade flows – looking not only at central and eastern Europe but also at the EU economies – and have critically assessed the Europe Agreements between the EU and CEE countries. Here, our concern is simply with some of the main characteristics of trade flows with central and eastern Europe, focusing on the EU as the major trading partner of the region, and the extent to which the pattern of trade flows reflects or otherwise the pattern of FDI flows. Trade and FDI patterns are, of course, not identical but, as with FDI, the highest levels of EU trade are with the Czech Republic, Hungary and Poland. However, Germany plays a dominant role, while the United States is less important in trade than with FDI.

Table 3.17 sets out EU trade with the CEE 5 from 1989 to 1994 for the EU as a whole and for the largest four exporting member states. The table also includes Austria's exports to central and eastern Europe, which exceed those of both the UK and France. The high rates of growth in both exports and imports since 1989 are set out – the annual average growth rate of exports from 1990 to 1994 is 24 per cent. However, annual rates vary, with a substantial slowdown in the

Table 3.17 EU trade with CEE, 1989–94[a] (US$m)

	1989	1990	1991	1992	1993	1994
Exports						
Germany	6,884	11,464	11,904	15,093	16,092	19,137
Italy	1,459	2,162	2,378	3,490	4,283	5,379
France	1,161	1,348	2,011	2,582	2,355	2,761
UK	932	1,094	1,244	1,919	2,115	2,451
EU 12 total	12,627	18,618	21,658	27,802	30,231	35,934
% annual	15.77	47.45	16.33	28.37	8.74	18.86
Austria	1,625	2,309	2,891	3,442	3,527	4,114
Imports						
Germany	5,657	8,646	11,081	14,229	13,857	17,517
Italy	2,438	2,462	2,526	3,254	2,959	4,164
France	1,542	1,815	1,825	1,937	1,758	2,168
UK	1,223	1,268	1,140	1,333	1,528	2,051
EU 12 total	12,401	17,398	20,159	24,524	23,717	30,753
% annual	7.60	29.83	15.87	21.65	−3.29	29.67
Austria	1,536	1,885	2,207	2,608	2,509	3,125

[a] Bulgaria, Czechoslovakia (to 1992), Czech Republic (from 1993), Hungary, Poland, Romania and Slovakia (from 1993).

Source: IMF Trade Statistics Yearbook 1995, Washington DC: IMF.

Table 3.18 Shares of EU exports to CEE (%)[a]

	1989	1994
Germany	54.5	53.2
Italy	11.5	14.9
France	9.1	7.6
UK	7.3	6.6
The Netherlands	6.68	5.4
Other	10.67	12.07
Total EU	100.00	100.00

[a] Bulgaria, Czechoslovakia (to 1992), Czech Republic (from 1993), Hungary, Poland, Romania and Slovakia (from 1993).

Source: IMF Trade Statistics Yearbook 1995, Washington DC: IMF.

recession year of 1993. Prospects are for continued high growth rates.

Table 3.18 sets out the shares of EU member states' exports to central and eastern Europe in 1989 and 1994. Despite the high rates of growth, Germany's share has remained almost constant at around 53

Table 3.19 EU exports to CEE as percentage of total extra-EU exports by country, 1994

	1994
EU	5.5
France	3.4
Germany	10.0
Italy	7.8
UK	2.9

Source: IMF Trade Statistics Yearbook 1995, Washington DC: IMF.

per cent of total EU exports – substantially higher than both its FDI share, and its overall export shares. Italy has the second highest share, showing a strong trade orientation to the region which is so far much more pronounced than in its FDI. France and the UK have smaller shares, closely followed by The Netherlands. Nonetheless, although the rankings vary, the largest five EU exporters to central and eastern Europe are also the largest five EU FDI source countries for the EU 12, i.e. excluding Austria, whose relatively high FDI share is complemented by a higher export share.

Table 3.19 shows the importance of exports to central and eastern Europe as a percentage of total extra-EU trade. For the EU as a whole, it is just over 5 per cent, with Germany at twice the EU average and Italy also relatively high, while the UK is about half the average. There is clearly substantial variation in the importance of CEE trade to EU member states, both absolutely and relatively, with the UK having a particularly low share.

Table 3.20 sets out the net trade balances of the EU 12 with the CEE 5 from 1989 to 1994. The EU trade balance shifts from deficit to surplus in 1990 and has remained in surplus – a fact which has led to some criticism that EU markets have not been opened sufficiently fast. However, transition economies may expect to face deficits if they are importing substantial amounts of investment goods. Furthermore, some individual CEE countries have a surplus with the EU – Slovakia, Latvia, Lithuania and Romania in 1994 and all 10 CEE Europe Agreement countries have surpluses with some EU member states (Grabbe and Hughes, 1997).

Table 3.21 sets out US exports and imports to the CEE 10 in 1994. As with the FDI data, Poland is the most important market for the United States. However, US trade with the region is low. Substantial amounts of its FDI flows appear to have been managed by US subsidiaries in western Europe – US companies may primarily also be

Table 3.20 EU 12 net trade balance with CEE 5 (US$m)[a]

	1989	1990	1991	1992	1993	1994
EU 12 total	−774	1,220	1,499	3,278	6,514	5,181
Germany	1,227	2,818	823	864	2,235	1,620
Italy	−979	−300	−148	236	1,324	1,215
France	−381	−467	186	645	597	593
UK	−291	−174	104	586	587	400

[a] Bulgaria, Czechoslovakia (to 1992), Czech Republic (from 1993), Hungary, Poland, Romania and Slovakia (from 1993).

Source: IMF Trade Statistics Yearbook 1995, Washington DC: IMF.

Table 3.21 US exports and imports to CEE (US$m)

	1989	1994
Exports		
CEE 10	927	1,992
Poland	414	625
Hungary	122	309
Czech Republic	0	297
Imports		
CEE 10	1,334	2,521
Poland	424	704
Hungary	361	503
Czech Republic	0	335
Net trade		
CEE 10	−407	−529
Poland	−10	−79
Hungary	−239	−194
Czech Republic	0	−38

Source: IMF Trade Statistics Yearbook 1995, Washington DC: IMF.

trading with central and eastern Europe from western Europe and this will not be picked up in US trade flows.

Tables 3.22 to 3.24 set out for the Czech Republic, Hungary and Poland their main trading partners between 1993 and the first quarter of 1995. In all three, the dominant importance of the trading relationship with Germany for both imports and exports is apparent. Other trading partners vary, but Italy and Russia are in the top five traders for all three, while Austria is second for Hungary and third for the Czech Republic. The UK is the fifth largest exporter for Poland but otherwise does not figure in the largest five for the other two countries.

Table 3.22 Czech Republic: main trading partners, percentage of total imports and exports, 1993–1995/Q1

Country	Exports			Imports		
	1993	1994	1995/Q1	1993	1994	1995/Q1
Germany	26.9	29.3	32.3	25.1	25.4	25.9
Slovakia	20.0	16.3	16.7	17.7	14.2	13.1
Austria	6.2	7.2	6.5	7.7	8.1	6.9
Russia	6.0	3.9	–	11.5	8.5	9.7
Italy	5.1	4.9	4.3	4.7	5.3	5.5
Poland	–	–	4.6	–	–	–
Others	35.8	38.5	35.6	33.3	38.5	38.9

Note: 1995/Q1 = first quarter of 1995.

Source: Statistical Bulletin, Prague, 1994/Q1 and 1995/Q1.

Table 3.23 Hungary: main trading partners, percentage of total exports and imports, 1993–1995/Q1

Country	Exports			Imports		
	1993	1994	1995/Q1	1993	1994	1995/Q1
Germany	26.6	28.2	27.8	21.6	23.4	23.8
Russia	15.3	7.5	5.6	22.2	12.0	13.0
Austria	10.1	10.9	11.1	11.6	12.0	11.1
Italy	8.0	8.5	9.4	6.0	7.0	7.7
United States	4.2	–	–	3.9	–	–
Others	35.8	40.6	41.8	34.7	41.6	40.4

Note: 1995/Q1 = first quarter of 1995.

Source: Statistical Bulletin, Prague, 1994/Q1 and 1995/Q1.

Table 3.24 Poland: main trading partners, percentage of total exports and imports, 1993–1995/Q1

Country	Exports			Imports		
	1993	1994	1995/Q1	1993	1994	1995/Q1
Germany	36.3	35.7	38.3	28.0	27.5	27.3
The Netherlands	5.9	5.9	5.8	4.7	4.6	4.8
Italy	5.2	4.9	5.0	7.8	8.4	8.1
Russia	4.6	5.4	5.0	6.8	6.8	7.1
UK	4.3	4.6	4.3	5.8	5.3	5.0
Others	43.7	43.5	41.6	46.9	47.4	47.7

Note: 1995/Q1 = first quarter of 1995.

Source: Statistical Bulletin, Prague, 1994/Q1 and 1995/Q1.

Overall, the trade statistics tell a similar story to the FDI statistics in terms of the relative importance of different western countries in the region. The lesser importance of the United States in the trade data may reflect the fact that US companies are trading with the region from their EU subsidiaries – as with their FDI – and this trade is not reflected in the US trade statistics. On the basis of the data presented, Germany stands out as the most important economic actor in the region in terms of its joint trade and FDI involvement. Although the macro-level picture, therefore, varies across Western countries according to their involvement in central and eastern Europe, the micro-level picture may or may not vary across source countries, i.e. in terms of motivations, behaviour and experience of MNEs from different Western countries when investing in central and eastern Europe. It is with this micro-level picture that the cases set out in the following chapters are concerned.

Conclusion

This chapter has analysed the data on FDI in central and eastern Europe together with some of the main trade data. By 1995, FDI flows into the region were high and rising particularly in those countries that are relatively advanced in their transitions and that have relatively large markets. The two main source countries of the FDI are the United States and Germany, and the main recipients are the Czech Republic, Hungary and Poland. FDI flows per head into the CEE countries receiving most FDI are comparable to those into most of the EU cohesion countries and are higher than those into most of the top FDI-recipient developing countries. Flows into the Czech Republic and Hungary in 1995 match absolute flows into some of the top developing countries. The analysis, therefore, shows that as transition has developed, FDI flows have grown. FDI may have a substantial impact on transition in those countries where it is high, and there are prospects for substantial growth of FDI in other CEE countries as their transitions progress.

As Chapter 2 discussed, motivations for these investments include markets, market share and costs. The transition economies offer low costs and high growth potential and some have large markets. However, there are also questions concerning the negative impact of the legacy of planning, actual and perceived stability, and the level of institutional and infrastructure development. The Czech Republic, Hungary and Poland are all relatively advanced in their transitions, especially compared to Bulgaria and Romania, and offer larger markets than the Baltic States, Slovenia and Slovakia. This may, in part, explain the larger flows into the Czech Republic, Hungary and Poland. However, the broad statistics presented in this chapter can only give limited insight into the determinants of FDI flows and their impact on transition. The more detailed micro-level analysis through a case study approach – as set out in subsequent chapters – provides a greater understanding of motivation and impact of the relationship between FDI and transition.

Part II

4

Framework for the Case Studies

Introduction

It is apparent from the discussion in Chapter 3 of the level and distribution of foreign direct investment (FDI) flows into central and eastern Europe (CEE) that existing data cannot fully answer the key questions concerning motivation for, and impact of, FDI with which we are concerned. In order to analyse the experience and role of FDI in the transition as set out in the analytical framework developed in Chapter 2, a more micro-level analysis is required. The case study approach provides the means to do this. A case study approach is also appropriate to the analysis of FDI and transition because of the uncertainty and ongoing change associated with the transition processes. Firms investing at different points in time may have different experiences of entry into and operation in a transition economy and consequently may also have different impacts. The case study approach, therefore, allows an in-depth consideration of motivations and behaviour of Western multinationals in investing in central and eastern Europe and of their direct and indirect impact on the host countries. The case study methodology is, inevitably, constrained by the standard question of the extent to which it is possible to generalize on the basis of a small number of cases. Nonetheless, in this context, the advantages of cases strongly outweigh the disadvantages. Chapter 15 assesses the general lessons from the cases together with an assessment of the extent and causes of variation in FDI behaviour across our case study sample. In this chapter, we set out our approach to the selection and undertaking of the case studies.

Case study selection

Case study selection focused on the questions first of which host and home countries to focus on and second of which range of sectors to select. Given a limited number of cases (a final sample of 10), it was decided to focus on the three main host countries for FDI in central and eastern Europe – the Czech Republic, Hungary and Poland (as discussed in Chapter 3). These three countries account for over two-thirds of the FDI into the former Soviet bloc and for about 80 per cent of FDI inflows into the 10 Europe Agreement countries. They have, however, also attracted different levels of FDI, especially relative to their overall economic size, and, while being relatively advanced in their transitions (as we saw in Chapter 2), have also had different experiences of transition. The focus on these three countries, therefore, makes it possible to both focus on the countries receiving the main FDI inflows and to compare FDI experiences in different transition economies.

In addition to assessing any differences across transition economies, we were also concerned to assess whether nationality of home country had any apparent impact on FDI motivations and behaviour. As shown in Chapter 3, the largest four home countries for FDI – in terms of global capital stock – are the United States, the UK, Japan and Germany. However, in central and eastern Europe, US and German investments dominate, UK investments are relatively low and Japanese investments minimal. The study, therefore, focused on UK, German and US FDI into central and eastern Europe. This allowed an analysis of the behaviour of the largest two investing countries into central and eastern Europe and of the largest two investing countries globally. Furthermore, it enabled the study to compare the behaviour of multinationals from the largest two European countries, in terms of FDI stock, and to consider why UK investment is relatively low. A number of reasons for the latter were put forward in Chapter 3, but an interesting question for the cases is whether those UK firms that did choose to invest in central and eastern Europe differed in impact, motivation or behaviour from the two larger investing countries of the United States and Germany.

With this sample of three home and three host countries, we aimed in our case study selection to identify one case from each home country in each host country. With the 10 cases undertaken, this was achieved as set out in Table 4.1 – in each of the Czech Republic, Hungary and Poland we have one case from each of the United States, UK and Germany, with one additional UK case in Hungary.

In selecting sectors, one aim was to be able to make intra-sectoral comparisons within and across countries as well as inter-sectoral comparisons. A second aim was to identify sectors where the CEE countries tended to have either some comparative advantage or

Table 4.1 Distribution of cases by sector and host country

Sector	Host country		
	Czech Republic	Hungary	Poland
Food and drink (low technology)		Schöller (Germany) United Biscuits (UK)	General Bottlers (US)
Pharmaceuticals (high technology)	Glaxo (UK)		
Engineering (medium technology)	Otis (USA) Pyramid (Germany)	Lycett (UK)	Volkswagen Bordnetze (Germany)
Bulk intermediates Glass (low technology)		Guardian (US	
Chemicals (medium technology)			British Vita (UK)

specialization and where multinational activity is commonly observed. With a limited sample, the range of desirable sector characteristics and variation that could be specified was inevitably limited, but further aims included that of having some variation across sectors by technology intensity – high, medium and low – and by intermediate and consumer good sector.

The ability to achieve all these different sectoral aims was limited not only by the sample size but also by the fact that in some sectors there were a very small number of investments from our three selected home countries and by the need to approach a number of companies in order to identify firms willing to act at as cases. In selecting cases, an initial distribution of sectors meeting the above criteria was selected. Information on foreign investments in the chosen CEE countries was collected from a variety of sources, including the investment agencies in the CEE countries, the commercial offices and embassies of the Western countries in the CEE countries and relevant government ministries in the home countries. This enabled compilation of lists of investing firms in each country, although, due to the provisional nature of much FDI information, such lists were not completely accurate in identifying firms that had already invested. On the basis of our initial sector selection and these lists, companies were approached to participate in the study. The acceptance rate of participation in the study was about one per four applications (with a higher ratio for

Germany), reflecting in part commercial sensitivity and in part lack of experience of the case study methodology. As in some sectors there were no more than one or two firms from the three Western home countries, the final sector distribution did not reflect a perfect distribution of sectors, cases and countries, but nonetheless the sector distribution as indicated in Table 4.1 does meet the main criteria we had established.

As Table 4.1 shows, there are four main sector groupings. The sector distribution of the cases focuses primarily on medium- and low-technology cases, which reflects the comparative advantage of these economies. Furthermore, the food and drink and engineering sectors are important industries in all these CEE economies and are sectors where there is substantial multinational activity on a global level. In the food and drink sector, we can make intra-sectoral comparisons both within Hungary and between Hungary and Poland, while in engineering it is possible to make intra-sectoral comparisons across all three of our CEE host countries. The sectors also represent a mixture of consumer and intermediate good sectors.

Finally, three of the 10 cases are small and medium sized enterprises (SMEs) – the inclusion of smaller firms was a deliberate aim, given the unusual phenomenon in the central and eastern European case of large numbers of small firms investing, primarily cross-border from Germany and Austria.

Case study approach

To understand the decision-making and behaviour of a multinational in a particular country, it is necessary to analyse its overall global structure and strategy and not simply the behaviour of its subsidiary. The case study approach we adopted, therefore, focused not only on the subsidiary in the CEE country but also on the headquarters (in some cases regional headquarters) of the investing multinational. Interviews were carried out for each case both in the headquarters and in the subsidiary. Numbers of interviews varied substantially from case to case; this primarily related to overall size of company and size of the subsidiary. On average, about four or five interviews were undertaken in headquarters and six to eight in the subsidiaries.

Prior to the case study interviews, a series of interviews were undertaken in the three CEE countries with relevant government ministries, academics, Western chambers of commerce and embassies to obtain an initial overview of opinions about the nature and experience of multinational companies in each country. These interviews were reinforced through further interviews in the UK and Germany and with relevant international organizations.

The case study interviews were based on a semi-structured questionnaire to ensure comparability across cases while allowing sufficient flexibility to incorporate the company-specific aspects of each case. Separate questionnaires were developed for the headquarters and subsidiary interviews respectively (the questionnaires are reproduced in Appendix 1). The questionnaires were developed on the basis of the analytical framework on FDI and transition set out in Chapter 2. In the headquarters interviews, the aim was to obtain an overview of company global structure and strategy and then to consider first how decisions were taken on new subsidiaries generally and second how and why decisions were taken to invest in central and eastern Europe. The interviews then addressed issues of experience in central and eastern Europe and relations between the headquarters and the CEE subsidiary. The CEE subsidiary interviews focused more directly on the experience of establishing and operating the subsidiary, including the subsidiary's views of headquarters motivation and relations with headquarters.

Chapters 5 to 14 present the individual cases – three in the Czech Republic, four in Hungary and three in Poland. Chapter 15 then assesses the lessons from the cases.

5

Glaxo-Wellcome plc

Overview

This is the case of a large UK multinational enterprise – Glaxo[1] – and its investment in the Czech Republic. The company is, since its recent merger with Wellcome, the world's largest pharmaceutical manufacturer. Its biggest market is the United States and it has subsidiaries in 56 countries. The company's activities in eastern Europe represent strategic investments aimed at establishing and expanding market share in these emerging markets. In the Czech Republic, Glaxo established a subsidiary as a limited liability company in 1993 – previously, there had only been a representative office. This is a case of a company aiming to establish and expand market share in a market that offers new sales opportunities not only because the Czech economy has become a more open market economy but also because the combined processes of political and economic transition have led to changes in the structure, organization and regulation of the health sector. The particular characteristics of the health sector mean that pharmaceutical companies, in addition to an emphasis on brand name, marketing and research and development (R&D), have to respond and act strategically with respect to government and regulatory structures, and with respect to the learning and knowledge base of their customers – doctors and patients. In the case of investment in the Czech Republic, this set of issues – government, regulation, marketing, brand name, R&D and education – is also strongly influenced by the process of transition.

Glaxo worldwide

The industrial sector

The pharmaceutical industry is oligopolistic and R&D-intensive. The time needed for bringing the developed product to the market is much longer than in other industries, due to the demanding testing and registration procedures. Intellectual property rights – in particular, patent protection – are therefore critical for companies if the long lead-times and high R&D expenditures are to be profitably recouped. The pharmaceuticals sector is highly regulated in most countries. The regulations are mostly concerned with prices, drug approval procedures and marketing techniques such as promotion and distribution.

Two main groups of competitors in the sector can be identified: producers of original products based on their own extensive R&D, and producers of generic (unbranded) products based on the expired patents of major drugs. Competition between the large multinationals producing original drugs is characterized by different product portfolios, as the cost implications of developing new drugs mean that firms have to concentrate on a small core of products. Hence, firms will tend to have different competitors for each drug in their portfolio. Competition from the generic manufacturers is cost-based and, because R&D costs are not involved, the multinationals will tend to find it impossible to match their prices overall. In spite of high costs and delayed payoffs, successful companies from the R&D-intensive group are potentially highly profitable because high costs of product development, patents and government regulations provide barriers to entry, while the generic producers may also benefit from regulatory barriers.

Government policies on reimbursement of drugs are crucial to the success or failure of a company in any country, but particularly in low- and middle-income countries, where the ability of the patient to pay for drugs is significantly reduced. Policies on private health insurance and the extent to which they exist at all are also of great significance. The effectiveness of legal protection for intellectual property rights is a central issue for the R&D-intensive companies.

A general trend of greater patient involvement and self-medication has increased the market in non-prescription drugs, in comparison to the market in ethical drugs, which are available only through a physician's prescription.

Growth has decelerated somewhat towards the mid-1990s. Total growth was 6 per cent in the year to 31 March 1994, compared to 10 per cent a year before, in a market worth £130 billion globally. The deceleration was most pronounced in the major industrialized nations of western Europe, the United States and Japan (which collectively form 84 per cent of the world market), as governments and health care providers attempted to reduce the rate of growth in their expenditure on health care.

Competitors

The major global competitors for Glaxo are SmithKline Beecham, Merck, Astra Pharmaceuticals, Schering, Eli Lilly and Bayer. Competition among these companies is essentially based on product characteristics and speed of innovation. Generic manufacturers exist in every country. As they have no R&D costs to recoup, producers of generic pharmaceuticals are able to undercut prices significantly. The quality of their products may not be of an equivalent standard across the full product range but they have a huge cost advantage, especially in the case of some of the state-owned pharmaceutical firms in central and eastern Europe (CEE), who have often sold at a loss. Hence, any competition between a research-based company and generic manufacturers cannot be price-based and must instead focus on issues such as quality, reduced treatment time and fewer side-effects, with the aim of ensuring full reimbursement from the government and preferential choice of their drugs by doctors.

Glaxo's share of the world market increased to 3.9 per cent in 1994 from 3.8 per cent in the previous year. Glaxo shares the position of largest prescription medicine company in the world with Merck.

Products, portfolio and sales

There are five categories of drugs that make up Glaxo's global portfolio (Figure 5.1):

- gastrointestinal drugs, including Glaxo's anti-ulcerant Zantac;
- respiratory drugs, including Ventolin, Becotide, Flixotide, Serevent, bronchodilators and corticosteroids;
- systemic antibiotics, including Zinnat, an oral cephalosporin, and Fortum and Zinacef, injectable and powder treatments for bacterial infections;
- anti-emesis drugs, including Zofran, Glaxo's 5-HT_3 antagonist for the prevention of nausea and vomiting associated with chemotherapy used in the treatment of cancer;
- anti-migraine drugs, including Imigran/Imitrex, which offers therapy for severe or frequent migraine and cluster headaches.

Glaxo's portfolio of drugs is dominated by Zantac, which is the world's best-selling medicine by a large margin. Its share of the world anti-ulcerant market in the 1994 was 35 per cent, which was a decrease

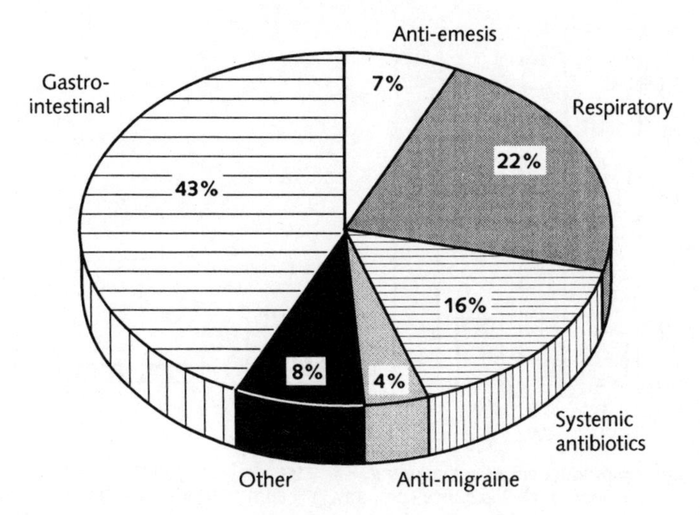

Figure 5.1 Percentage of sales from each category of drug

of 1.8 percentage points on the previous year. Glaxo has five products in the world's top 50 medicines, including Zantac. Sales are concentrated in the United States; CEE accounts for only 1 per cent of sales worldwide (Figure 5.2), though it is nonetheless an important region for Glaxo. One important part of Glaxo's strategy is to develop its portfolio of drugs in order to maintain its market share when the Zantac patent expires.

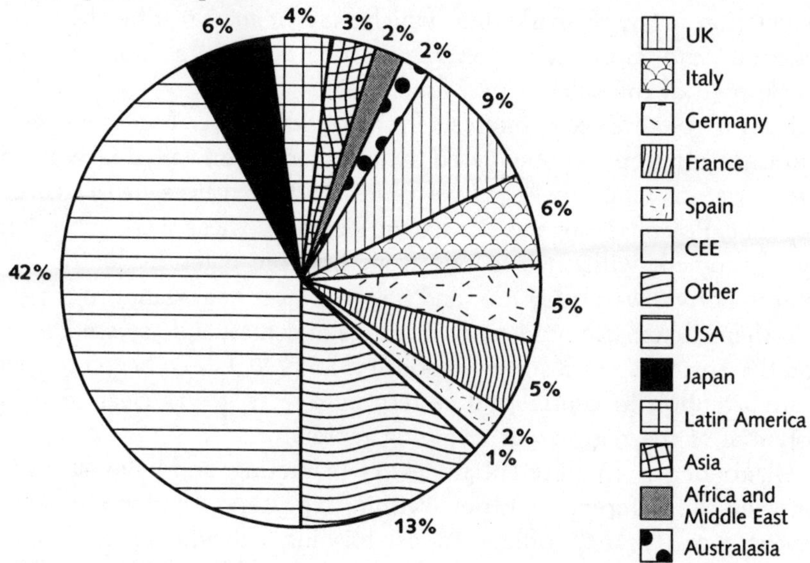

Figure 5.2 Geographical distribution of sales

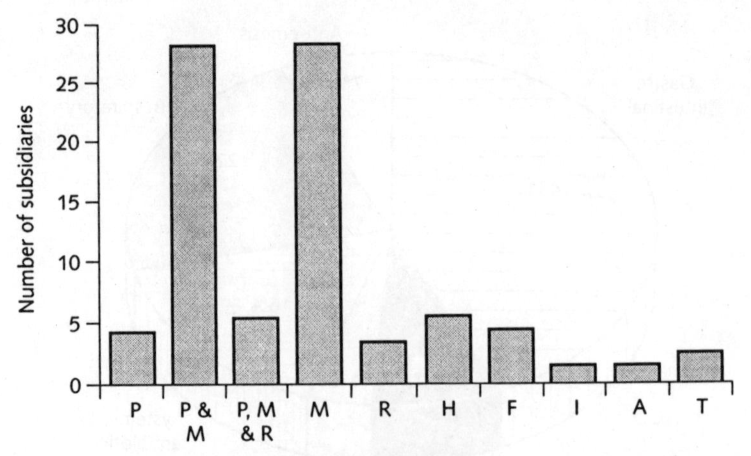

Figure 5.3 Functions of the Glaxo offices

Organisational structure

Glaxo's head office is in the UK and it has offices in a number of strategic locations responsible for the interests of different geographical areas. There are 82 subsidiaries, of which 37 are involved with production, 61 with marketing, which may or may not be their sole function, and eight with R&D. Figure 5.3 gives a more specific breakdown of the subsidiaries' functions.

Prior to 1989, Glaxo's interests in the Middle East, Africa and central and eastern Europe were covered by an organization called Glaxomed. Glaxo had a minor presence via representative offices in the Czech Republic, Poland, Hungary, Russia and Bulgaria. These were controlled by Glaxomed, with instructions from London. Sales in central and eastern Europe were very low, and only the most important drugs were sold there. Glaxo did not licence its drugs to central and eastern Europe and the area was not a strategic priority. In 1990, Glaxo began to give more attention to central and eastern Europe as it was clear that the potential of the region was changing rapidly.

Glaxo began to differentiate in its marketing and sales strategy between the different countries. Within two years it had moved from having small branch offices to establishing subsidiaries as limited liability companies in Hungary, the Czech Republic and Poland. The new subsidiaries were fully integrated into Glaxo's structures and had substantial responsibility and scope at a local level.

The decision to invest in the Czech Republic

Glaxo decided to establish a subsidiary in the Czech Republic in 1993 to take advantage of the expanding market opportunities there. Central and eastern Europe – and China – are seen to represent major market opportunities, while competition is intensifying in Western markets. Glaxo had had a representative office in Czechoslovakia for 15 years prior to the decision to establish a subsidiary. Although this was only a small office and sales were not large, this prior experience was beneficial when the subsidiary was established, both as the office already had some knowledge of the country and the market, and as Glaxo already had an established image and its name and products were known to some extent in the country.

Glaxo's decision to establish a full subsidiary presence in the Czech Republic was, therefore, primarily driven by market opportunities. It was also seen as important to have a physical presence in the country, even though the Czech operation was only for marketing and sales, and not for production. The market was not considered large enough to justify a production base; furthermore, Glaxo had sufficient spare capacity in its other production sites to supply the market.

The importance of locating in the market relates to various characteristics of the pharmaceuticals market. Government regulation of the market – including drug registration, reimbursement categories and patent protection – is central. If a company is located in the market, it is in a better position to establish contacts and to enter into discussions with the government. This is particularly important during a period of major change in the health sector, as companies wish both to be up to date on regulatory and organizational changes, and to have the opportunity to present their views on desirable structures and changes. A local presence contributes substantially to marketing and sales strategy, which requires both an understanding of the market and a strategy of educating and persuading the market. Local knowledge is always important but, in a period of major transition, local interaction, understanding and influence is central. This local knowledge is important for all levels of the company, from senior management through to the sales force. Furthermore, a local company is able to control and develop an effective and efficient sales force, well integrated into overall corporate strategy, whereas if a company is only importing, marketing may be much more diffuse.

Structure of the Czech subsidiary

Initially there was one office for the whole of Czechoslovakia. When the country split at the beginning of 1993, it was decided that the two countries would still be treated as one entity for operational purposes. Hence, when the limited liability Czech company was established on 19 April 1993, a branch office was formed in the Slovak Republic; this office is a separate entity but reports directly to the general manager of Glaxo in Prague. There are 82 people in the Czech Republic office and 22 in the Slovak Republic office. Finance and administration are separate functions in each operation, while human resource management and information technology are partly shared but mainly local. The medical side is closely interlinked, as the requirements for dossiers for the registration of drugs and for clinical trials are very similar. There are separate sales forces for the two countries, though they come together for training. Marketing is done for both markets in the same way, although there are regional differences. The general manager, commercial manager and finance manager are all expatriates; other management positions are filled by local managers.

Organizational links to head office

After 1989, strategic responsibility for the development of Glaxo's activities in central and eastern Europe and the CIS was located in Glaxo's Rome office. From May 1995, this responsibility was moved back to the London headquarters.

The area director for Glaxo Central and Eastern Europe in Rome reported back directly to the chief executive or to one of the board of directors of Glaxo in the UK. The Rome office was small – at its largest, it comprised five people. It was a purely managerial, strategy-focused organization – necessary services were provided from the UK whenever they were required. The Rome office's responsibilities ranged from management recruitment to strategy development. Given its small size, its function can be seen in some ways as similar to that of a consultancy agency, in providing assistance and expertise, but with overall authority and decision-making powers. The main focus of the Rome office concerned overall strategy, marketing and finance. There was also some organization of management training.

Each local manager in central and eastern Europe is responsible for producing – on an annual basis – a five-year strategic plan covering sales plans, products, marketing, staff and financial resources, and so forth. This plan was then discussed and agreed with the Rome office. Proposals for investments come from the subsidiaries but were agreed with the Rome office and, from there, with the Glaxo headquarters. Thus, although the Rome office had overall responsibility, the subsidiaries were given substantial autonomy and the main aim of the Rome office was to facilitate rather than control. The Rome office communicated with the subsidiaries through phone, fax and electronic mail and through frequent travel to the region. It also organized meetings to bring together some of the managers from the different CEE countries and organized workshops with the Product Strategy Group.

The financing arrangements of the Czech subsidiary are linked directly to the head office in London. The subsidiary reports to London with the product costs, monthly cash flow and accounts, quarterly expenses, annual budget and five-year budget plan. The finance managers for all the branches need to be approved by London. There is a lot of regulation on the financial side and they receive support from head office for the treasury and legal assets of the business.

Cash management is centralized and the subsidiary is not allowed to run cash balances. All cash balances must be sent back to London. Glaxo as a company has always been very cash liquid and the head office has financed everything. Hence the Czech subsidiary has no loans or overdrafts with local or foreign banks.

Company strategy in the Czech Republic

Glaxo's main strategies are aimed first at reinforcing the physical presence of the group in markets where it already sells its products – this includes diffusing product information and knowledge to doctors. Second, its pricing strategy allows decisions about pricing of drugs to be flexible within guidelines set by the company. This allows some local autonomy. Similarly, promotion and marketing are based on the same ethical principles in all countries but, within these strict guidelines, marketing companies can vary priorities and tactics according to local circumstances.

Products

Glaxo worldwide has a portfolio largely biased toward its key drug, Zantac. This could have been granted patent protection in the Czech or Slovak Republics in the 1980s and early 1990s according to previous patent legislation. From 1991, the legislation changed and it became possible to file for patents in Czechoslovakia only if the drug had not been sold before in the country or if no generic was already available. A Czech company had launched a generic before 1991, and so patenting was not possible; the Czech company also sells at close to production cost.

Glaxo has therefore had to find a strategy to compete without Zantac in the Czech Republic. Initially, Glaxo sold two main products, Fortum (an antibiotic) and Zofran (an anti-emetic). These were very successful. The technology for Fortum is quite advanced and this makes it difficult to copy; Glaxo is optimistic that this will protect it. Some other Glaxo products, such as Zinnat (an oral antibiotic), a range of anti-asthmatics and one injectable antibiotic, do not have the life-saving features of Fortum and Zofran. Therefore they were replaced with similar or inferior drugs in the past. Hence, marketing these drugs requires more communication with doctors about their characteristics and performance, and so a greater learning period is needed. Their overall aim in the Czech Republic is to build a balanced portfolio of products which will include anti-asthmatics, antibiotics and new chemical entities. Despite the popularity of Fortum and Zofran, Glaxo is reducing their relative weight in the portfolio to make it more balanced, and is increasing the share of other drugs. This strategy is being observed with interest by other parts of Glaxo as one potential model that could be followed once Glaxo has to reduce its dependence on Zantac.

Market share and competition

Glaxo's sales in the Czech Republic are growing and the company is performing successfully. However, according to Czech law, companies selling imported drugs cannot make a gross profit, as the system permits only a minimum mark-up. This legislation is resulting in the Czech government losing corporation tax. Glaxo's market share in 1995 was about 1.3 per cent. In 1994 it was in third position among the Western companies and probably in the top 12 overall. In value terms, Czech and Slovak manufacturers have together about 73 per cent of the market, and, in volume, about 39 per cent. The generic manufacturers, therefore, have a dominant presence. Some of these Czech companies have formed joint ventures with Western companies, but Glaxo has decided not to produce in the market at present. Some Czech companies are technically quite good but most production units still do not comply with the standards of good manufacturing practice. Given government interest in their survival, they should be able to continue to stay in the market. It is, in fact, in the interests of foreign companies that there is a strong local industry, because of the role of government policy and government funding in the health care sector. Government funding policies might be different if the industry constituted only foreign companies. In Russia, for example, the local industry has collapsed; unless it revives, drug purchasing may focus on cheap, developing country suppliers.

Reimbursement of drugs and relations to government

The ability to sell pharmaceutical products in any market depends to a large extent on the level of reimbursement of the drug and prescribing limitations. If a drug is fully reimbursed, this means that the government – or insurance company – agrees to pay the drug company in full for the drug that is prescribed. Less than full reimbursement implies that the patient will have to pay a percentage of the cost. If a drug is totally delisted, then the full burden of the drug cost falls to the patient.

When Glaxo started in the Czech Republic, there was no reimbursement or insurance system in place. A reimbursement system began in 1992 and problems were immediately created because technical resources were limited and the government had difficulties producing a decree and implementing such a system. The first issue for Glaxo was to get all its drugs onto the reimbursement lists and then to ensure that they received the highest possible amount of reimbursement. Typically, drugs classified as essential are completely reimbursed, and for others there are various limits – the range of reimbursement can be anything from 0 to 100 per cent. If there is a generic drug available, then it is used as the standard benchmark for pricing, and usually it is impossible to compete with the price that the generic manufacturer is charging. In the Czech Republic, as in other transitional economies, a drug that is not fully reimbursed is difficult to market. Often the doctor will not even give the patient the option of buying the drug; instead, a generic will be prescribed which will usually be much cheaper.

There is one large health insurance company in the Czech Republic and approximately 30 smaller ones. The policy of reimbursement is dealt with by the Ministry of Health in collaboration with the largest company. The general manager and the chief medical officer of the Glaxo subsidiary have regular contact and discussion with the government to try to explain the characteristics and qualities of their drugs and why they justify the additional costs relative to cheaper options. A further issue is whether drugs are confined to hospital use or can also be prescribed by general practitioners or sold over the counter. Glaxo has been successful in getting its major products reimbursed; however, the system is not static. Health insurance regulations change quite often, which means that the company has to keep reassessing its strategy and keep up to date. Furthermore, not only is the Czech Republic a relatively poor country, but there was already a system of fairly strong constraints on prescribing which has influenced current regulations limiting the number of prescriptions that may be issued. Overall, the governments in central and eastern Europe are seen to have understood the politics and economics of the health care market very quickly, including how to restrain consumption and prices. Apart from the lower income levels, the health care markets in the Czech Republic, Hungary, Poland and Slovakia are already seen to be very similar to Western markets in terms of rules, competition and health care.

Marketing and sales

Marketing is a key component of Glaxo's activities. Given its high-quality and innovative products, and balanced product portfolio, marketing and diffusion of information is central. Marketing has to be interpreted broadly in the context of the pharmaceuticals sector: it involves a critical role for the government in terms of registration and reimbursement (as discussed above), contact and interaction with the medical profession, and, to some extent, the final consumer – the patient. The role of the sales force in communicating with doctors is particularly important. Much of the emphasis in marketing has to be on information and education, unlike in many other sectors, where persuasion has the central emphasis. The companies are dealing with highly educated and skilled people – both in government and in the medical profession – and are selling products which affect the public's health. Marketing therefore has to emphasize and explain the characteristics of the product, and its performance relative to competing options. This requires a sophisticated, well-trained sales force (as discussed further below) and a well-developed sales and marketing strategy.

Given the close interconnections between marketing and sales, these are brought together in the Czech Republic in one department headed by a commercial manager. Glaxo's overall aim is to widen the knowledge base of the medical sector about its products and to change outdated prescribing habits. There is seen to be substantial scope to do this as, prior to 1989, both information on, and availability of, drugs was limited. Nonetheless, one of the biggest challenges is to persuade doctors to use new procedures and drugs. There is also a question of whether doctors will advise patients that they should spend their own money on a higher-quality drug where full reimbursement is not available. Differences in attitudes across markets are also seen. Glaxo sees, for example, some similarities between the UK and the Czech Republic in their use of older – first-line – antibiotics, while in Slovakia there is wider use of more modern antibiotics.

Glaxo is taking a 'twin-track' approach to marketing in the Czech Republic. On the one hand, it has a structure of product managers and area managers who develop and implement the marketing and sales strategy and, on the other hand, it has a specific and more indirect strategy of promoting health care information and education through a separate entity that it has established called Mediforum. The product managers are responsible for developing the sales strategy and the area managers are responsible for its implementation. There need to be close links between these managers. Glaxo separates the Czech Republic into six areas to implement its sales strategy. There is a sales force of 30, and six area managers or team leaders. The company employs sales representatives who have some medical training, but further training is provided, as discussed below. The activities of the sales force are carefully monitored – the number of calls and visits made, the range of specialists, hospitals and doctors visited – and this information is fed into the monthly meetings of the sales and marketing managers and teams.

Mediforum, although a part of Glaxo, is separate from its day-to-day commercial environment, and Glaxo has no commercial interest in it. The role of Mediforum, which stands for medical forum, is as a general health information organization. Glaxo sees it as important to share and expand medical knowledge in an emerging market. Furthermore, Mediforum indicates long-run commitment by Glaxo and may help to create goodwill. To the extent that doctors do not respond well to direct marketing and sales methods, it may also provide a more indirect way of influencing prescribing towards higher-quality but higher-price drugs. This indirect and more long-term approach is relevant to the transitional economies; it is not a typical approach in Glaxo's Western markets. Most of Glaxo's competitors, it believes, are not doing anything as in-depth as this.

The overall aim of Mediforum is to share knowledge with doctors in major therapy areas, to set up projects concerning new treatments, to provide guidelines and information and to cascade this down to the vast majority of prescribers. There are two major programmes undertaken by Mediforum, one on antibiotics prescribing, which is done within the guidelines of the Czech government, and an asthma education programme. Education in the field of asthma diagnosis and treatment is at a low level globally, not just in the Czech Republic. The main focus of the education programme in this field is to try and change the attitudes of the doctors about the type of drugs that they should prescribe. For example, the Czech Republic tends to follow the older methods of treatment in taking tablets for asthma, instead of the newer types of treatment involving inhaled products, which 80 per cent of the world's asthma sufferers use.

One of the advantages of Mediforum is that it provides a chance to bring together doctors from both the Czech and the Slovak Republics. Often these doctors have studied and worked together for years, and they welcome the opportunity to meet again at conferences.

Training

Glaxo has found that doctors in the Czech Republic respond more positively to sales staff who have a medical background. Hence it has been important to recruit people with at least a secondary medical education or those who have worked as nurses, scientists and, in some instances, as doctors themselves. It is possible to recruit such high-calibre staff for sales jobs, as state salaries are relatively low. Training on sales and marketing – and on finance – is particularly important, as these are areas where there is a lack of relevant previous experience. Sales representatives are given six weeks of initial training. There is then additional training four or five times a year. Throughout the company, the training needs of individuals are assessed in the context of their departments. Training is divided into three main areas: medical, marketing and selling skills. Training is given on management skills, time management and presentation skills, product training and clinical trials. More generally, staff have to learn, and be encouraged to take, responsibility.

Wages

Salary levels are about two to three times the average level for the Czech Republic. However, although Glaxo's wage levels are good, it is not the highest payer in the sector. In Prague, where unemployment is low, it can have difficulties in attracting skilled staff. There are no trade unions. The general manager is responsible for decisions on wages, based on the recommendations of department managers. Sales representatives and area and product managers receive a basic wage and a bonus according to performance.

R&D and product development

There is no substantive R&D in the Czech Republic, but medical trials are undertaken, and have been an important part of Glaxo's work in the Czech Republic. The Czech and Slovak subsidiaries assist with trials of both new and old drugs. Trials for old drugs are important as, even after a drug has been approved, there can be new indications, adverse events or responses – perhaps only once in 10,000 cases. Trials can also provide further information on the efficiency of drugs over time.

There are two reasons for undertaking trials in the Czech Republic: first, there are more subjects for trials in the Czech and Slovak Federal Republics and trials are cheaper to administer than in western Europe. Second, clinical trials undertaken in the Czech Republic may help to encourage prescribers to become more familiar with the product.

The Czech subsidiary works with Glaxo's central R&D department in its drug trials. For new drug trials, there are always both Glaxo central R&D and local monitors. Procedures for clinical trials were already in place prior to 1989, as the key physicians in Czechoslovakia were able to visit the United States and return to implement US practices, which were subsequently developed.

Conclusion

This is a case of a company responding swiftly to new market growth opportunities in central and eastern Europe. The case illustrates, in particular, the challenges posed in expanding in a high-technology, highly regulated sector in a transitional economy. There are strong interdependencies between regulation, marketing and education, and benefits to be gained from locating in the market. Glaxo has applied its existing marketing and managerial expertise and has also developed specific marketing strategies appropriate to the Czech Republic, with successful results.

Note

1. This case study was undertaken before the logistics of the Glaxo merger with Wellcome had taken place; hence the company will be referred to throughout as 'Glaxo', as the case focuses on the running of only Glaxo's venture in the Czech Republic and not on the merger of the two firms.

6

United Technologies Otis Division

Overview

This is the case of the US multinational enterprise – United Technologies – that is the world's largest manufacturer of lifts (elevators). United Technologies (UTC) invested in the Czech Republic through its Otis division to take advantage both of the market opportunities post-1989 and of cheap labour and material costs. The company entered relatively early – it was the third large investment in Czechoslovakia with the aim of securing market share both in new lifts and in lift-servicing contracts. By investing in the market, it also avoided import tariffs, although this is now no longer possible. Otis formed a joint venture with an existing Czech company which needed extensive restructuring. The strategy for the joint venture – Tranza-Otis – is that it should be the main production location for central and eastern Europe (CEE), and not only for the Czech Republic.

United Technologies

UTC is a holding company that comprises five operating divisions: Pratt & Whitney, which produces commercial and military jet engines and other related services for aircraft; Flight Systems, a company producing military and commercial helicopters and controls and propellers systems for jet engines; Carrier, which manufactures heating, ventilating and air-conditioning equipment for industrial and residential buildings; Automotive, which produces automotive electrical distribution systems; and Otis, concerned with the production of lifts, escalators and shuttle systems, and their installation, maintenance, repair and modernization.

Otis: market share and competition

Otis was founded in 1853. Now it is the world's largest manufacturer and servicer of lifts and escalators. At the end of 1993, the company's share of the global market for new equipment (in dollar terms) was 21 per cent, and this was about twice that of its nearest competitor. More than 80 per cent of Otis's revenues are generated from outside the United States, and it has been very active in establishing operations in emerging markets. In Europe, it has a permanent market share of about 25–30 per cent.

Otis's main competitors in Europe are Thyssen, Schindler and Kone – they are all producers of lifts and are also involved with servicing. There are some small companies that produce parts for lifts, located mainly in Italy. There are also a few medium-sized German lift manufacturers. The large companies also have many small competitors on the lift-servicing side of the market in most countries.

Organizational structure

There are four operational divisions of Otis: North America and Canada; Pacific and Asia; Latin America; and Europe – European Trans-continental Operations (ETO). The overall headquarters of Otis is also located in the United States where it has a small staff which coordinates the four regional divisions, and a central research and development (R&D) facility. The European headquarters is located in Paris and is responsible not only for Europe, but also for the CIS, the Middle East and parts of Africa.

Within Europe, the Austrian subsidiary is responsible for exports to all territories of CEE where there is no Otis company or assigned company for exports. The Austrian subsidiary deals with Albania, the former Yugoslavia, Romania, Bulgaria, Slovenia, Hungary, Poland the Czech Republic and Slovakia.

There are four vice-presidents together with the European president in the Paris headquarters; the vice-presidents are responsible respectively for northern Europe, western Europe, central and eastern Europe and the Middle East. Otis has about 35 operating companies in about 20 countries in Europe. The headquarters has several main coordinating functions, including: marketing, finance, human resources, legal, field activities, quality and manufacturing. This current organizational structure reflects a restructuring in the early 1990s, done largely in response to mixed patterns of growth and recession in

European operations and independently of the general restructuring of UTC in 1992. In western Europe in 1991–2 there had been some recession, especially in the new equipment market in the UK, but this did not inhibit the strategy in central and eastern Europe.

The managing director of each subsidiary is responsible for the profit and loss outcome of the subsidiary, and reports to the appropriate area vice-president. The subsidiaries also have lines of communication from their functional specialists, such as marketing, to the headquarters' functional directors. The local managing directors can approve small investments; larger investments will go to the Otis vice-presidents, the Otis president and, finally, for the largest investments, back to UTC.

Company strategy

The overall Otis European strategy, as the market leader, is to act to maintain and improve its position as market leader, and its market share. Globally, it sets internal targets regarding the areas and countries in which it needs to improve, and from this it develops a broad overall global strategy. Within each of the four regional operations there are different approaches, as the markets and countries are different and strategies must be localized. The strategy on the regional operational level needs to be complementary with each individual country strategy.

Otis believes that it has a number of competitive strengths. These strengths include the following.

- *Size.* The scale of manufacturing for new equipment is important. Within Europe, this means that different factories concentrate on certain specialities in order to gain economies of scale.
- *Service competitiveness.* Otis has a good service network and a very good call-out record. It tries to make call-outs within 10–20 minutes and within a maximum of one hour.
- *Consistent strategy.* Otis has a stable workforce and expertise. Consistency and continuity help it to understand the markets within which it is operating and to make its business professional.
- *Technology and innovation* are two of Otis's big strengths; it has a wide range of products, from high-speed lifts for skyscrapers to dumb-waiters for the hotel and catering industry.
- *Quality.* Competition is on both price and quality, and Otis puts an emphasis on achieving high quality standards.

Otis has a global human resource strategy for its top management, coordinated from the United States. Managers may be moved all over the world, and this is seen as providing new blood and dynamism.

The decision to invest in central and eastern Europe and in the Czech Republic

Otis had experience of operating in eastern Europe and Russia prior to 1989. Primarily, it exported to the region, but it also had some collaboration with local companies and some local offices. This was managed from the Austrian subsidiary. Consequently, Otis already had some knowledge of these markets, and top management was very open to the opportunities that developed from the late 1980s. In 1987, discussions were already underway with a company in the Soviet Union on forming a joint venture. From 1989, it was clear that there were many new opportunities for investment. Otis, therefore, saw the decision to invest as one of how, rather than whether, to enter the market. Its first joint ventures were in the former East Germany and in Hungary in 1990, followed by the Soviet Union in July 1990.

The agreement to form a joint venture in the former Czechoslovakia was made in September 1991 after about a year of negotiation. Otis was looking for a location in central Europe to act as a major production site for the area. Czechoslovakia was considered attractive both because of the stability of its transition process and because it had more installed lifts, about 110,000, than Poland, despite its smaller population. Low labour costs were an attractive and important feature of the country and there were other advantages to local production, both avoiding tariff barriers and forming strong local links to establish a good servicing network. Equally important, despite 45 years of communism, Czechoslovakia still had a strong industrial tradition.

Tranza, the joint venture partner, was the major lift manufacturer, having a monopolistic position in the market, and so appeared to provide a promising way of entering the market. Otis now has joint ventures in Russia, Ukraine, Hungary, Poland and the Czech Republic, and the Czech Republic is seen as the key production site for central Europe.

Otis gathers relevant data and information on each country before investing, to assess political and economic stability, credit rating, support from the World Bank and so forth. Investment incentives are not seen as important. Apart from local production costs, key issues are the expected future development of the housing market, which relates strongly to changes in income per head and to the overall population size. Otis tends to enter markets through joint ventures, although it does have some greenfield sites. Joint ventures provide a better means of acquiring market share and market information, and of building up local service networks. Existing firms will have existing customers and networks which can provide an important base, and this is more important than the particular production characteristics of the joint venture partner.

The joint venture negotiations and the investment

Tranza was the biggest manufacturer of lifts in Czechoslovakia. It had some of the best facilities of any firm in eastern Europe. The company was created in 1989 when a previous state monopoly, Chudim, was dismantled. Tranza consisted of four plants: Pragolift in Prague; a lift- and escalator-manufacturing plant in Břeclav; an escalator-manufacturing plant and foundry in Poštorná; and a small elevator and electromechanical components manufacturer in Brno. The main plant of interest to Otis was the lift production plant in Břeclav. The facilities were far from Western standards. The buildings were crumbling and there were lifts rusting in the forecourt. The technology being used was obsolete by Western standards and there was only one type of lift produced.

In 1990, Pragolift became independent and formed a joint venture with Kone. Both Otis and its competitors, Schindler and Kone, approached Tranza to form a joint venture for the remaining plants. Tranza was facing potential bankruptcy in the new market environment. It was aware that much of its technology was obsolete. With the privatization legislation being developed, the only way it could survive was by having a strong partner. Saving jobs was its top priority. The Tranza management was keen to move quickly to establish a joint venture, as the legislation was due to change at the end of 1991, creating uncertainty.

Tranza decided that it wanted to negotiate with Otis. It evaluated what it knew about the three companies, Otis, Schindler and Kone, and spoke to some of Otis's customers to see if they were satisfied with their service, and then chose Otis. Otis was not interested in the plant in Poštorná and negotiations were undertaken for a joint venture with the Břeclav and Brno plants. Discussions were rather lengthy, taking about one year.

The joint venture agreement was signed in September 1991, and restructuring began in October. The joint venture was called Tranza-

Otis; Otis had a 51 per cent share and Tranza 49 per cent. Tranza-Otis included the two lift companies in Brno and Břeclav, and Tranza retained ownership of the conveyors plant in Poštorná and the foundry. Tranza itself was not privatized until 1994.

During the joint venture negotiations, the two sides worked on a feasibility study showing how the joint venture could operate in the new environment. The joint venture agreement went through the Ministry of Privatization, and other ministries (Industry and Trade, and Finance) were also involved. Negotiations focused on the feasibility plan and on what Otis said it was going to invest in Tranza, on the one hand, and on what Tranza was contributing, on the other. Discussions on Tranza's contribution revolved around the valuation of the plant, equipment, receivables, work-in-progress and buildings. The final agreement was that Otis would pay $13.5 million for a 51 per cent share in the joint venture. This money would be used for restructuring and was not, therefore, simply a price paid for ownership. Otis was not willing to make a commitment not to lay off any workers, and this was accepted.

Tranza itself was privatized through the voucher privatization process and is now owned partly by private shareholders (23 per cent), and partly by a reserve fund (5 per cent), the remainder being split between four investment funds. Eighty per cent of Tranza's assets are accounted for by its 49 per cent share in Tranza-Otis. Otis might increase its ownership share by purchasing shares from Tranza, but it currently achieves sufficient control through its 51 per cent share.

Once the package was finalized, the joint venture was started and Otis immediately introduced a new business plan and started the restructuring programme, not just in the factory but in all areas: finance, administration and marketing.

Markets and competition

In terms of market share in the Czech Republic, there are two parameters to be considered, the number of units with maintenance contracts and the number of new units sold. The total market for units in the Czech and Slovak Republics is around 1,500 per year and there are around 110,000 units that require servicing.

Otis maintains 11,500 units and produces 500 new units a year. Schindler maintains 15,000 units and produces 120–150 new units a year. Kone maintains around 8,000 units and installs less than 100 new units a year. Otis, therefore, has a market share of about 9 per cent in servicing and 30 per cent in new lifts. Exports are about one-fifth of sales. The industry is very competitive because of the large number of small local companies, about 600, mainly service oriented. This market structure means that it is more difficult to build up a nationwide sales team for maintenance contracts, but Otis has done so. Nonetheless, competition in each local area is strong. Government decisions have also affected the structure of the market. Otis aimed at one point to buy a company servicing elevators in Prague, but the government decided to let Schindler buy it, because of Otis's existing strength in the market.

Tranza-Otis company strategy

The initial phase of Otis's plan was a radical restructuring of the plant, the production facilities, the finance department and the sales department. The strategy was to produce for the domestic market, to service lifts within the Czech and Slovak Republics and to supply other markets in central Europe, both elevators and spare parts. However, there was a large (and larger than expected) fall in the demand for lifts. The market fell from about 6,000 to 1,500 new units a year in the former Czechoslovakia. Otis had expected a possible 50 per cent fall. This large fall was due in part to a collapse in the social housing market; government was actually closing flats and so maintenance possibilities were also reduced. Tranza had previously produced about 5,000 lifts a year (85 per cent of the market). Furthermore, the restitution process in the Czech Republic meant that people were often unsure about who owned property, and so it was unclear who was responsible for lift maintenance. Other, new owners of property often did not have the money to pay for maintenance. This led to Otis being in a situation where it was producing at less than 50 per cent of capacity and so it looked elsewhere to gain contracts for the Czech plant as well as implementing its restructuring strategy.

In 1993 it had an opportunity to supply to Otis's German subsidiary near Hannover, which made escalators and travelators and was looking for subcontractors to make the structure of the escalator, which is labour-intensive. Tranza had previously been producing conveyors but the market for them had collapsed. Currently Tranza-Otis is supplying 75 per cent of the German company's requirements; this will probably increase to 100 per cent.

Restructuring

A restructuring strategy was implemented in 1991, immediately after the joint venture, Tranza-Otis, had been agreed. The restructuring strategy involved swift changes in finance, sales and marketing, restructuring of the plants and the establishment of a branch service network. Otis introduced expatriate managers, 'twinned' with Czech managers, in the three key areas of production, finance and overall general management. Initially, there was a local Czech general manager, but this was not successful and an expatriate manager took over.

Otis created a commercial department to cover sales and marketing. Previously, Tranza had no understanding of marketing or of what constituted a proper sales contract. Otis acted quickly to create proper contracts with a well-defined payments system. Tranza had about 450 lifts in stock, which it said were manufactured on a contract basis.

Upon asking for contracts, Otis was shown a few letters of intent and a few letters asking for quotations but nothing that constituted a proper contract. It created contracts and divided the payments system into three parts: downpayment, payment when the materials arrived and payment after installation. It was a six-month process to make people understand the necessity of the contracting system. Financially, Tranza was suffering from poor cash management, with about $4 million in receivables outstanding in the balance sheet and a lack of cash flow. Under the guidance of the expatriate finance manager, a task force was immediately created to collect all the money owed to the company. The collectors were paid a percentage of the money collected as an incentive; 70 per cent of the total debt was collected. Billing was immediately transferred from sales to finance and automated within a week. Over the first six months, a finance manager from Tranza shadowed the expatriate manager and learnt as he slowly introduced all the Otis accountancy procedures. The local manager is now in charge of running the finances in the Czech Republic, while there is an expatriate finance manager responsible for a number of CEE countries. Overall, the new financial structures and the physical restructuring have substantially improved the position of Tranza-Otis and not all the $13.5 million invested has yet been used.

Closing the Brno factory and retrenchment at Břeclav

At the time of the joint venture, Tranza-Otis consisted of two factories, one in Břeclav and one in Brno. Given the market prospects, this was seen as representing too great a production capacity. The joint venture started on 1 October 1991. The Brno plant produced the electro-mechanical parts (spare parts); hence the aim was to transfer the spare parts production to Břeclav. Otis did not close the Brno plant until September 1992, after production had been transferred. At the same time, the Břeclav plant was restructured to increase efficiency, which also involved job losses. Two hundred people lost their jobs in Brno and 92 in Břeclav.

The closure was a shock for the workforce. Czech law for closing a plant is quite ambiguous. If a company wants to downsize the workforce in a plant, then certain vulnerable people are protected, e.g. the disabled and those close to retirement age. However, if a company closes a factory there is no protection for these groups of people. The first thing Otis needed to do was to convince the management team that this was the right thing to do, and that there was no other choice. Then it needed to make the team believe that it could technically transfer the production process and finally that it could manage the social plan (i.e. redundancies) without too many drawbacks for the employees. Discussions took place in autumn 1991 and the production was fully transferred by June–July 1992. Two people from Brno were kept on and everyone else found a new job very quickly. Otis started an out-placement service and almost no one used it. They informed the employment office; this was the first time that any company had informed it of impending redundancies.

The restructuring and job losses in a small town like Břeclav were more difficult. Otis has had two waves of retrenchment at Břeclav and each time it has had to explain it to the employment offices. The employees were given a good redundancy package and, in general, were paid six months' salary. The restructuring cost of the closure of the Brno plant was approximately $0.4 million but produced a saving of $1 million.

Restructuring the factory

Restructuring the Břeclav factory first required scrapping the large quantities of rusty raw materials that Tranza had kept in order to secure its input supplies. The whole factory was cleaned, and rubbish and unusable raw materials amounting to an entire train load removed. There was only one reason why Otis had considered not closing the Brno factory, and this was the concern about the lack of space at Břeclav; after cleaning, it had more space than it needed.

Otis then substantially reconstructed the factory. It felt that it could not ask for, and explain the importance of, safety, quality and efficiency if the floor was dirty, the lighting did not work and there were holes in the roof. It spent $2 million upgrading offices, painting walls and putting in new floor covering; machines were painted, and new telephones, lighting and heating installed. New technology was introduced throughout the production process. Although the old technology in the plant was seen as largely redundant, it was decided that a substantial number of the old drilling machines could still be used, which meant that the original investment plans could be scaled back.

Otis redesigned all the lines of production and increased quality, the aim being to be more competitive with price and quality. It took the best of the Czech designs and remodelled them. It managed to launch a full range of products in one and a half years. (Within Otis, it normally takes three to five years to launch a new range.)

Otis intends to invest a further $1 million in a new powder painting line. This type of painting has the same quality as metallic painting.

All Otis factories are specialized in part of Otis's overall range in order to benefit from scale economies and learning, and to promote higher quality. The Czech factory is most similar to the French one, focusing on metalwork, although the French one also does some software. Berlin specializes in electronics for the whole of Europe.

Another immediate action undertaken by Otis was to stop the construction of the huge components store (for new equipment), nicknamed the 'cathedral', that was half-way towards completion. Otis introduced the just-in-time concept and, with the fall in demand for lift maintenance, the workshop was no longer needed. The cost of demolishing the 'cathedral' was approximately $15 million, including the write-off of the investment. The issue has become an important one for Otis because the tax authorities are not prepared to give a tax deduction on it. Their attitude is that Otis took the decision to demolish the service centre and so it cannot be deducted from tax. Otis's argument is that it did not take a decision to demolish the building to gain any tax advantage, and if it had not demolished it, it would have been allowed amortization cost and maintenance costs against tax. Otis has now brought this to the attention of the Ministry of Finance and is still hoping to receive some tax concessions.

The total cost of the restructuring was $8 million in investment and $2 million in expenses; consequently, Tranza-Otis has substantial funds from the joint venture agreement for future investment.

Labour force

The labour force is seen as having a good level of technical ability; there are more weaknesses in the sales, commercial, finance and general management areas, where capabilities were initially overestimated. People also need to learn, and be trained, to take more responsibility. Absenteeism is about 8 per cent. There are trade unions representing the labour force, and this system is seen to operate well. Salaries are at an average level for the sector and area; they do experience some problems in attracting staff, both as they are near the Austrian border and as there are two other higher-paying multinationals in the area.

Performance

Tranza-Otis had sales of about $20 million in 1994. Its performance has been better than Otis predicted; the initial three years were expected to be loss-making, with a 7–8-year payback period, but the company was profitable under US accounting standards in the second year and thereafter, and will also show a profit under Czech accounting standards in 1995–6. The difference between the Czech and US outcomes is largely due to writing off the demolition costs of the 'cathedral'.

Development of branch organizations

The Otis worldwide strategy is to be a service company; and, since the demand for new lifts in the Czech Republic is limited, servicing is an increasingly important side of the business. Tranza-Otis acquired some contacts with maintenance companies when the state-owned maintenance companies broke up. Some of the former employees had customers and set up on their own, while others thought that it would be better for them to join a big company. Otis rapidly created 11 branches and managed to jump from servicing 4,000 units to servicing 10,000 units. Around 300–400 people joined the company. This was a quick but unstable process because each local organization had its own type of work method. People were expecting to get a salary but remain the top person in the region. It was difficult to get all the people to work together and this has not yet been fully achieved. Otis invested substantially in training and evaluation aimed at clarifying who had responsibility in different areas.

Conclusions

This is a case of a company moving rapidly into the Czech Republic after 1989 for markets, market share and cost reasons. As the first foreign entrant into the market, Otis benefited from first-mover advantages and has the largest share of production, although it has a slightly lower share of the servicing market than its main competitor, Schindler. Otis undertook substantial restructuring of the joint venture that it established. Performance of the joint venture has been good (better than expected) and the company is profitable under US accounting standards. The housing market, however, is still weak and no upturn is expected in the short term. Nevertheless, the company can look both to better prospects in the medium term and to supplying much of central Europe from its base in the Czech Republic.

7

Pyramid Junger GmbH

This is the case of a small German company, Pyramid Junger Gmbh, which established a subsidiary in the Czech Republic in 1991. The company produces strings for musical instruments of all kinds, except key instruments like the piano, and it produces pitch-pipes for tuning instruments.

Overview

Pyramid is a small firm of about 30 employees located in Bavaria, southern Germany. It is a family firm originally established in the nineteenth century and currently owned by the two Junger brothers. Although small, it is highly competitive in its niche and is a world leader in the production of pitch pipes. This firm may in many ways be seen as a typical example of the successful German small and medium-sized enterprise (SME) sector – the Mittelstand. Many German – and also Austrian – SMEs have invested in central and Eastern Europe (CEE) since 1989, in particular, through investments to nearby locations – from southern Germany to the Czech Republic, from eastern Germany to Poland and from Austria to western Hungary. This represents a rather unusual phenomenon of small firms becoming multinationals, and as such is related particularly to the specific features of the transition in central and eastern Europe and its relationship to the economies of western Europe. This case provides an illustration of this phenomenon.

This is a case of a small firm that competes in and supplies to a large number of international markets. It has faced increasing competition in those markets, in part due to increasing cost competition, particularly from US producers, and also due to lack of effective patent and intellectual property rights protection in certain markets. In order to continue to compete both on price and on quality, this firm invested in the Czech Republic in order to reduce its costs substantially. This has proved to be a successful strategy. The close location of the Czech subsidiary to the parent firm is one part of the success of this strategy.

The musical instruments and equipment sector

This is a sector with a large number of SMEs as well as some large firms and where competition is frequently in niches or subsectors within the sector. Competition is both on price and quality, and name, reputation and trademarks can be important competitive advantages. The importance of quality varies according to the target consumer – in some cases quality is of prime importance and in others less so. Producers may also specialize, therefore, in different niches according to levels of quality. Competition is international. US producers have been benefiting in particular in recent years from the low dollar, making their products much more cost competitive. Once markets have been lost, re-entry can be difficult and costly.

Pyramid is located in Bavaria, which has a long tradition of producing musical instruments and parts, as does the neighbouring region of western Bohemia in the Czech Republic. Although classified in the musical instruments sector, the firm can also be seen as – more generally – a metalworking engineering firm.

Ownership and organizational structure

The elder of the two brothers who own the firm (Herr Junger) is the general manager, and the younger brother is a development engineer with an international reputation as a stringed instrument expert. There is a relatively large white-collar staff, which is necessary mainly because of the large and complex export business.

The Czech subsidiary is managed directly from the German headquarters. There is a part-time overseer for the Czech operation who assists in ensuring smooth day-to-day operation. All sales and marketing, including exports, is carried out from the parent firm. Consequently, all the Czech production is re-exported back to the parent and does not attract import or export duties.

The products and production process

Pyramid Junger Gmbh produces a wide variety of strings for musical instruments. It does not undertake any mass production but has an extremely wide range of specialities, such as strings for medieval instruments. It has a range of more than 2,000 products and uses a variety of materials for their strings, from nylon to silver. It will also make individual designs on request and fulfil orders for unusual instruments. It is said to be the world leader for strings for medieval and Renaissance instruments. It also produces pitch-pipes for tuning instruments and is the world leader for this product.

It has about 30 input suppliers; most of them are German, but some come from the United States, e.g. for nylon inputs. It uses a wide variety of different types of metal wires, including zinc, steel, copper, silver and silver-plated wires, nickel and other alloys, and also some plastic fabrics. The machine tools that it uses are traditional, mechanical machine tools. The US manufacturers tend to have expensive electronic tools; however, these are not the critical factor in quality. Technical innovation tends to come from the use of particular raw materials, not from the techniques of production.

The production skills can be learnt within a short period of time – one to three months. The workforce is largely female – this partly reflects the fact that this is low-wage work, but the work is also considered by the management to be better done by women, as they are better at the fast and nimble manual work that is required. The German factory does use part-time labour but there are no specific shifts, as each worker has a machine and can allocate her time independently. New employees have a three-month probation period where they learn the basics of the job and demonstrate their competence. The firm is not unionized but does pay the union agreed rate in the area.

Prior to the investment in the Czech Republic, the firm had had a larger number of employees and had used a substantial number of homeworkers. The homeworkers had been given a machine and could produce the strings effectively at home. The employees in the parent company are aware of the international competitive pressures facing the firm and understand the need to expand and shift production to the Czech Republic.

Strategy

Pyramid's name, reputation and know-how represent important competitive strengths which it aims to maintain and build on in maintaining and expanding its position in its various markets. It has an export/sales ratio of about 70 per cent and exports its internationally known brand – Pyramid – to more than 100 countries. Its customers are wholesalers, musical instrument manufacturers and individual retailers.

Pyramid's strongest competition in recent years has come from two main sources. First, it faces intense competition from large US companies with high-technology equipment and relatively low wages who are now also benefiting from a weak dollar. These companies have entered German and international markets with high levels of advertising. In addition, German wholesalers buy directly in the United States and get discounts. Second, competition has come from the Pacific Rim area, and in recent years the company has lost about 85 per cent of its markets in East Asia – Indonesia, Malaysia and Singapore, China and Taiwan. As a result, annual company sales went down from DM 3 million to DM 2 million. This was due not only to cost competition from these countries but also in some cases to imitation of brands – copies are of lower quality but better than they used to be. Customers who place a premium on quality recognize the difference, but nonetheless Pyramid has lost sales.

Despite these lost markets, the firm has a strategy to expand, given the cost advantages it has gained from its Czech operations. Its market share is already expanding once again – particular prospects are seen for the South American market, where previously Pyramid could not compete on price with the US products. There is also growing demand in the new markets in central and eastern Europe. Pyramid's strengths include a brand name and reputation for excellent quality, and flexible production of speciality and niche products.

As a small company, Pyramid is not in a position to spend a large amount on advertising. Its main marketing tools are, first, its English–German catalogue, which it sends all over the world, and second, its participation in international trade fairs. There are two main musical equipment trade fairs, one in Frankfurt and one in California, and Pyramid participates in both with its own stand in a modern pyramid design. Personal contacts are also important. Furthermore, the younger Junger brother also carries out research in the area and gives talks and publishes articles – among his audience are many young professional musicians who are aware of the Pyramid brand.

The decision to invest in the Czech Republic

The decision to invest in the Czech Republic was driven by the need to reduce costs in the face of the competitive pressures described above. Pyramid had initially tried to reduce costs by investment in more capital-intensive machinery but, in the context of the continuing fall in the dollar, this did not result in a sufficient reduction in costs. It therefore began to consider the option of investing in the Czech Republic. Herr Junger already knew some other local entrepreneurs who had invested there and was aware that a number of SMEs from Bavaria had invested in the Czech Republic. Furthermore, Herr Junger, as a Sudeten German, already had some understanding of the area. In addition to the low costs of producing in the Czech Republic, locational issues were important. The Czech subsidiary that Pyramid established is only 2½ hours from the parent company by car. Poland would have been too far.

The Czech Republic still has a musical instruments industry and there would have been the possibility to acquire or establish a joint venture with an existing firm. Pyramid chose in preference to establish a greenfield operation. This enabled a small-scale operation to be established without any pre-existing commitments.

Herr Junger went to a small private office in the Czech Republic that specializes in company tax and administrative procedures for assistance in investing. A business acquaintance who had already invested in the Czech Republic had informed him about this office. Pyramid initially started discussions with this office in summer 1990. It was found very helpful to have the assistance of this office in dealing with the Czech authorities and in establishing a greenfield operation. Through the office Pyramid was put in contact with someone who spoke good German (in fact the father of the office manager), who found a set of rooms which Pyramid could use as a small workshop, and who identified potential employees. This person subsequently became the part-time overseer of the subsidiary. The agency continues to manage Pyramid's local administrative issues, including dealing with export and customs documentation. It is clear that informal and personal contacts were particularly important in this investment process, and these contacts were found to be of more assistance than more formal institutions such as the local chamber of commerce.

Pyramid invested the minimum required to establish a limited liability company in the Czech Republic – 100,000 Czech Crowns, about DM 6,000 – and an additional amount to cover the first month of wages. In addition, capital equipment and inputs were supplied from the parent company. The initial investment was, therefore, small. The aim was to establish a small operation and develop slowly in order to ensure that the strategy was sound, and not to become overcommitted either financially or in terms of making commitments to the local community that could not be kept. For financial dealings with the subsidiary, Pyramid uses a local Czech bank where it has a Deutschmark account.

Experience of operating in the Czech Republic

The subsidiary in the Czech Republic is very small – there are six female workers and a part-time overseer. It is essentially managed directly from the headquarters in Germany. Day-to-day coordination is carried out by phone and fax. In addition to the part-time overseer, one of the workforce acts as a forewoman. Production requirements are set out on schedules that are brought from the headquarters. Herr Junger himself visits the subsidiary about every six to eight weeks, and other members of staff visit every two weeks or so. There have been some language problems but the overseer speaks German and normally acts as a translator.

In establishing the subsidiary, old machines were transported from Germany to the workshop. Subsequently, newer machines were taken over. At the time of establishing the subsidiary, it was possible to import used machines without paying any tariffs or taxes but there is currently a bill, which may become law in the Czech Republic, that would require such tariffs to be paid.

Before production started in the Czech subsidiary, the Czech workforce was brought to Germany for a couple of days to learn the basics of the production process. None of the workers had any previous experience but the processes are relatively easy to acquire and, as long as workers have the necessary manual dexterity, substantial learning occurs over a period of about three months. When additional training is needed, the forewoman goes to Germany for a day to learn any new procedures and then trains the other workers in the subsidiary.

The workforce normally works from 5.30 a.m. to 2 p.m. for five days a week. However, as each worker works at a different machine, part-time work is possible. The wage rate in 1995 was 38 Czech Crowns, about DM 2.3, compared to wages of around DM 16 in the headquarters. In the Czech Republic, Pyramid must pay about 50 per cent of the wage costs to social insurance, but this percentage is higher in Germany. The labour cost advantages are, therefore, substantial. The wages are relatively high for female labour in the Czech Republic and so it has been straightforward to attract labour. Pyramid does not expect substantial wage increases due to inflation in the coming period. Transport costs also have to be taken into account but these are not substantial relative to the labour cost advantage. Goods have to go via a longer route than is possible by car, for customs reasons, but the time required is still only about four hours. Overall, the reduction in costs achieved through expansion to the Czech Republic has allowed Pyramid not simply to survive in highly competitive international markets but to increase its competitiveness and its sales.

Productivity in the subsidiary was initially lower than in the headquarters, which reflects both learning and older machines, but is now higher in the Czech Republic. This higher productivity is a result of the subsidiary concentrating on the simpler and larger-volume products. The parent company produces the more complex and specialized parts and the smaller orders. All the inputs to the subsidiary are supplied from the parent company and the output is re-exported to the parent company. Consequently, there are no import or export tariffs – customs documentation does, nonetheless, still have to be completed. This documentation is one reason why production for small, specialized orders is done in Germany.

Quality levels are satisfactory for the types of product that the subsidiary is producing. In the medium term, Pyramid aims to expand in the US market in particular, in producing strings for stringed instruments. This will require very high quality but low costs, and additional training for the Czech workforce will be necessary. Final quality control is carried out in the parent company and it is possible to identify the workers responsible for particular pieces of output and so to identify any quality problems. Overall, the work ethic of the workforce is seen to be good and performance is high.

The infrastructure in the Czech Republic is considered to be adequate for Pyramid's operating needs. The legal framework is also developing quite quickly and is fairly similar in many ways to the German system.

Conclusion

This is a case of a small German firm making a cross-border investment in the Czech Republic in order to reduce its costs. This investment has been a successful one for the company, enabling it to compete in international markets and, in particular, to compete with low-cost US producers. The close geographical location of the subsidiary, together with the fact that its production is entirely for the parent company, has contributed to the smooth management of this international expansion by an SME.

8

Guardian Industries Limited

This is the case of Guardian Industries, one of the largest manufacturers of float glass in the world, and its investment in Hungary, which was the first big foreign investment in that country. The investment was undertaken prior to 1989 and represented a strategic decision to supply to the COMECON market and Hungary's neighbouring countries. The company initially had to form a joint venture with a Hungarian company but in the end used few of the partner's facilities. Instead, it rebuilt the entire plant almost from scratch. This is an example of what can be termed 'brownfield' development. This strategy was made feasible by reforms in Hungary which allowed foreign firms wholly to own subsidiaries; once the legislation was introduced, Guardian acted to buy out its joint venture partner. With the changes in 1989 and the unforeseeable collapse of its anticipated markets, Guardian has had to find new areas to sell to and to shift production to higher-value-added products. These changes made the investment more costly than was originally expected, but the pessimistic outlook of 1991–2 has now turned around. Guardian expects its Hungarian subsidiary to be profitable in the near future, and now plans further expansion into central and eastern Europe (CEE).

Sector and products

Guardian's main product is float glass, which is produced in varying thicknesses for different uses. The global sector is dominated by five firms: Pilkington (UK), Saint-Gobain (France), PPG (United States), Asahi (Japan) and Guardian (US). The same firms dominate the European market, led by Saint-Gobain and Pilkington.

Until the 1950s, the major production techniques for the production of glass were the sheet and plate glass methods. These methods were labour-intensive and produced an inconsistent quality of glass. A technological breakthrough in the 1950s was developed by Pilkington, which patented the float glass method. This is a far more cost-efficient method which produces glass of a high quality. Float glass is now the key technology, and is still licensed by Pilkington. However, there is now a range of products and quality levels, and technological changes have allowed a variety of glass types and processes to emerge.

For float glass, there is a minimum efficient scale of production of about 450 tonnes per day. Once a float line has been constructed, most costs derive from raw materials and energy. Production is continuous, as once the furnace has reached the required temperature for production, it is expensive to shut the plant down. Transport costs are high relative to value added, so most production is sold near the market (a radius of 300–500 km is the furthest that most glass can efficiently be transported). Given approximately constant returns in variable costs, and high costs of shutdown, storage and transport, it is important for glass firms to be able to sell their output relatively locally.

The sector is oligopolistic. Competition is based on price and quality of product, and also on the range of products sold and the sales tactics. The closer to the factory the glass can be sold, to the larger the company's profit margin will be. In the 1970s there may have been implicit collusion between firms in Europe, which aimed to maintain prices by restricting capacity. Pilkington controlled the licences for the production of float glass and allowed very few companies to have access to the technology. Those firms producing float glass may have understood that it was not in their best interests to compete aggressively with one another. There were structural changes in the European market in the 1970 and 1980s. One European manufacturer, BSN, was bought by PPG, while new entrants Asahi and Guardian came into the market. If there was implicit collusion, it probably ended as the competition increased from the new entrants.

Company structure

Guardian is a US multinational enterprise operating in the United States, Europe and Asia. It is now privately owned by William Davidson, who founded the company and bought it back from the market during the 1980s. Guardian has 15 float plants worldwide, five of which are in Europe, two in Luxembourg, two in Spain, and one in Hungary. One new float plant is under construction in Germany. Sales are around $1.5 billion and the firm is currently the world's fifth largest producer of float glass.

The company has a fairly flat organizational structure; for example, the European headquarters employs 15 people in total (including administrative staff). Guardian Europe has about seven senior managers. It has a subsidiary in Luxembourg which is responsible for research and engineering, and plant construction. The managing director is based in the United States.

Decision-making in Guardian is largely devolved – day-to-day production and local sales are local management responsibilities – but investment, finance and non-local sales decisions are centralized, first in the area headquarters (i.e. Europe) and then through to the United States. Guardian has approximately a 14 per cent market share in the United States and Europe. This has been rising very quickly – the company only went into Europe in the early 1980s and the share has been increasing at around 1 percentage point per annum since then. European employment is approximately 2,500 and sales are $500 million. This is about 35 per cent of Guardian's global turnover, and approximately 40 per cent of profits.

Guardian has had a very effective entry strategy into the European market. The company offers a wide range of products but probably not as wide as those of its competitors; it is less vertically integrated than other firms. Management has chosen to concentrate on the production of float glass and cutting and preparation of glass in strategic areas, such as for the manufacture of windscreens and for picture framing. One of the implications of restricting production to large-volume items is that Guardian is reputed to be the lowest-cost producer. Operating margins are of the order of 15 per cent, compared with an average of 10 per cent for other major glass-makers in the United States. Unlike some competitors, such as Pilkington, Guardian has not diversified downstream into areas such as double-glazing, because it believes that margins are too low as a result of stiff competition in such sectors of the market. This approach of 'capturing' markets rather than competing in them by high-cost acquisition also leads, in the Guardian view, to unnecessarily high levels of leveraging.

Guardian strategy

Guardian Europe has a strategy of steady expansion in the number of plants with the aim of increasing its market share. It has already opened six factories in Europe, and more are due. For existing plants, the strategy is, first, to sell all their output, and second, gradually to move to higher-value-added products (e.g. mirror glass and 2 mm glass), given the fixed capacity of any one plant. Given its strategic growth objective, Guardian focuses on selling its glass by operating on both price and quality. The company is very competitive in its market behaviour; prices, for example, will be cut if necessary to sell output and the firm has been prepared to sell at a loss in order to move its stock and ensure continued production. For example, Guardian was the only European supplier in the recession not to close any plants, thus avoiding the losses associated with shutdown.

Guardian takes a long term view of its strategy and investment returns. It is exploiting its current position of being relatively small – compared to competitors – and so is able to be flexible in its approach to the market. The firm is also now private – it was bought back by Mr Davidson in a leveraged buyout of $305 million in 1985. The firm has since then been slowly reducing the debt/capital ratio from an initial level of 70 per cent to below 30 per cent by the early 1990s.

In addition to low-cost production and high-quality products, Guardian's strategy depends on its sales organization. The company does not store products for more than two months, and tries to 'sell out' its production by a combination of altering prices and attracting new customers. The factories and the sales activities, unusually for the industry, are very closely linked. Manufacture is therefore brought very close to the market, and stress is laid on the ability to sell the product. Just-in-time delivery, price flexibility, 24-hour service and total reliability are key elements in the company's rapid expansion in European market share. The company also avoids areas where its competitors are strong; it learns about the marketplace from its customers. It also 'cherry-picks' customers that it wants, using a combination of price, quality and other conditions to make an irresistible deal.

A key element of Guardian's strategy is, therefore, to maintain close customer and supplier relations. The company does not have marketing departments, either at headquarters or in the individual factories, distinct from its production activities. The sales people have substantial authority to make decisions and, as we have noted, maintain exceptionally close links back to production. Sales outside each plant's local area (this area may cover several neighbouring countries) are centralized, so that local sales people do not go to the same customers as those from other factories.

Guardian views itself as being comparable with US steel mini-mills, i.e. it benefits from being a smaller, lower-cost producer. It is a deliberate strategy to be less vertically integrated, as by doing so Guardian is able to get all the independent customers. In this way it manages to retain flexibility.

Guardian is a 'lean company'. It does not try to do everything in the glass market, but instead concentrates on a few highly profitable areas. The organization is also lean: 'European head office has 15 people managing $500 million revenue'. Management is convinced that it also has more flexibility and a longer-term outlook because the company is privately owned. One example is investment strategy, which is different to that of other companies. Guardian tends to finance investments when the market is in a downswing, because at this point it will be cheaper. This can have the effect of alienating its competitors, who have a more cautious stance and are concerned about the market being flooded with glass during a recession.

Guardian has therefore developed considerable experience in investing in western Europe which it had hoped would apply to central and eastern Europe. In its approach, key categories assessed when an investment site is chosen would be:

- proximity to an established market, since transport costs are high;
- location of competitors, as the domestic market, especially in a medium-sized economy such as that of Hungary, would have a finite demand for glass;
- ability to obtain the necessary raw materials and energy for glass production;
- adequate provision of infrastructure, particularly of roads, gas supplies (required for the production process), and telecommunications.

The key issue for Guardian in Europe has therefore been the ability to sell glass. The company tends to establish a market presence first, building a reputation based on quality, reliability and service as well as competitive pricing. Once it feels that potential sales are sufficient to support a production facility, it investigates investment opportunities.

The decision to invest in Hungary

Guardian had been importing to the central and eastern European region prior to investing there. It chose to invest in Hungary primarily because it was by far the most politically stable of the countries in the region. The economy had been radically opened up and the market for investment was deregulated and provided a range of opportunities, particularly for joint ventures. State subsidies still existed, and the government, keen to obtain hard currency investment, was willing to offer tax breaks to potential investors.

Some Guardian investments are based on obvious market needs or opportunities. The company's two plants in Luxembourg, which service Belgium, France and Germany, fall into this category. However, in Hungary, the company was approached to take part in a deal which was felt to be advantageous. Guardian believed that the opportunity offered to it in Hungary pre-reform provided a way to learn about central and eastern Europe and the Soviet market. In fact, Guardian had considered investing in central and eastern Europe from as early as the early 1980s, because it saw the market opportunities for a low-cost float glass manufacturer in an area still underdeveloped. However, it was not until 1986 that an opportunity presented itself, when Hungarian Glass Works (HGW) contacted Guardian to discuss the possibility of forming a joint venture. Management claims that the company did not expect to make money from the deal in the short term; the learning experience was always an important element.

At the time when HGW approached Guardian to form a joint venture, Guardian Europe was in fact short of glass to supply its customers in the region and elsewhere in Europe. The attractions were that the Hunguard deal seemed to offer both entry to a new, virgin market before any competitors, and as an additional supply of glass to relieve shortages elsewhere in Europe.

Hungarian investment

Hungarian Glass Works (Magyar Üvegipari Mûvek) was created in 1948, when the two sheet glass factories in Hungary, one in Orosháza (in the southeast of Hungary, about 50 kilometres from the border with Romania) and one in Salgótarján, were nationalized. It managed these and six other glass plants which produced glass tubes, glass containers and sheet glass fabrications. The activities of the sheet glass manufacturers were always limited to base glass production and they used the rolled glass technique. This is a very labour-intensive form of production, requiring approximately 800 people to operate a plant as opposed to around 160 people for a float glass factory.

In 1986 the two manufacturing plants and the fabrications plants were split up and the factory in Orosháza was then referred to as Hungarian Glass Works (HGW). The opening of the Hungarian economy to foreign investors at this time meant that HGW was able to search for a partner to form a joint venture. The Hungarian management of the plant realized that the technology in the plant was old and the quality of the glass poor. The efficiency of the plant in terms of energy consumption was not good and the system of production used was not competitive with float glass manufacturing. HGW knew that it could buy Pilkington's float glass technology but realized that this alone would not be sufficient to ensure survival in the face of competition. To achieve this aim, it felt that it also needed to acquire Western sales, managerial and financial skills.

Eventually, HGW chose to work with Guardian. It had also talked with Asahi, Pilkington and PPG. The main motivation for this choice was that Guardian had already successfully converted a sheet glass plant in Spain, which had used rolled glass technology, to the float glass technique. The letter of intent was signed in late 1986 – before the reform process proper had begun, though by then Hungary had been the most market-oriented communist country for almost twenty years. By 1987 the agreement had been drawn up for the basic design of the joint venture. The aim of the venture initially was to convert the existing sheet glass manufacturing facility in Orosháza to a modern 500 tonnes/day float glass plant, with the aim of production commencing by the end of 1990.

The deal was completed and signed in November 1988, by which time Hungary was already embarking on some degree of real reform, though the Berlin Wall was still a year from falling. The government gave Guardian certain concessions and agreed to construct a road from the plant. Guardian was the first big foreign investor in Hungary. This caused some problems for Guardian, which had no other large investors with which to talk to discuss the potential pitfalls. However, it did provide an advantage in the negotiations with the government, which was keen to ensure that the deal ran smoothly.

The history of the joint venture

The joint venture was created as a separate entity from HGW. There were clearly benefits to the Hungarian side from the deal. HGW continued to function as an autonomous company, though problems of overmanning and the necessity for restructuring persisted. Given the governmental legislation at the time, Guardian initially was only allowed to have a 49 per cent stake in the joint venture. In April 1990, after a change in policy, HGW initiated a change in the ownership structure and Guardian acquired a controlling 80 per cent stake in the joint venture company, which had been named Hunguard Float Glass

Limited. HGW proved unable to resolve the problems of the large, traditional, glass-manufacturing side of the business, and was unable to participate financially in the fuller development of the joint venture. In effect, the partner was bankrupt and Guardian attempted to increase its stake to 100 per cent. However, HGW did not want to sell, because its only asset of value was its stake in Hunguard. There were protracted negotiations with the government, and Guardian involved the media to argue its case, stressing its role as the first, and one of the major, foreign direct investors into Hungary. By 1992 Guardian had won its battle and owned 100 per cent of the company.

Finance

The financing of Guardian's deal with the Hungarian government was rather complex. The firm had to pay a capital sum for its share in the joint venture, which cost in the order of $14 million in cash. HGW's contribution was a 'contribution in kind', where it brought assets to the venture instead of cash. (The estimated market value of these assets was far lower than the amount paid by Guardian.) However, Guardian's immediate investment was in fact very small because, in a deal typical of pre-reform communism, HGW simultaneously signed a contract with Guardian with a fee for the construction of the new plant, which was done by Guardian. (HGW did not have the expertise to build a float plant.) Both partners in the joint venture were part of the fee structure, where fees were paid for work done in relation to the building of the plant, and later for contributions to the company (Hunguard).

The cost of building the plant was approximately $120 million, which does not include Guardian's capital investment or the payment for outstanding shares. Half of this was initially financed by loans.

The project was initially funded by two loans from Hungarian banks: Budapest Bank and OKHB. Deutsche Bank also gave two loans of $21 million and $20.2 million. The loans have now been restructured using internal funds to avoid the high interest rate charged by the Hungarian banks. The reason why Guardian had used Hungarian banks in the first place was that their joint venture partner had insisted, but once they had total control over the firm, this was no longer necessary.

Guardian's equity in the company is therefore now over $70 million. Domestic debt is still $9 million, foreign outside hard currency debt is $10 million and there is $38 million of inter-company debt. Its

Spanish plant cost around $80 million because it was built in a recession; and normal costs are closer to $110 million.

Choice of investment

With the experience of hindsight, Guardian managers say that they probably would not have gone into Hungary through the joint venture route and they would not have invested in Orosháza, a location which is very remote. Of course, a variety of options was not available in eastern Europe in 1988; Guardian had to accept what it was offered. But there were problems in the way that the deal worked out almost from the outset, which had serious implications for profitability, and the reforms affected in a negative way both the operating cost calculations and Guardian's ability to sell glass as planned.

The HGW plant was almost completely rebuilt. Hence the advantages of going in as a joint venture were access to the market and a local workforce with an existing knowledge of glass production. The disadvantage proved to be the location (due to long transportation to markets). One of HGW's factories was located in southeast Hungary, and the government had wanted the glass production to remain there. The Hungarian management team of the joint venture partner had limited experience. However, HGW and Guardian went ahead with the joint venture and created Hunguard. All employees of Hunguard were Hunguard employees and not HGW employees, although some came from HGW. Hunguard created its own management team and was not managed by HGW.

(Re)building Hunguard

The plant was 'converted', i.e. effectively rebuilt along the lines of the Spanish plant. The joint venture retained only the original oven from the HGW plant. There was a nine-month gap in production in 1990–1, while construction occurred; during this time, Guardian used existing stocks to fulfil customer orders. Construction went as well as it had in Spain, where a similar transformation had been undertaken.

Guardian's investment was therefore neither exactly acquisition nor greenfield. This phenomenon of 'brownfield' investment is surprisingly common in transitional economies. The firm, in fact, used very little from its partner company, though it clearly drew on the local expertise and labour force.

Post-1989 impact on decision strategy

The original aim of the production facility in Orosháza was to supply an area within a 1000-kilometre radius. This is a wider area than usual for a Guardian factory, but the limited size of the Hungarian market meant that Guardian had to sell to other countries. This was part of the company's broader strategy to use Hungary as a springboard for expansion in the whole region, notably Bulgaria, Romania and Yugoslavia (as it was then) at the outset, as well as to provide some glass for western Europe. The plan was to sell 55 per cent of production to the COMECON countries, including Hungary, and the remaining 45 per cent to western Europe in order to generate hard currency for Hungary.

The 1989 changes in central and eastern Europe both undermined the strategic motive of the investment and changed fundamentally the underlying economic conditions. Central and eastern European trade collapsed with the disintegration of CMEA, so there were no trading advantages in selling to, for example, Romania from Hungary. Even more significantly in the short term, the very steep recession across the entire region from 1990 deeply affected the demand for glass. Only 10 per cent of Hunguard's output could be sold in Hungary, and almost none in the other transition economies, so the rest had to be sold in the west. This is a much higher proportion than was planned to be sold to markets where transport costs were very high – 26 per cent. This can be seen in Table 8.1. There were also different political expectations of economic change and foreign direct investment (FDI).

Given that the strategy had collapsed, Guardian could have pulled out of Hungary altogether, but the company did not do so because it was felt that this would have been damaging for the Guardian image in Europe, and would damage other deals that were being negotiated at the time. Management anticipated that the Hungarian project would now require a long-term approach, and the expected payback period had to be radically revised. Financial performance is now gradually improving, but Hunguard is now only breaking even after high losses in the early years. The normal payback period for a Guardian factory is two years in normal trading conditions and up to four and a half years if conditions are poor. However, Hunguard will still not pay back in the near future.

Table 8.1 Breakdown of production costs

	(%) post-1989
Transportation costs	26
Material costs	20
Wage costs	4
Company overheads	31
Packaging	9
Costs from sales	6
Other	4

Turnover and markets

Guardian had managed to turn the situation around by 1995, though, as we noted above, the project has proved very expensive. The turnover of Hunguard in 1995 will be approximately $60 million per year. The company has achieved a 90 per cent share of the Hungarian market. Thick glass constitutes 65 per cent of production. One-third of its sales are in Hungary and the remainder are spread thinly across the regions in Austria, southeast Germany, Romania, former Yugoslavia and Slovenia. As we have seen, this is very different from the envisaged markets and, for a while, when demand locally was at its lowest, Hunguard had to sell at a loss in Italy to ensure that all production was sold.

An important element in Hunguard's strategy to resolve the problems posed by the fall of the Berlin Wall was to alter the production mix. The idea was to make Hunguard the European base for manufacture of high-value-added glass which can be transported further distances. This appears to have been successful. Hunguard focuses on the production of 2 mm glass for use in picture frames; this represents about 35 per cent of production. There are not many plants in Europe that produce thin glass, and so a higher price can be charged. The thin glass is transported further, and most of the sales for this are in western Europe, even as far as the UK.

Hunguard needs to sell all of its output rather quickly because there are limited storage facilities and the manufacturing process is continuous. Like the rest of Guardian Europe, the company has an aggressive pricing strategy to achieve this goal. A secondary aim is to increase the value-added component. As we have seen, it has been successful in this, increasing the percentage of 2 mm glass produced and sold and installing a cutting and grinding facility in Orosháza. The main focus of the company in the long term is to be selling to closer markets.

In terms of competitors, Hunguard does now dominate the Hungarian market. Guardian is also establishing a new plant in (eastern) Germany as part of its strategy for Poland and central and eastern Europe more generally. It is possible that the Hungarian experience offered some benefits here, though the particular problems faced will probably not be repeated elsewhere. Other competitors has also entered the region. Pilkington has a plant in Poland, although it has yet to start production, and Asahi has made an acquisition in the Czech Republic.

Management

Guardian uses local managers and workers all over Europe and has applied the same policy in Hungary. At the management level, the finance and sales managers in Hunguard are expatriates, although these posts are seen as temporary. A few more expatriates did work at the plant when it opened. The managing director was chosen from HGW; he impressed Guardian managers by being a tough negotiator on the other side in the early phases. The plant manager was sent around Guardian's other plants to be trained.

According to the managers, it took some time before Hunguard employees understood the idea of devolving decisions and accepting responsibility. The language issue was also a problem at the beginning, although now all the senior managers speak English.

Workforce

Hunguard employs about 315 people in four shifts. Most of these were chosen from HGW, so they already had experience of working with glass. Guardian trained the key people in Luxembourg for a month. Wages are set above average for the area and a bonus system is given for attendance, so there is low absenteeism. The overall unemployment in the region is high (about 13 per cent). There is little alternative employment in Orosháza. The other two sizeable firms in the area are a glass-bottling plant (which used to be part of the sheet glass factory) and a chicken-plucking factory.

The management discourages trade unions and no one in the plant is a member of one. There is a works council, but its functions are very unclear; management does not promote worker representation and prefers 'open communication structures'. In general, Guardian is happy with the workforce, and the local management has now got full control. The workers are trained on the job, and health and safety issues are emphasized.

Production and technology

The production facility in Hungary is similar to others owned by Guardian. All the equipment installed is the latest and most high-technology machinery available. The technology is the same as that used in the most modern of Guardian's Luxembourg plants. The only differences in the plants are in their capacities. The Hunguard plant is currently running at full capacity but if it had the same structure as the Luxembourg plant it could produce 15–20 tonnes more glass per day. The difference in the structure is a result of the types of glass being produced. Hunguard is carving itself a niche in 2 mm glass, which is much more sensitive, so an increase in production volume is not possible. In Europe, Hunguard is one of only a very few float lines that can produce 2 mm glass in any bulk and still maintain the quality; as the tonnage of 2 mm glass increases, the quality normally falls.

Sales

The sales department is run by an expatriate manager because sales is still viewed as being a major skills gap in Hungary, especially in this particular area of the country. Hunguard has an internal and an external sales force constructed in the same way as those of the other Guardian plants. Management has found it difficult to recruit the right calibre of people, partly because of the location of the plant and partly because the types of skills required are difficult to find. It is usually unable to find anyone with previous selling experience, although this is not a major problem, as employees are trained on the job. More important, though, since the sales staff will need to sell to people from various different countries, is finding people with the relevant language skills. The company provides language lessons for four different languages.

Infrastructure

The Guardian plant is very isolated, and the distances to be travelled to the regions emerging as the main markets are substantial. One of the biggest problems with the infrastructure in southeast Hungary is the poor condition of the roads. The company negotiated with the government, which has agreed to lay 35 kilometres of new roads. Telecommunications have also been a problem, although they are now much improved. Gas supplies have given cause for concern, both from the aspect of quality and because of the huge increase in prices as the government withdrew its subsidies.

Conclusions

Overall, Guardian has been a very successful company in Europe. Its Hungarian expansion turned out to be costly, given the timing and the location of the plant. However, the deal has given it an almost total share in the Hungarian market and it will be well placed for the emerging CEE markets (Bulgaria, Russia, former Yugoslavia) when those economies pick up. The joint venture was probably the only way for Guardian to enter the Hungarian market, especially given the early date, but the original logic of the investment was almost immediately overtaken by events. Once the company had established full control over the joint venture, the local plant adapted and functioned well; but the collapse of the market created serious problems which a shift to a more specialized product mix and the gradual upturn are only now beginning to resolve.

9

Lycett Danubius Limited

Overview

This is the case of a small UK company, working primarily for a single UK heavy vehicle manufacturer, which invested in Hungary to obtain access to cheap steel and labour. The investment may have been relatively successful in its own terms, though there were serious labour problems and the expected cost advantages were never fully established. The investment was the cause of a conflict between Lycett and its major customer which led to Lycett being put into Administration. This was Lycett's first experience of manufacturing outside the UK, and the company probably did not have the resources of manpower, or capital, to finance the full costs of learning how to manage multinational operations.

The sector and the firm

History of Lycett

Lycett manufactures in the steel fabrication industry, an industry mainly comprising small to middle-sized companies in the UK, and facing strong competition, especially from Germany and the Far East. Lycett originally made steel columns but has more recently diversified into parts for construction equipment and materials-handling equipment. Lycett is a relatively small company; in 1994, employment in the UK was around 400 people in three facilities. The company was formed as a management buyout in 1982 of Lycett Fabrications in Tamworth, near Birmingham, which manufactured steel roof supports for the UK mining industry. Turnover in 1982 was around £1 million. The company diversified because the prospects for the UK mining sector were viewed at that date by management as being poor (this was around the period of the miners' strike, when the coal industry was being run down). Nonetheless, the steel roof support business did grow in the 1980s – largely because much of the competition left the market – and Lycett in 1994 had 60 per cent of UK sales, as well as exports to Australia and the United States. Turnover had increased at Tamworth to £2.5 million in 1994, when the company was sold by the Administrators. The Hungarian subsidiary of Lycett supported the management buyout of Tamworth and is currently a minority investor. In its first year of operation (to 31 December 1995) the subsidiary had a turnover of £3.7 million and made a profit of £304,000.

Lycett's diversification occurred primarily within the boundaries of the steel fabrication sector. The company moved initially into construction equipment, developing an offshoot of an existing Lycett company to make chassis for aluminium trains (for ABB). It also attempted to integrate forwards, and in 1991 acquired a manufacturer of lorry bodies. This proved in the end to be unsuccessful, because Lycett management did not have experience of marketing or dealing with a variety of customers. Steel fabrication takes the form of a very small customer base, perhaps two or three firms, each spending a high proportion of revenue, while there are typically rather more customers downstream. On its own account, Lycett failed, primarily on the marketing side, and ultimately sold the business in 1994 at a loss of £1.5 million to £2 million.

Another expansion was into construction equipment and materials-handling equipment; at the peak of the business, the company supplied Caterpillar, JCB, Boss and Lansing. In 1990, Lycett already had a total turnover in this part of the company of around £9 million, with factories in Mansfield and Burton-on-Trent as well as its original plant in Tamworth. This activity generated the bulk of Lycett's revenue even prior to its expansion into Hungary in the early 1990s.

Competitors and customers

The business is, of course, highly cyclical, along with the rest of the construction industry. Lycett was selling mainly within the UK market, though from an early date there were plans to expand into continental Europe. Competition within the UK does not seem to have been great; Lycett was probably the largest player in the UK market, though there were a number of other smaller private firms. Some German companies, typically also small and private, were selling on the UK market, as well as one large Belgian firm.

According to Lycett's management, the key to success in the metal fabrication business is managing relations with customers. Though Lycett was initially selling to a number of construction equipment manufacturers, its involvement with Caterpillar became increasingly close. After negotiations with Caterpillar, Lycett was persuaded to acquire a large plant in Nottingham of a company devoted to supplying Caterpillar. The Nottingham plant employed 300 people, approximately as many people as the three other Lycett sites combined. As a result, the Burton plant was closed down and its manufacture shifted to Nottingham, but, according to managers, Lycett found it difficult to transfer its corporate culture to its large new acquisition. Of course, the tie with Caterpillar also became much closer. The relationship underpinned an enormous increase in turnover, which went up to £22.5 million by 1993.

Company structure and strategy

Lycett Industries is organized as a number of manufacturing facilities around the UK (and after 1992 in Hungary) with, from 1992, a central logistics function at Stonehouse. Robert Armitage is one of its main owners, and the managing director, and appears to make strategic decisions largely alone, though with the assistance of support staff.

In its prospectus for the Hungarian project, Lycett Industries viewed its main strengths as being:

- marketing – in particular, knowledge of the market and existing relationships with the relatively narrow European customer base;
- production and engineering – cost-effective methods;
- logistics – development of supply systems and materials control;
- quality – achieving international quality standards in metal fabrication.

Armitage strongly believed in 1990 that for the company successfully to expand further, it needed to extend its markets to new geographical areas. The forward integration route was also attempted simultaneously, but, as we have seen, proved to be a costly failure. He believed that the appropriate place for such expansion was central and eastern Europe (CEE), because competition from these countries was already beginning to put pressure on his margins in the UK. Labour and steel costs in the region were low, and in his view economic reform created the prospects for growth as the countries of eastern

Europe tried to catch up with the West in terms of infrastructure. His original plan was to go to a small site in eastern Europe, and develop it slowly, simultaneously extending market links with firms in continental Europe. In Armitage's view, continental customers would be unlikely to place orders with a UK firm in the UK, but might look to purchase from one based in eastern Europe. He also believes that the metal fabrication industry will disappear in the long term from the UK altogether, because the customers themselves will largely move to Southeast Asia, continental and eastern Europe and the Americas.

As we have noted, the company operated with some success in the UK metal fabrication sector in the 1980s, apparently maintaining close customer relations on the basis of high-quality control and just-in-time delivery systems. However, despite its claimed European or even global medium-term strategy, Lycett in practice had virtually no international experience. More importantly, the very rapid post-1990 expansion derived from the relationship with a single customer – Caterpillar – which was simultaneously developing its own European strategy, as well as plans for expansion into eastern Europe.

How the decision was made

Lycett's objective was to shift production from the UK to lower-cost areas within Europe. This would allow it both to meet the downward price pressure from its customers and to broaden its customer base within Europe. Armitage decided to buy a plant in central Europe, where Lycett could purchase steel and cut it, before transporting it to Nottingham for welding and delivery to the customers. The logistics would have been fearsome once the two plants operated near capacity (at peak, with capacity around 70 per cent in both plants, Lycett had 12 lorries a week going to the UK and was making 55 machines per day in Nottingham). But Armitage still considered the logistics worthwhile because of the lower costs of labour and, especially, steel in Hungary, and also because he was so pessimistic about the future of the industry in the UK, and therefore sought to establish Lycett on the continent.

Lycett is a small firm with short chains of command and no boards to satisfy. In effect, Armitage travelled around central Europe until he found a company that he liked enough to make an offer. It took him two and a half years, from making the decision to explore the region, until the deal was signed. Given the difficulties that he encountered, he believes that the process would not have been brought to fruition in a public company. It is possible, however, that a larger organization would have taken a more methodical and cost-effective approach.

Choice of firm

Armitage quickly realized that Lycett probably did not need to buy a whole eastern European company to obtain the required manufacturing capacity, but just a part of a company. Socialist firms had been highly integrated, so while many manufacturing firms had metal fabrication units within them, few or none of these were free-standing enterprises for sale on their own. It appeared that Lycett could probably only get into the region by unbundling an existing firm, and in the early transition climate such deals were exceedingly hard to negotiate. This was because ownership rights, and especially land ownership rights, were poorly defined, so it was unclear who had the authority to enter into such negotiations. Moreover, the sellers were often very uncertain about privatizing a small part of a firm if the sale might in any way place in jeopardy the sale of the enterprise as a whole. Armitage also looked at a few small fabrication companies, but found them to be so technologically backward or overmanned (or both) that Lycett was unwilling to contemplate taking them on; the company calculated that overmanning was of the order of 10:1, relative to UK standards.

Choice of Hungary

Lycett started its search with the UK embassy, which arranged for someone to show Armitage manufacturing plants around the country. Other UK institutions provided little help, however, because Lycett was already well ahead of the game in 1990. Its contact from the Hungarian embassy in London is now on the Lycett Danubius board. Armitage built up his own network of contacts within the country, though the process was very time-consuming. He worked initially via an agent in Budapest, and via a completely owned local subsidiary that he set up to buy components for Lycett's UK operators. Turnover in the subsidiary was small (£600,000 per year), but the subsidiary was a vehicle to learn about the people and the markets.

Armitage travelled to Poland, Czechoslovakia and Hungary in search of appropriate deals. The determining factor in the choice of a Hungarian site seems to have been that the division of Danubius on offer was the most appropriate for Lycett's needs. However, Armitage also believed that Hungary offered the most stable political environment, with no threat of a return to communism. He also felt Budapest to be at the centre of Europe, with good communications. Finally, he noted the strong engineering traditions. It is unclear how many of these points were correct, or were really influential in the decision in practice. Armitage has since said 'If I were to do it again, I would go to Poland or Slovakia'.

Lycett actually seems to have entered into negotiations with east European companies several times, and indeed got a considerable way towards purchasing several factories. For example, one potential joint venture with a company on the border with Slovakia went almost to completion, before it was rejected by the works council because of the threatened job losses (Lycett offered work for 80 of the 800 employees). Compared with other firms entering the region, Lycett's approach seems to have been very inefficient and costly in terms of top managerial resources. This is probably not only because of its relative inexperience in the region.

The Hungarian partner

In the end, Lycett bought a division of the Ganz shipbuilding group to form Lycett Danubius. The Hungarian division which they finally purchased, Danubius, was founded in 1835 as a shipbuilder. It was merged with the Ganz shipyards upon nationalization in 1948, and the whole enterprise was privatized in 1991. The division had since been searching for foreign partners, for several years. It was hoped that foreigners would bring investment, and a clarification of their ownership situation relative to Ganz, especially concerning land and buildings. The managing director of the division prior to the purchase, Joszef Pappert, is still production manager, and was personally involved in the search for foreign partners in the early 1990s. He had even left pamphlets at embassies which explained the firm's capabilities. Other companies had been interested in buying the division, including a firm which had made the engineering equipment (but this had gone bankrupt) and a German company. According to Pappert, Lycett's interest was greater and it was impressed with the quality of the sample made for it. Local managers took the view that Lycett was the right partner, because it brought big orders from important customers, such as Caterpillar.

Negotiations

The negotiations were long and complex, in part, according to Lycett, because no one in authority on the Hungarian side wanted to make decisions. The management of Ganz and the shipbuilding subsidiary had mixed views about the sale: some were keen on a partner, while others wanted to go back to how things used to be. But the key people in the division were in favour of the link with Lycett, and this seems to have been decisive. The division's works council was not involved in the negotiation.

Lycett entered the negotiations with the objective of a joint venture, and at first the agreement was on this basis. But Armitage came to believe that there was potential for too many things to go wrong in such an arrangement, especially since many Hungarian companies were undertaking multiple joint ventures at that time, and conflicts of interest, as well as administrative and organization overload, seemed likely to occur. Lycett decided that if it was going to run the Hungarian division, it would also have to control it itself. In Lycett's case, the main issue was that no one would make good joint venture partners with it, because there was no understanding of key concepts from Lycett's perspective, such as quality or just-in-time delivery. According to Armitage, 'we had not expected them to understand all the Western ideas but were not prepared for just how little knowledge they had about marketing and quality control'.

The negotiations were in fact mainly with the SHC (State Holding Company) and SPA (the State Property Agency), which between them owned the state's 100 per cent shareholding, rather than with Ganz. Dealings with the SHC were straightforward, though apparently Armitage usually found the meetings to be very long because of disagreements about who should be there; the Hungarian side often sent seven or eight people, not always in agreement.

Finance

In the end, it was the SHC shares that Lycett bought. It paid £1 million for a 70 per cent stake in the division. The shares were bought in four equal instalments over four years. The SPA never actually made a decision on the matter of whether to sell, and indeed refused to talk about the price at all because it had not taken a decision in principle about whether or not the firm should be sold. Lycett obtained the remaining shares via a deal with Ganz – it swapped a debt with Ganz for the remaining 30 per cent of the shares, but these remained non-voting. This debt-for-equity swap was expensive on paper but very cheap in practice, because Ganz was effectively bankrupt, and thus unlikely to be able ever to repay the debt.

Valuation was contentious. The Hungarian side insisted upon an independent valuation, but the valuers did not use the method of earnings-based valuation, rather an asset basis, and the balance sheet indicated a £6 million valuation. In hindsight, Armitage believes that the price Lycett paid was still too high, though the firm was valued in 1994 at £2.5 million.

Operations in eastern Europe

Early performance

Lycett Danubius Rt, as the division was known, grew extraordinarily rapidly on the back of orders from Caterpillar. The economic data are summarized in Table 9.1, which shows that sales increased more than 10-fold between 1992 and 1994, the vast majority of output being exported back to the UK, to the Nottingham plant. Employment rose by around 275 per cent, and the company had an operating profit by 1994. Given that the firm was paying Hungarian wages, it was in fact much cheaper to manufacture in Hungary. Armitage calculated that Lycett could make and transport the finished product for 15 per cent less than in the UK. In addition to cheaper steel, the reason was low labour costs. An unskilled worker earned around £40 per week in Hungary, and a welder around £1.24 per hour. Even after the hefty social security payments took this to £2.90 per hour, this compared favourably with £6.60 (including national insurance) in the UK. Finally, there were signs that by 1994 the original marketing concept was beginning to pay off. Lycett Danubius obtained new contracts from CASE, in France, Mitsubishi and, more recently, from South Korean firms, all in continental Europe. Tony Holman, the general manager, was of the view that 'the strategy was a good one'.

Strategy in practice

The concept behind Lycett's Hungarian connection was to use cheap eastern European steel and labour to manufacture much of its supply

Table 9.1 Lycett Danubius Rt

HUF '000	1991	1992	1993	1994
Sales	102,677	135,380	555,553	1,467,933
Exports	101,027	116,699	441,411	1,399,584
Employment				
(year end)	104	148	189	279
Manual	61	120	170	164
Non-manual	43	28	19	25
Guest	–	–	40	90
Profits				
Gross operating profit/loss	–38,400	–53,105	–43,717	113,506
Net loss	–55,625	–25,471	–43,782	–97,599
Investment	–	81,010	16,029	69,690
Fixed assets	382,757	365,880	358,250	393,229
Gross wages and salaries	–	58,649	121,118	157,312
Capital employed	463,631	438,160	394,377	324,778
Issued capital	515,000	515,000	515,000	543,000

HUF = Hungarian forints.

to Caterpillar, rather than simply to buy steel cheaply in the east, and manufacture in Nottingham. Lycett planned to part-manufacture near the steel supply in Budapest, and transport parts for construction equipment back to the UK; hence the extremely high export-to-sales ratio in Table 9.1. (At one point, in 1994, Lycett became one of the top 20 exporters from Hungary.) Construction equipment has a production process in two parts: cutting, which has relatively low value added, and welding, which has higher value added. The original plan was to cut in Budapest, flat pack the steel and ship it by lorry to Nottingham, where the plates would be assembled and painted. Most managers in 1995 still felt that the underlying concept was sound, but the logistics were fearsome, increasingly so as Caterpillar's demands built up. At one point, Lycett was shipping 12 lorries per week between Budapest and Nottingham, where output had risen from 15 machines in mid-1992 to 55 machines per day in 1994. Nonetheless, neither plant was yet operating at full capacity. One estimate was that production reached only around 70 per cent capacity in each plant.

The strategy ended in failure. Lycett was put into Administration in the UK in 1994 and Lycett Danubius was soon also forced into bankruptcy as a consequence. One can distinguish three causal elements in these two linked bankruptcies: unexpected market and environmental factors; problems within Lycett and Lycett Danubius;

and Lycett's relationship with Caterpillar. We shall deal with each in turn.

Market and environmental factors

The Hungarian economy went into deep recession with economic reforms and the collapse of the CMEA market in 1991, and did not recover before 1994. Table 9.2 charts the problems, with declines in output and industrial output for every year after 1990, and construction being particularly hard hit. While it was never part of Lycett's original plan to sell initially to the Hungarian market, the recession no doubt restricted the possibilities when such an option might have helped in 1994.

The second problem was the price of steel. Initially, this was very low – for example, it was $250 per tonne in Slovakia compared with $450 in the UK. Steel costs represented around 40 per cent of the UK selling price in 1993 using UK manufacturing and prices, but only 33 per cent using Budapest as a base. But there was a steel crisis in July 1994, with such a shortage that according to Armitage, even eastern European manufacturers were able to name their prices. Prices increased by more than 10 per cent and there were problems for Lycett in obtaining adequate supplies. One might have expected Lycett, which had operated with success in the steel fabrication business for so many years, to have a better feel for the input price risks in sourcing most material supplies from eastern Europe.

Finally, Lycett encountered profound and unexpected difficulties in transferring its corporate culture from the UK to Hungary. There were

Table 9.2 Hungarian economic performance, 1986-93

Year	Gross domestic product	Industry	Construction	Agriculture
1986	101.5	99.5	100.1	103.5
1987	104.1	103.2	107.8	97.0
1988	99.9	98.5	94.5	107.4
1989	100.7	98.0	108.3	98.8
1990	96.5	92.3	78.3	95.3
1991	88.1	82.1	85.0	91.8
1992	95.7	92.1	99.2	86.1
1993	97.7	99.7	96.1	85.3

Base year 1985 = 100.

initial cultural difficulties because the British involved did not understand the history and complexity of the region. These were exacerbated by problems in recruiting and keeping staff, and in the growing use of expatriate management. Lycett management regarded one of its competitive strengths as being its training- and incentive-based corporate culture, but the underlying principles did not transfer successfully to the Hungarian operation, which was run as a UK outpost by expatriates who did not speak the language or learn much about Hungarian methods and culture.

Problems within Lycett Danubius

Lycett's Hungarian operation started very well. The UK company put considerable investment into new machinery, e.g. Pullman plasma cutters, Whitney machines and Japanese cutters. The transfer of technology proved very successful, and Pappert, now the production manager, is confident of the firm's technical levels and capacity to satisfy customer demand at world standards. The strong traditions of the Ganz shipyards also served the new company well in terms of the technical skills of the labour force; the workers had no problems working from UK technical drawings, and learnt quickly and effectively, so that productivity levels quickly became quite close to those attained in the UK.

There were three fundamental areas of difficulty for the operations of the Hungarian subsidiary, however, in terms of finance, of the labour force and of management. Each of these contributed to the fact that it was more expensive than expected for Lycett to run two plants than one, especially in terms of working capital, financing the set-up costs of the new plant and scarce managerial resources. This problem is indicated by the fact that, at the end of 1992, Lycett was making operating losses despite the enormously increasing volumes. According to Armitage, in the construction equipment business the prices paid by the main customer, Caterpillar, were less than costs by around 20 per cent. It seems likely that these financial burdens in the UK were exacerbated by problems in the failed lorry company.

Labour

We have seen that the manual labour force in Budapest was skilled, yet relatively cheap. However, Lycett encountered very serious labour problems, because it found it very hard to hire Hungarian blue-collar labour. When the firm had 300 workers, in 1994, around 150 were guests from other countries, primarily Poland and Slovakia. This was apparently traditional in Hungary – welders from there had usually worked in Germany, and their jobs in Hungary were filled by Polish migrants. At one point, of 100 welders in the firm, only six were Hungarian. Pappert did not regard the cultural heterogeneity of the labour force as a problem – he claimed that communication could occur between most workers in German and that there were few serious problems. The UK managers were much more concerned about the reliance on guest workers, and the possible threat by the Hungarian government, in the face of rising unemployment, to ban them. They also stressed the communication costs and the impossibility of developing any sense of corporate identity among the labour force.

As a result, labour turnover was very high. On average, four people per week left the company and 7–8% per cent were on sick leave. According to Pappert, this was largely because the pace of work was fast, and many workers were unable to perform at these levels. The British managers also felt it to be a serious problem that many workers had more than one job, and that there was a widespread black market which was pushing up wages semi-legally. Lycett has been unwilling to hire people in this way, avoiding tax and social security payments, and as a result loses people who can earn more elsewhere. The company paid about 20 per cent above the market average, however. The impermanence of guest workers was also a major source of high labour turnover. The company reacted by introducing a performance-based piecework system, rising through three categories of employee, depending on how many machines each worker could work. Though this helped to reduce labour turnover somewhat, it remained very high.

Management

Lycett immediately introduced new capital into its new subsidiary, and attempted to introduce much higher quality control and just-in-time delivery systems. Cultural problems were serious with the latter innovations. According to Armitage: 'they did not work ... the Hungarians we had were not up to it. We put in expatriates when there were problems in production, but this caused worse difficulties because they had to deal with suppliers who did not speak English.' The production problems were linked to the very rapid increase in sales between 1992 and 1994. The whole strategy relied on successful logistics – in purchasing supplies, organizing finance, ensuring production quality and arranging transport logistics – but there proved to be operational problems on all fronts, and most of these can be traced back to personnel difficulties. Lycett found it extremely hard to recruit suitable Hungarian staff in all areas and increasingly came to rely on expatriate workers. However, this drained the resources of the UK company. Moreover, it did not entirely solve the most serious problems, because language and cultural differences persisted, especially, for example, in the purchase of inputs. For instance, one of Lycett's aims had been to develop a network of suppliers as it had done in the UK, but this proved to be impossible for the expatriate managers to achieve, and Lycett was unable to recruit the sort of people whom it sought locally.

Armitage's original intention was to send out one person from the UK to Hungary (with his family) to work on logistics. Within a few months, the company had to send its finance director as well, originally for two months. He has now returned (though he now works for another company). They then sent out their quality director, who stayed, and then more and more operational directors and production people. According to Armitage: 'we stripped out the best management in the UK and sent them to Hungary. This meant neither business ran very effectively'. For example, the operational director found it hard to get things repaired. In the end, Armitage found that it needed around eight to ten expatriate managers to operate the Hungarian division. None managed to learn the language properly. Training, upon which the UK company put great stress, was restricted by the linguistic and labour turnover difficulties. Nonetheless, Lycett did train the foreman and all people in positions higher than that, and brought shopfloor workers from the UK to show their Budapest counterparts how to work the machines over a period of four to six weeks.

Finance

These problems all led back to the bottom line, and to working capital needs. Set-up costs and learning costs were much higher than originally envisaged. Lycett in the UK was making losses on the margin and by 1994 was not able to finance them. The parent company had a cash crisis, and since half its turnover came from Lycett Danubius, this affected the Hungarian company's creditworthiness. The original finance for the expansion of the Hungarian company had been borrowed from the Budapest Bank in 1993, on the basis of the five-year contract that the parent Lycett company had made with Caterpillar. Lycett was unable to provide the assets itself. According to Armitage, raising loans in Hungary was very hard for the company: 'the Hungarians expect inward investors to bring everything with them ... getting finance is virtually impossible'.

The Budapest Bank proved willing in 1993 to lend Lycett Danubius large amounts of money; the maximum facility reached $2.7 million. But Lycett Danubius was unable to make its first repayment, due in January 1994, because of the parent company's cash problems. Caterpillar eventually advanced considerable sums to finance the 1993 loss, perhaps as much as £4 million. However, the Budapest Bank had lost confidence in the subsidiary and was unwilling to advance further amounts, even though Lycett Danubius managed to keep up all later repayments. Other banks in Hungary were unwilling to negotiate with Lycett, apparently because it was with Budapest Bank. This was the period, from mid-1993 to mid-1994, when turnover of the subsidiary more than doubled, and there was a large increase in the required working capital. Budapest Bank had agreed that there were to be no repayments of the loan between July and August 1994, but then asked that the entire loan be repaid at the end of October 1994, a date later extended to 31 January 1995.

According to the finance director, Phil Sage, the bank did not understand the concept of lending on security – the loan from the bank was in fact only around 20 per cent of the Lycett Danubius secured assets: 'they had decided they did not like Lycett and wanted them to go away and pay up'. The problems were exacerbated when Lycett went into administration in the UK, and the Caterpillar contract on which everything was originally based became null and void. It became from that point onwards impossible to get export finance without an ongoing contract, and impossible to get a contract without working capital. Though the company has the capacity to produce £1.5 million of output per month, it produced in March 1995 only £130,000, and the labour force has dwindled to its technical minimum of 65 on the shopfloor. The last remaining orders are with Mitsubishi and Boss.

Lycett Industries UK and Caterpillar

Behind this sorry tale is the deteriorating relationship between Lycett and Caterpillar. Problems began once operating losses emerged in the Caterpillar contract in 1992. According to Armitage, 'the more the volume increased, the greater the losses'. Lycett asked Caterpillar for a price increase, which was agreed on a temporary basis, giving Lycett 'time to sort things out'.

Conflict over the Budapest plant

Armitage decided that the only way to achieve the output prices Caterpillar wanted was to cut one of the two plants: Nottingham or

Budapest. Given Armitage's view of the long-term prospects for the industry in the UK, he chose to keep the Budapest facility. However, Caterpillar wanted to retain the Nottingham factory. The company wanted to keep a facility close by it, and was dubious about Lycett's ability to achieve just-in-time delivery from Budapest. Caterpillar was also expanding itself into eastern Europe, and it probably did not fit its strategy to undertake such developments in partnership with its UK supplier. It is possible that Caterpillar was also beginning to believe that it had become too reliant on Lycett for its UK operation, though after Lycett went into administration, the Nottingham plant was sold and has continued to supply Caterpillar under the new owners. Caterpillar stated that it would start to dual-source its supplies; however, it continues to single-source from a UK factory.

Liquidation

Whatever the reason, Caterpillar withdrew first its financial support, and then its custom, driving Lycett into administration in November 1994. Armitage initially hoped that Lycett would be given one year to repay the large outstanding debt of £4 million to Caterpillar, so that it could continue to operate from Budapest on a contract from CASE (Caterpillar's main competitor in Europe), which would offer Lycett greater recovery of overheads. Lycett had thought that it would be feasible to repay the loan, but could only raise £600,000. Even this it wanted to invest in a paint plant, not use to repay debt; a plan which seemed to be accepted by Caterpillar on 1 October 1994. However, Caterpillar suddenly attempted to put the company into liquidation on 1 November 1994. At that time, Lycett had assets in excess of the debt: its site alone was worth £5 million. However, the company still went into administration on 11 November, and, within two hours, the administrators dismissed the manager at Lycett Danubius, though the order had been to save that company. In fact, the managers re-formed the company and re-employed everyone, but morale did not recover.

Evaluation

This is the case of a UK engineering company moving to central and eastern Europe to save labour and raw material costs, and to access new and expanding markets. The underlying concept may have been sound but the company had neither the resources nor the experience to carry the project through successfully. The increasing reliance on

Caterpillar, and the conflicting strategic commitments in eastern Europe, were the final nails in the coffin of an overambitious and underfinanced project. To quote Armitage, 'We were too small a company to take on a position which meant that we became the largest UK-owned employer in Hungary'.

Postscript

Since this study was undertaken, the chairman of Lycett Danubius, Robert Armitage, has been able to buy back the share capital of Lycett Danubius Rt from the administrators and is now the major shareholder in the company. He has restructured and reduced the size of the operation and now operates with only two expatriates, but has rebuilt the workforce to 185. The order book is strong and the company is trading profitably on a month-to-month basis. Armitage has secured orders from the UK, Sweden, Holland and Germany. However, the future of the business remains very uncertain because of the residue of creditors that Lycett has agreed to repay in Hungary. It is the chairman's intention to maintain the business at a much smaller level and to have limited horizons for growth; even so, the order book for the next year will provide Lycett with a turnover in excess of £6 million.

10

Schöller Lebensmittel GmbH & Co. KG

This is the case of Schöller Lebensmittel GmbH & Co. KG and its investment in Hungary. It is an ice cream and frozen foods manufacturer with its headquarters in Germany.

Overview

Schöller was a family-owned firm until 1994, when the majority ownership was transferred to Südzucker AG, one of Europe's largest sugar producers. This is a case of a firm that is in a strong position in its domestic market, has a number of subsidiaries in western Europe looking for new and expanding markets, and is moving quickly to take advantage of the opportunities that have opened up in central and eastern Europe. The case involves a joint venture with an existing firm in Hungary rather than a greenfield investment, as this was seen as the best way to obtain substantial market share rapidly. However, the joint venture involved high levels of new investment and may be best described as a 'brownfield' investment. Although Schöller was the first major ice cream producer investing in the Hungarian market, Unilever entered the market as a relatively fast second entrant and rapidly overtook Schöller in terms of domestic market share. This case, therefore, also demonstrates the dynamics of competition for market share between established western companies in central and eastern Europe. It also illustrates the importance of advertising and marketing both in obtaining market share and in trying to change and develop consumer tastes from existing patterns. Overall, the investment in Hungary is seen by Schöller as a success, and subsequent investments have been made in Poland and the Czech Republic (although in the latter case not for production).

Sector background

The food and drink sector in general is a maturing market in western Europe and this is also true for the ice cream segment of the sector. Key strategies for firms are, consequently, to increase added value by marketing higher-quality or innovative products. This is a sector and subsector where advertising and brand name are of substantial importance. The characteristics of the market also mean that it is relatively difficult and costly to enter new western markets, given established competition, as this would require very high levels of advertising expenditure. The percentage of overall expenditure accounted for by marketing is in some instances higher in eastern Europe than in western markets, but absolute figures may be smaller. Through this situation, investors hope to gain a significant market share quickly and then grow with the market later on. Together with marketing and advertising, quality and product range are also key features. Access to, and control of, distribution networks is also of major importance.

The food and drink sector as a whole is a competitive environment dominated by a small number of multinational enterprises, but there is high regional variation and the relative roles of small and large firms vary by country. The sector – and the ice cream subsector – can be broadly defined as low technology; however, there have been developments in the processing machinery used. In particular, there has been a demand for more efficient and more flexible machinery. Application of computer control processes to production has been one important development. These result in faster speed of production and higher quality. However, apart from such developments, the basic technology involved in producing ice cream has remained substantially the same for many years. The bottleneck in the process is the packaging stage, as the packaging machines operate relatively slowly.

Ownership and organizational structure

Schöller was a family firm in which the strategy and development of the firm were strongly influenced and directed by the family owners. The Schöller family maintained a majority share ownership until October 1994 – immediately prior to this, Herr Schöller held 51 per cent of the equity and Südzucker held 49 per cent. From October 1994, Südzucker took control of 65 per cent of the equity and Schöller retained a share of only 35 per cent. It is relatively early to see the impact of this ownership change on the structure and strategy of Schöller GmbH, but changes are probably due to the shift from the direct entrepreneurial involvement of the dominant owner to the dominant owner being a large existing company – one likely outcome is more decision-making by committee at senior management and board level.

In addition to its Hungarian subsidiary, Schöller has production subsidiaries in Belgium, Austria, France and Poland. It has marketing and distribution subsidiaries in a number of other countries, including the Czech Republic, and controls many distribution outlets. In Germany it has the second largest market share after Unilever, its overall market share being about 29 per cent. In Austria, it has a market share of just over 20 per cent but its market share in other western countries is relatively small. It also exports to a large number of countries. Its total turnover is between DM 1.5 billion and DM 2 billion, and total employment is about 6,500.

The Schöller headquarters is in Nuremberg, where central management functions are located, together with a large production facility. Management functions in the headquarters include: sales, commerce, production and technology, personnel, finance and marketing. Schöller aims to be relatively decentralized and to give some local decision-making autonomy to its subsidiaries. However, annual budgets and investment plans are agreed with the headquarters, and there is central influence and advice in other key functional areas, especially marketing. In general, there is closer central management communication and coordination with the subsidiaries in central and eastern Europe than with the western European subsidiaries. The relative time allocation to eastern subsidiaries is about twice as large as that to western subsidiaries. This in part reflects the learning processes in the subsidiaries in central and eastern Europe, it also reflects the fact that market change in eastern Europe tends to happen at a much faster pace than in western markets. The subsidiaries in the eastern countries tend to be more communicative with the parent company than the western subsidiaries.

Subsidiaries report every month to the headquarters: a sales report, consolidated profit and loss statement and balance sheet are produced. The profit and loss calculation is the key measure for monitoring and comparing subsidiaries' performance.

The organization of labour relations varies across its subsidiaries. In the headquarters, the workforce is represented by the German food and tobacco union. Wages in Germany are at the level of the average wage.

Products and production process

Schöller produces ice creams and frozen food products, with a range of about 160 different products. The market has broadly three segments: traditional trade, retail trade and restaurants. Traditional trade refers to sales from locations such as kiosks and petrol stations – so-called 'impulse' sales. The minimum efficient scale in production of impulse ice cream is 25 million units per year. However, lower quantities may be produced in order to provide adequate variety and product mix. Quality, product differentiation and marketing and advertising, together with distribution networks, are all important and interdependent aspects of production and sales.

The basic principles behind ice cream manufacture have remained virtually the same for many years. Major changes are mainly due to the use of computers, resulting in increased speed and higher quality. Over time, there has been change in the form of presentation, such as whether there is a chocolate cover or an almond cover, but, for example, there have been only slight changes in the taste of standard vanilla ice cream. Packaging machines operate relatively slowly and represent a bottleneck in the production process. There are three main functions or issues for packaging: hygiene/protection, visual impact, and environmental considerations (recycling). Packaging must also contain information on ingredients according to the relevant legal requirements.

Strategy

Schöller's main strategic orientation is to focus on market share as its key aim and indicator. Maintaining and expanding market share depends both on quality and on advertising – these are, in general, of greater importance than price, though this varies by market. It is also a question of targeting the right markets. Schöller aims to have a consumer and market orientation rather than a production orientation. This represents a conscious shift in strategy over the last two to three years. This has been reflected in some organizational changes – a marketing coordination department was created which is responsible for brand name and the overall value chain, while the subsidiaries are responsible for local marketing, which will need to vary to take account of local circumstances.

As western markets are maturing, the main prospects for market share and market growth lie in central and eastern Europe – these are seen as the markets for the future.

Competitive strengths and position

Schöller has the second largest market share in Germany, at about 29 per cent, compared to Unilever, which is responsible for about half the market. They have approximately equal market shares in the traditional trade segment but Unilever has a larger market share in the retail and restaurant segments.

One of Schöller's main competitive strengths is its quality and product variety. In the high-quality product range, its Mövenpick range holds the quality leadership. The marketing strategy defines and promotes a different 'ice cream of the year' every year, during which period one or two different or new tastes form the marketing focus. Schöller is market leader in this premier segment, with 44 per cent market share.

The decision to invest in Hungary

The decision to invest in Hungary was a strategic one motivated by the aim of establishing new markets and market share in central and east European countries. This decision reflected both the new market opportunities that opened up in eastern Europe after 1989 and the lack of opportunities for substantial new growth in western markets. The main initial information required to assess markets was the overall market size, i.e. population, income etc. and existing sales in ice cream. There were various reasons for choosing Hungary as the initial location – the assessment of the Hungarian market was that it was most developed, and Schöller had a subsidiary in Austria which was, therefore, close and could support the project. The aim was both to produce for the Hungarian market and to use the investment as a basis for expanding into markets further east through exports.

The decision to invest through a joint venture was taken both because this would allow faster access to the market and because Schöller could benefit from the existing market share of the joint venture partner. The existence of a suitable partner in Hungary added to the motivation for the initial selection of Hungary. In contrast, in Czechoslovakia no existing producer was the appropriate size, while in Poland, a greenfield investment was made, motivated in part by the high import tariffs which made local production more profitable.

Joint venture negotiations

There were two main ice cream manufacturers in Hungary in 1989 – one was a state-owned company, and one, Budatej, was owned by a cooperative of 12 agricultural companies. Budatej was the market leader and was also the closest to Budapest. Schöller first visited Hungary in September 1989, responding rapidly to the developments in central and eastern Europe. Schöller decided to focus on Budatej, and negotiations and discussions were conducted over one year. Discussions were simplified by the ownership structure of Budatej, since there was no need to go through the government via the State Property Agency. Schöller did have to have discussions with all 12 companies but, as agricultural prices were falling, the companies were keen to negotiate. It was apparent to the Budatej management that it could not compete with the western competition entering the Hungarian market, particularly Unilever and Schöller. It was therefore positively inclined to negotiate with Schöller.

Budatej was founded in the early 1970s to produce mainly milk products; from the late 1970s, it started to produce ice cream. It had a distribution network involving 12 subsidiaries across Hungary and provided retail outlets with freezers. This distribution network was also one of the attractions of the company to Schöller. By the late 1980s, Budatej had a Hungarian market share of 55 per cent.

In December 1990, Schöller signed a letter of intent to form a joint venture with Budatej. The final agreement was made in autumn 1991. Initial ownership was Schöller 51 per cent and Budatej 49 per cent. In 1992, Schöller increased its share capital and bought out all the Hungarian owners except one, giving Schöller 97 per cent ownership. This subsequently increased to 98 per cent, and in April 1995 increased to 100 per cent ownership. The joint venture was called Schöller-Budatej BT. The increase in ownership to 98 per cent reflected a desire by Schöller for full control and some dissatisfaction with working with the joint venture partner.

Schöller did also receive some incentives for investing in Hungary. In particular, it was given tax advantages by the government in the form of 60 per cent tax relief on profits provided that they were reinvested in Hungary. This is not seen as a major advantage, as high profits would not be predicted in the early stages of such an investment. A second incentive was permission to bring machines into the country without paying import tariffs. This could only be done under the condition that the machines formed part of the equity of the company. This was important because of the need to import freezers.

However, as discussed further below, major difficulties arose around this issue.

In 1992, Schöller made a second investment in Hungary, acquiring a frozen foods manufacturer – Mirsa. Here, it was given 100 per cent tax relief for 10 years. However, subsequently, levels of tax relief have been reduced in Hungary.

Investment and restructuring

The Schöller investment in Hungary may best be described as a 'brownfield' investment, since, although a joint venture was formed with an existing firm, Schöller effectively reconstructed the factory and introduced four new production lines, so that there is only one remaining old – Danish – production line. The total cost of the investment was DM 80 million. In addition to changing the production lines, the infrastructure was also altered – the sewage and water systems were changed, as were the electrical wiring and energy systems. The distribution warehouses were also rebuilt, and new freezers were provided to shops. Rebuilding started in September 1991 and production started in June 1992. In the interim period, Schöller serviced the market through exports. The production technology is the same in Hungary as in Germany.

There were substantial changes to the workforce. In production, the workforce was reduced by 60 per cent and administrative employees were also reduced. However, there was a large increase in the sales force as part of the important need to build up the distribution network. Schöller was not prepared to give any employment guarantees during its negotiations to establish the joint venture and subsequently a milk-bottling plant which belonged to the firm was closed down. Overall, as indicated in Table 10.1, employment has increased. Sales fell in 1991, but recovered in 1992 as the joint venture got underway. In real terms, sales were roughly constant from 1992 to 1994.

Table 10.1 Sales and employment in Schöller-Budatej

	1990	1991	1992	1993	1994
Sales (HUF '000s)	1,191,715	715,345	2,142,994	2,403,256	2,995,356
Employment	264	286	328	357	392

HUF = Hungarian forints.

Management

There are three German managers in Schöller-Budatej. As in the Polish subsidiary, there are two joint managing directors – one German and one local (Hungarian). The Hungarian joint managing director was the previous director of Budatej and had impressed Schöller during the joint venture negotiations. There have never been more than three German managers in Schöller-Budatej. However, there are three managers stationed in Germany who specialize respectively in the three main market segments – traditional, restaurants and retail – and who visit Hungary for two days each month. From the summer of 1995, the Hungarian subsidiary was given more independence and only one manager continued to visit the firm, on a less frequent basis. Marketing was until very recently seen as a function where a Western background is central. However, a Hungarian marketing manager is now employed and several marketing positions in Nuremberg which dealt with marketing in CEE have been eliminated. The ability to take a medium-term strategic view of marketing – a vision to the year 2000 – is seen as central, and something that a Western manager is currently more capable of doing. Upper levels of Hungarian management are expected to be able to speak German.

During the first two or three years of the joint venture, there was substantial management control from the Nuremberg headquarters. The subsidiary now has more autonomy in a number of decision areas. However, organizational change and learning are not yet complete, and headquarters managers spend relatively more time on communication with their eastern than their western subsidiaries. This is more due to the faster development of the market and the competition than any inability on the part of the management.

Schöller has experienced some difficulties in transferring its German management system to Hungary and considers that this may have initially been done too quickly without taking sufficiently into account local characteristics of production and sales. One important and difficult issue in developing local managers is developing decision-making abilities and the idea of management as constructive leadership rather than based on hierarchy and authority. In general, the younger generation is seen as more open to these concepts. Even so, it is difficult to promote managers from the third or fourth grade to the first grade.

Finance

The investments in Schöller-Budatej were financed from Schöller's own funds and from borrowing in Germany. The loans were then given to the subsidiary initially, but from the beginning of 1994 the subsidiary financed itself through banks in Hungary. Schöller did not apply for any German government support or credit insurance. This was because the total sum invested may have been too large, because it would have been too time-consuming and because Schöller did not want to give up any independence in decision-making. Schöller-Budatej had an initial equity base of DM 21.5 million in 1991; by 1995, DM 80 million had been invested in it.

The overall financial evaluation of the Schöller-Budatej investment is done by Schöller headquarters. The budget is produced annually and agreed between the headquarters and the subsidiary. Because of the large seasonal aspect of sales, financial flows vary throughout the year and there is a large short-term financing need in winter and spring. The company borrows locally using Hungarian banks in both DM and Hungarian forints. The two major banks have in one case a Dutch parent company and in the other a German parent company. A Hungarian bank without a foreign parent company was the main bank connection for Schöller-Budatej, but due to poor service and conditions the local management changed its banking relationships completely. It has a substantial equity base (about 90 per cent of assets), which the parent company believes to be important. The commercial director in the subsidiary is responsible for the budget and finance – there is no separate financial director in the CEE subsidiaries.

Distribution network

An efficient distribution network is a central element of competitiveness in this sector. One key part of developing the distribution network was to ensure that modern freezers were installed at supply points. This was critical for ensuring that products are stored at a sufficiently low temperature, to maintain quality, and for ensuring control over whose products are stored in the freezer – the aim is to ensure that only Schöller products are stored in Schöller-supplied freezers. When Schöller initially invested, fixed assets necessary for the production process could be brought in without import duties as long as they stayed in the firm for at least three years. The letter of intent establishing the joint venture had stated the number of freezers to be brought in.

The government then announced its intention to collect an import duty on the freezers. This bill would have been DM 7 million for two years. Schöller was involved in long and hard discussions with the Hungarian government over this issue and obtained some support from its own local government in Germany. The dispute was reported in the media, and Schöller finally compromised on paying a negligible amount rather than prolonging the discussion and damaging client relations through further media exposure. This problem occupied senior management time in the Hungarian firm for a number of months.

Market share and competition

Schöller was the first Western firm into the market and initially had a market share of 55 per cent. Unilever entered the market second in 1992 through the acquisition of the state-owned ice cream firm – Veszpremtej – although it was exporting into the market from 1990. Remaining competition was from small domestic firms. Schöller lost market share relatively rapidly to Unilever, although in real terms Schöller's sales were roughly constant from 1992 to 1994. Unilever was, therefore, taking a larger share of a growing market. Current market shares are, approximately, Unilever 55 per cent, Schöller 35 per cent. There appear to be a number of reasons for this.

Unilever was aware that it was coming second into the Hungarian market and made very strong marketing efforts in a deliberate marketing strategy to obtain market share. It spent over three times as much on advertising in Hungary as did Schöller – the Unilever advertising budget for Hungary is about DM 3.6 million. Unilever also had a high-quality, well-qualified sales team that took a very aggressive approach. Schöller's sales force was initially less experienced. Unilever also adopted a different approach to products. In particular, it introduced and placed great emphasis on its top brand, Magnum, which was a success. In contrast, Schöller had placed less emphasis on its top brand, Macao, considering it to be expensive for the Hungarian market. Pricing policies – discussed further below – may also have contributed to the initial loss of market share. Schöller's prices were initially 20–25 per cent higher than typical Hungarian ice cream prices, but quality is not yet paid for with a significant price premium in Hungary. Developing a strategy appropriate for the particular characteristics of the Hungarian market is, therefore, important.

Market shares now appear to have stabilized and roughly reflect Western market shares in Germany. Whether Schöller can recapture market share in Hungary remains to be seen. Hungarian consumption levels of ice cream are about one-third of German levels and so there remains scope for substantial market growth and for changing market shares as this growth appears. Furthermore, despite its loss of market share, Schöller expects to break even overall before Unilever. As the goal for 1995 was to gain market share, so the results of the profit and loss account were not very good, taking into account the relatively large amount of hard currency invested. From a profit perspective this is not a satisfactory situation, but it may be typical for many Western investors in the consumer goods industry.

Products and pricing strategy

Schöller-Budatej produces three groups of products which can be differentiated by both price and quality. The first group is the premium-quality range – Mövenpick – and prices for this range are relatively high. The second group is Schöller's standard range. The third group is a lower-price group which includes the brand range previously produced by Budatej – an ice cream range called 'Leo'. The technology and the standards of production for 'Leo' have improved but the price remains low. Initially, the company removed this brand, but it subsequently recognized both consumer attachment to the brand and the importance of having a low-price brand in a market where consumer incomes were low and declining. It reintroduced Leo as an ice cream name, with Schöller as the overall brand name. Identifying the best product names is another important competitive element.

The relatively low incomes and low ice cream consumption per capita in Hungary are two of the important characteristics of the market. Hungarian consumption is estimated to be about 3 litres per head, while in Germany it is about 8.5 litres per head, and in the United States over 20 litres per head. Hungarian consumption did increase by about 40–50 per cent from 1991 to 1995. Although production costs are about the same as in Germany despite lower labour costs, prices in Hungary are lower (by about 25 per cent or more). Production costs are about the same because most of the raw material inputs have to be imported and import duties increase their cost. Per capita consumption is seen as currently developing in a manner similar to that in Germany in the 1950s and 1960s. Hungarian consumption patterns also are more biased seasonally than in Western countries, with relatively less consumed in winter compared to a smaller decline in Western countries. Production and sales patterns are not, therefore, identical – rather, sales exceed production in summer and production exceeds sales in the rest of the year. Product and pricing strategies, therefore, have to take into account these characteristics of the market, both in supplying it and in developing current and future marketing and advertising strategies. In particular, at present it is important to ensure reasonable quality but at a competitive prices given consumer income levels. Costs have been increasing while income levels have been falling but purchasing power is expected to start rising again. Tariff increases which affect costs cannot currently be passed on to the consumer. Additionally, the depreciation costs are relatively high in Hungary, as large-scale machines for the production of ice cream can only be purchased from hard currency countries. Raw materials also represent a proportionately high cost; although many products (e.g. milk, butter, milk powder and sugar) are usually available in Hungary, they are normally sold at world market prices.

About 90 per cent of production is for the domestic market and 10 per cent is exported to other CEE markets, including Bulgaria, the Czech Republic, Russia, Romania and Slovakia.

Production

Production has to be flexible. In early 1995, two shifts were working a five-day week at about 75 per cent capacity. Capacity utilization can increase to respond to both seasonal demand changes and to market growth. The company has a capacity of about 60,000 litres of ice cream per day – about 20 million litres a year. From autumn to spring, it produces both for the market and for the freezer store. Production levels during this period depend on future sales estimates made by the sales department. At the start of the joint venture, Schöller headquarters would make the overall decisions about production levels but subsequently the subsidiary has been given total control of and responsibility for its production decisions. It changes the product range every year, adding new products and removing products that do not sell well.

Schöller aims if possible in its subsidiaries to obtain inputs locally, but this depends on raw product quality levels. In particular, fruit quality is often as yet not of sufficient quality in eastern Europe. In general, the quality of the fruit in Hungary is not high enough for ice cream and so must be imported, though they are hoping to begin to use some domestic substitutes. High-quality chocolate is also imported, while most of the chocolate for the cheaper ranges comes from Hungary. Packaging materials were mostly imported initially but now Schöller has identified higher-quality Hungarian producers and so will be able to source more from Hungary.

Improving quality standards of production, including cleanliness and hygiene, was an important initial task for Schöller. Improved quality depends in part on management and training, as discussed further below, and also on investment in new machines and technology. As described above, major investments were made by Schöller, and four new production lines were installed, together with other investments in the factory and infrastructure. One set of expensive machine parts – for producing stick ice cream – is currently shared between Poland and Hungary, this is taken to and fro, and output placed in stock. Quality standards of the products are now considered to be equivalent to standards in Germany, and the same methods of production quality control are used as in Germany. Productivity levels are difficult to compare but, in general, performance is equal if measured by output per unit of time of a line operated by the same number of workers. This is achieved through the same machinery and the same training. The workforce has had to learn a lot in working with the new technology. Overall productivity has been a little lower than in Germany, reflecting learning, capacity utilization, and existence of old lines and different products.

There are differences in some of the legal regulations in eastern Europe which affect production, particularly labelling of ingredients on packaging. There is an EU regulation that states that a detailed declaration on ingredients is not required for ice cream portions of less than 200 ml. As yet, this regulation has not been adopted in eastern Europe. Hungarian food law is extensive and there is no complete interpretation of every detail, so firms must make their own practical interpretation.

Labour force and training

In Hungary, the labour force is full-time, in contrast to Poland, where substantial seasonal labour is used. Weekly working hours are less flexible in both Hungary and Poland than in Germany. Schöller has experienced problems in trying to negotiate agreement on allowing overtime with local government in Hungary – it has been difficult to obtain a clear written agreement and commitment, though in oral discussions it has appeared possible. At the start of the joint venture, the labour force was restructured, reducing the numbers in production and increasing the sales force. Training is considered important in all areas of the organization. The major emphasis has been placed on training and developing the sales force but there have also been other training initiatives – e.g. accountancy and book-keeping, and on standards of hygiene and cleanliness. When Schöller installed the new machines and technology, it took a number of the workforce to Austria and Germany to show them how it operated – the Hungarian labour force did already have substantial experience of ice cream production, which was an advantage.

One of the main challenges was to train the sales force. Schöller usually aims to use a 'cascade' system of training through 'training the trainer'. However, it has found until now that this system does not work very well in eastern Europe. Therefore, in 1995, Schöller set up a large central training programme where 500 sales people were trained in sales know-how in their own language. This aimed to introduce to the workforce new concepts, attitudes and approaches, whether for new or pre-existing jobs. For example, one key position here is that of the driver delivering products, who is the sole contact with the kiosk or outlet manager. Previously, this was a low-status job and there was no emphasis on marketing. Schöller has aimed to train drivers so that they communicate with the outlet manager about display, stock planning, promoting new varieties and not placing competitors' products in the freezer. Drivers are also trained concerning route planning. Schöller is now monitoring the outcome of this central training programme and will also continue the 'train the trainer' principle.

Work attitudes are considered to be between good and satisfactory. Employees in Hungary tend to be less committed to the company than those in Germany and there are other differences. Management experience is that employees are less able to take criticism and are less willing to make decisions and take responsibility, but many are beginning to learn. However, this remains a problem and employees tend to lack initiative. There is also no natural tendency to cooperate across groups and areas. Prior to the acquisition, the company was not sales-oriented, which affected attitudes in all areas.

Wages were initially set by headquarters in Germany, but the decisions are now taken locally. Schöller-Budatej used to pay above-average wages but wage levels are now average. It currently increases most wages by an amount far below the level of inflation, but where it sees a need for regrading this will be done and good performance will be rewarded. However, it does not in general have specific bonus schemes, as this could encourage an expectation that a bonus is always due. There are, however, bonus schemes in the sales department, and, to try to avoid wastage, in the production department.

Schöller-Budatej does not have a works council, though the workforce would be entitled to request the formation of one. As yet it has not done so, and Schöller tries to discuss labour issues directly with the workforce and encourages it to elect representatives to work for it. There is a preference for informal communication between management and workers.

Conclusion

This is a case of a company investing in a joint venture in order to obtain market share and future sales opportunities. Although it was a joint venture, there were substantial levels of new investment, and Schöller subsequently moved to 100 per cent ownership. The company now has a substantial market share in Hungary – but this is lower than its original share, due to strong competition from Unilever. The company is expecting to break even in the next two to three years.

11

United Biscuits (Holdings) plc

Overview

This is the case of a UK biscuit and snack food manufacturer, McVitie's Group, an operating division of United Biscuits, which is the second largest producer of biscuits in Europe. McVitie's undertook a joint venture with Hungary's largest biscuit manufacturer, Györi Keksz, and has subsequently undertaken a greenfield investment in a snack factory. The investment in eastern Europe was experimental; it was the first time that the company had invested in the region, and there were no established methods for operating in eastern European markets. The company had to be flexible and innovative in its approach, but took a risk-averse stance. The Hungarian company which it acquired had to be transformed to reach United Biscuits' high quality standards. Numerous operating problems emerged and have had to be overcome. However, the expansion into Hungary has eventually been successful and the joint venture and greenfield investment are now both profitable.

Sectoral setting

Biscuits and snacks are final consumption goods. The industry is oligopolistic within a country, due to the cost advantages that accrue to economies of scale, with tariffs forming a barrier to entry for importers. A decision about whether to produce within a country or import is liable to be based largely on the size of the population. The minimum efficient scale of production appears to be for a population of around 5 million people. A brand name or series of brand names can be considered intangible assets for biscuit and snack manufacturers, and the brand name, rather than the product name, will tend to be a major defining characteristic between companies, though some firms do have unique products that help to differentiate them from others.

United Biscuits (Holdings) plc

United Biscuits is a holding company with four operating divisions, each producing different products and covering different geographical areas. The divisions are: McVitie's Group, Europe's second largest biscuit manufacturer; KP Foods Group, the market leader in the production of savoury snack food in the UK, Australia and the Asia Pacific region (excluding Japan); and Ross Young's, the second largest UK frozen food manufacturer. Each division has its own management board, financial targets and strategic plans. United Biscuits was restructured and the operating divisions created in 1988. McVitie's Group's 'mission' is to be the most successful biscuit manufacturer in Europe. The group expanded in Europe throughout the 1980s and early 1990s, primarily through acquisition. Thus, in 1990 the group acquired Koninklijke Verkade, a Dutch firm which was the country's leading manufacturer of biscuits and chocolate. In 1991, the group purchased a controlling share in Oxford Biscuits of Denmark and a 49 per cent share in Fazer Biscuits in Finland. In 1993, a joint venture was agreed between McVitie's and Royal Brands, a Spanish biscuit manufacturer, and between United Biscuits and San, who hold the second position in the Polish biscuit market. The Hungarian venture – an 84 per cent stake in Györi Keksz – fits into this strategy.

Organizational structure of United Biscuits

United Biscuits has a number of central group functions, including: finance and accounting, business planning, personnel, company secretariat, pensions, legal affairs and corporate communications. There is an International Production Services department (IPS) that is responsible for organizing the quality aspects of the raw ingredients in the production process on behalf of the operating divisions. After the acquisition of a new firm, IPS performs key functions, ensuring that consistency of production is achieved and securing domestic suppliers for raw materials.

The managing directors of the individual divisions have total responsibility for targets, profitability, cash flow targets and return on capital; the operating results are driven by local management. The treasury, taxation and interest decisions are all head office functions. Within each division, the board will liaise with the managing directors of the various units that comprise the division in order to set targets. United Biscuits will agree with the division the amount of money that it is allowed for investment and it is up to the division to decide the allocation between subsidiaries. Finance required for capital expenditure and acquisition is considered separately.

In summary, the operating divisions have a considerable degree of autonomy over the day-to-day running of their business but United Biscuits runs a very centralized operation on the finance and treasury side. Divisions must gain approval for most investment decisions and are not allowed to run cash surpluses; all additional funds must be returned to the group treasury.

Corporate strategy

The company strategy is determined by the chief executive and board. Any change in the core activities of the group is always decided at this level, and they also decide the direction in which the operating divisions should focus. The overall strategy of the company is to be a world leader in the production and marketing of snack food, which includes: biscuits, salty and savoury snacks, the majority of the Ross Young's foods that need microwaving, chilled foods and possibly confectionery (though having recently sold the confectionery-producing division, Terry's, this is a less important area) Given resource limitations, the approach is to concentrate on markets where the company can have a rapid result in terms of market share. The company will often initially attempt to develop the local business by importing its products before attempting to establish a production facility, although this will depend on various factors, including the country, its flexibility and its tariff duties.

Competitors in Western markets

The snack food industry internationally comprises a few multinational firms and many local competitors in each country. Competition is not price-based, as prices tend to be fairly similar across the competitors. Rather, it is based primarily on quality, branding and efficiency of distribution.

United Biscuits' McVitie's and KP divisions produce primarily for the European market. In terms of snacks, PepsiCo and United Biscuits both have a 30 per cent market share in Europe. In the United States, PepsiCo is dominant, with 45 per cent of the market as opposed to United Biscuits' 2–3 per cent. PepsiCo is also strong in The

Netherlands and Spain, whereas United Biscuits' market share is higher in France, Belgium and Italy. In the biscuit market the major competitors are BSN and Bahlsen, who together hold around 20–25 per cent of the market. Pain Jacquet is strong in both France and Germany, Anheuser and Allied Lyons dominate the Spanish market, and Nestlé is also a major competitor across the region.

McVitie's Group

McVitie's has the responsibility within United Biscuits for developing the company's biscuit market in Europe. Its objective is to become the largest manufacturer of biscuits in Europe. McVitie's core market is the UK where it is market leader. It uses its prominence in the UK market to generate the capital for expansion. McVitie's progress in western Europe has been steady, though the market is mature and dramatic market growth is not to be expected. Though there is believed also to be potential for growth in the Mediterranean and Scandinavian countries, McVitie's is focusing on the eastern European markets because it believes that the opportunity for growth in this region is substantial. Biscuit manufacture is essentially a cottage industry in most countries of the region, but there are brand names that are well established and popular. This means that, in McVitie's view, the optimal strategy for entering such markets is by acquisition of one of the dominant firms. This was the strategy employed in both Hungary and Poland.

Evaluation of potential foreign direct investments

McVitie's has developed an internal decision-making process for evaluating new investments in central and eastern Europe (CEE) and the former Soviet Union. There are three stages:

- a country-screening process;
- an evaluation of the biscuit market;
- market entry options.

Country screening

Country screening addresses various key issues, including:

- Size of the population; this is important to ensure minimum efficient scale of production.

- The net wealth of the population and income distribution; if the majority of the population is living in poverty, it is less likely to be able to afford biscuits or snacks.
- The stability of government, the level of corruption and the bureaucracy involved in forming a joint venture or greenfield investment; future expropriation of property is also an issue.

Evaluation of the biscuit market

McVitie's will then analyse more closely the market-specific characteristics, which will include the following.

- Market stability, including: the ease of access to the market; telecommunications; linguistic difficulties; visa complications; legal and banking sector framework.
- The competitiveness of the market, which is important strategically.
- The number of competitors and their size will determine whether an optimal strategy might be to acquire a top brand, or, if none exists, a greenfield site.
- The eating habits of the population. The levels of per capita consumption and typical diet are analysed to see whether biscuits and snacks are traditionally products that the people have consumed. In central and eastern Europe, biscuits are part of the diet, though snacks and crisps that were fried instead of baked were almost unheard of prior to 1989.
- The availability of ingredients and the costs of importing those products which are not available. There are usually tariffs with the EU countries for agricultural goods and often a quota system is in operation. Quotas are particularly hard to circumvent and so if a crop fails there may be no way of importing the required ingredients.

McVitie's has also to decide whether it is feasible to run a company in the current business environment; it needs to be confident that it could work with the distributors or set up a distribution network where necessary.

Market entry options

McVitie's then analyses potential market entry routes. These include exporting, setting up a sales venture, or manufacturing. Import tariffs are an important consideration in investment (FDI) decisions. If they exist, then this makes foreign direct investment a more attractive alternative than importing, though other competitors may already be investing in the market. If there are tariffs, then McVitie's must form an opinion about their duration. As a manufacturer in a country, if it manages to secure a first mover advantage, import duties can provide a valuable period of protection, allowing the company to develop a defensible position prior to entry of its competitors. As an importer, tariff barriers often mean that it is impossible to compete on the domestic market without running at a loss. Where a brand already exists with a strong market position, the optimal strategy is likely to be an acquisition of that company.

McVitie's has found in some instances that companies in central and eastern Europe, knowing that they may not survive without a Western partner, have approached them to request a joint venture. At this stage, the company screening processes will be applied and aspects such as the ability to work with the management of the company, the level of technology at the firm, and the amount of investment required to bring the firm up to McVitie's standards, will be analysed. Consideration will also be given to the number of workers the firm has and their skill level.

If there is no brand available for it to invest in, or, as in the case of the snack market for Hungary, the product is new for the country, then McVitie's will consider greenfield investment. However, if a competitor has acquired the leading brand, it may have lost the valuable first mover advantage.

This decision-making, operationalized via a series of decision matrices, led McVitie's to choose Hungary for its first investment in central and eastern Europe. The market, of 10.3 million people, was smaller than some neighbouring countries, but was considered to be large enough to be profitable, yet small enough to be manageable. At the time the decision was made, in 1989, Hungary was widely regarded as politically the most stable country in the region and had been open to foreign investors since 1972. Within the biscuit market, 80 per cent tariffs were being levied on the importation of biscuits into Hungary and this would provide McVitie's with a limited period of time within which it could restructure a company and achieve a defensible market position. Hungary was also the country most open at that time to joint ventures with foreign firms. Moreover, greenfield investments which, because of property rights issues, were difficult to undertake elsewhere were feasible. Finally, Hungary was the country that looked least likely to ease off in its reform process.

Table 11.1 Output in the Hungarian food-processing industry for 1993

Sector	%
Meat and fish processing	19.2
Milk and dairy products	12.5
Fodder production	10.7
Fruit and vegetable processing	7.7
Poultry processing	7.2
Sugar	5.4
Beer	5.1
Tobacco	4.1
Vegetable oil	3.5
Soft drinks	2.9
Alcohol	2.8
Confectionery	2.7
Other	16.9
Total	100.0

Source: Reuters Business Briefing, 22 August 1994.

Experience in central and eastern Europe

Sectoral setting in Hungary

Sales in the Hungarian sweets and biscuits industry are approximately US$ 230 million. The latest detailed figures on the subsectors of the food industry are from 1993. In that year, confectionery accounted for 2.7 per cent of national output (Table 11.1). Market structure has become highly non-competitive since reforms began. Three firms dominated sales in 1991. The important players are Quintie Sweets Industry Ltd and Nestlé Hungary Ltd. These companies were, respectively, ranked (based on their net sales) 19 and 98 in the top 200 list of Hungarian firms in 1991. The next biscuit and sweets firm was Györi Keksz, the company acquired by United Biscuits, which was ranked 153. Nestlé Hungary Ltd was ranked 7 on a list based on the size of foreign-owned equity capital of Hungarian joint ventures, while Györi Keksz was ranked 20.

Competitors

Györi Keksz is the top biscuit manufacturer in Hungary, with a 50 per cent market share. Its current main competitors are Bahlsen,

Stollwerck, Burton's, Nestlé, Manner and Auer, all Western companies either exporting to or manufacturing within Hungary. Györi Keksz is also the market leader for boiled sweets, where Nestlé is the most important competitor.

Snack production using the Croky name (a brand name used by United Biscuits elsewhere in continental Europe) was started by McVitie's in 1993 and its market share is now 34 per cent. Its position is improving; it is second to Chio, a company owned by the Convent Group which recently acquired Zweiffel and Wolf, whose market share is around 36 per cent.

For all products there is a variety of smaller domestic Hungarian manufacturers that charge lower prices but provide lower quality. These manufacturers pose a threat for McVitie's because it is felt that Hungarians consider snacks to be luxuries, and are hence more likely to purchase the cheaper brands regardless of the differences in the quality and consistency of the product or its freshness. However, these manufacturers only produce on a small scale and represent threats only in small, localized areas.

Foreign direct investment in Hungary

McVitie's made its decision to invest in Hungary in 1989. The target company, Györi Keksz, generated profits in the past and had a market-oriented outlook. However, the decision to enter negotiations was not based on the location of the company, although Györ in the northwest of Hungary, half-way between Budapest and Vienna, is Hungary's second most important city for industry. Rather, it was based on the brand advantage and the market share that McVitie's would acquire. McVitie's visited the company in May 1989, and there was a year of discussions before the decision was made.

Györi Keksz was looking for a partner in the West to supply it with Western technology, management techniques and know-how. It knew that the company would be severely pressured by Western competition and that it would be privatized. Management decided to find a partner for itself rather than waiting for the government to act. It approached several companies, including United Biscuits. Following discussions, a tender was set up, and bid for by United Biscuits and Bahlsen. The management of Györi Keksz favoured United Biscuits, because it said it was prepared to continue with some of the Györi Keksz products and was felt to have the expertise required to ensure that Györi Keksz would be competitive in the

Hungarian market. The Hungarian management also believed that Bahlsen's products were too expensive for the Hungarian market. Finally, the management of Györi Keksz thought that it would prefer to work with a UK rather than a German firm.

In May 1990, McVitie's and the board of Györi Keksz presented a united front to the works council, explaining McVitie's' commitments laid out in its business plan:

- to preserve the Györi Keksz identity;
- to retain the existing board;
- to guarantee all jobs for at least one year;
- to create a national sales force;
- to build a greenfield crisps factory.

The support of the works council, the body which represented the workers of Györi Keksz, was crucial, in its own right and to obtain Hungarian government agreement. The works council's major concern was the job security of the employees, and it was reassured by McVitie's. In the autumn of 1990, the three parties went together to the State Property Agency (SPA) and presented it with an agreed proposal. The price was determined after negotiations with the SPA in April 1991.

Ownership structure

McVitie's paid £11.6 million for Györi Keksz, and promised to invest in a greenfield snacks factory at a later stage. United Biscuits subsequently invested a further £4 million in a greenfield snacks factory close to the biscuit plant in Györ. Just after the privatization, United Biscuits owned 84 per cent of the business shares, the SPA owned 5 per cent, the local government of Györ owned approximately 10 per cent and the local government of Jánossomorja owned approximately 2 per cent.

The SPA later offered the employees its shares, which it valued at 71 million Hungarian forints (HUF) ($710,000). The smallest unit that could be purchased was worth HUF 10,000 ($100) but employees only had to contribute half, and the fund for the employees of Györi Keksz provided interest-free loans of three years to help them pay for this. The remainder was given to them by the SPA. However, even with these financial incentives, less than 25 per cent of workers bought shares in the company. Hence the SPA sold 4 per cent of its shares to the employees and the other 1 per cent was purchased by United Biscuits.

United Biscuits promised not to pay a dividend on the Hungarian investment for five years. Most after-tax profits have since been used to increase its capital base, and this has also increased the value of the employee-owned shares. In 1993, United Biscuits bought out the 12 per cent owned by the governments of Györ and Jánossomorja, so the company now has a 96.5 per cent stake in Györi Keksz, with its employees owning 3.5 per cent.

Restructuring Györi Keksz

Background

Györi Keksz used to be a part of the Austrian company Kostlin, and the name was well known in Hungary and in Croatia. The company was established by Lajos Kostlin in 1900, and nationalized in 1949. The next major institutional change was in 1963, when all the chocolate, biscuits and sweets factories in Hungary were put under a Trust known as the Hungarian Sweets Works. This Trust existed until 1981, when a wave of decentralization in Hungary swept most of them away. Györi Keksz became an independent, state-owned firm, which had some autonomy over its own financial and investment decision-making. Györi Keksz invested heavily throughout the 1980s and, with a change in the law in 1988, was able to establish joint ventures with other Hungarian firms. It was one of the first Hungarian companies to do so.

Associated joint ventures and social assets

As a result of this history, McVitie's acquired a company that was in fact a small empire that the company had diversified into an array of ventures. Györi Keksz was the Hungarian market leader in the production of biscuits, wafers, sugar confectionery, steamed peanuts, pudding powders, coffee substitute and lemon tablets. The company owned a plant in Jánossamorja that produced chicory, barley sugar, pudding powders and baking powder. It had a 50 per cent stake in Hungercandi (where it produced Pez sweets) and a 50 per cent stake in Packet (packaging materials). It also owned a guest house in Balaton and another, 40 kilometres from Györ, in the mountains. There is another guest house in Györ that belongs to Györi Keksz itself and is now used for visitors from the UK. The company is still obliged by law to have a surgery with doctors, nurses, a dentist and a woman's doctor, though these people are not now directly employed by Györi Keksz.

Organizational restructuring

McVitie's made relatively few changes on the production and sales side to its new Hungarian subsidiary in the first two years. It was only in late 1992 that McVitie's started to seriously restructure the company. The loss of momentum meant that the changes became harder to instigate.

McVitie's first activities involved financial restructuring. Almost immediately, all the assets that did not fit into the core production strengths of United Biscuits were sold off. This included the chicory factory in Jánossamorja, which was sold to Multi-Extract, and the pudding powders part of the plant, which was sold to Dr Oetker (who had been a customer of the plant), plus the stake in Hungercandi and Packet. The confectionery side of the Györ plant was kept because it was a profitable operation. United Biscuits still owned Terry's, the confectionery company, and continues to develop confectionery businesses in certain territories.

The board of Györi Keksz was expanded by three directors: a commercial director, who is a second-generation Hungarian born in the UK, a production director from Finland and a Hungarian human resources director. The structure of Györi Keksz was consolidated and departments amalgamated to streamline the organizational structure.

Organizational change has been continuous, with major developments in the commercial, marketing and sales divisions. Some departments have been closed, whereas others have been merged to produce a more streamlined organization.

Business strategy for Györi Keksz

By 1993, McVitie's had begun to develop a new business strategy for Györi Keksz. This focused primarily on the domestic market, where the aim was to increase market share in snack production and to attempt to become the top producer in Hungary. In the biscuit, wafer and confectionery markets, the aim was to stabilize market position and maintain the market share, given the huge increase in competition. With regard to overseas sales, then 6 per cent of production, the aim was to increase sales.

Division of responsibilities

Györi Keksz is technically as independent as any of the manufacturing subsidiaries in the McVitie's Group. However, given the significant reorientation that was needed in the first years of the joint venture,

Györi Keksz has largely been following directives from the head office. As the venture has developed, McVitie's has allowed the Györi Keksz board to make more decisions autonomously, but not investment decisions or strategic decisions, e.g. the decision to build the greenfield snacks factory, which was agreed when McVitie's signed the contract to take over Györi Keksz. The decision to make further progress, which was made at the head office, was delayed considerably and not taken until 18 months after the restructuring of the plant commenced (three and a half years after take-over). This probably led to the loss of the first mover advantage in the market. A competitor entered the market first, and secured market leadership which McVitie's has since had to chase.

Restructuring the factory

Finance

McVitie's obtained all its funding for the acquisition from United Biscuits. In turn, United Biscuits raised the funds internally. As for Györi Keksz, it has no outstanding debts, and a high credit rating with the bank. There is a five-year annual financial plan, revised annually in April and approved by head office in the UK.

Technology

Technology in the company falls into three categories: equipment which existed prior to take-over in the biscuit factory; that which has subsequently been added to the biscuit factory; and the technology that was transferred to the snacks factory.

The biscuit factory

Technology levels here are mixed. Some of the plant is state of the art, while other areas house antiquated and inefficient machinery and require labour-intensive techniques to achieve simple tasks. The Hungarian company did make major investments in plant and machinery after 1981, reconstructing the biscuit factory with advanced lines from West Germany. However, there were also some ovens from Russia and machinery from East Germany. One of the ovens, which is Austrian, requires the workers to manually load and unload the trays of biscuits. However, the products made in this way do not feature in the long-term portfolio of biscuits that Györi Keksz intends to produce.

In 1988, Györi Keksz reconstructed its wafer plant and installed the best product line from the world's premier wafer producer, linked to an Italian packaging line. In 1989–90 the company installed a Bosch confectionery line, which was the world's leading model and is capable of producing five different types of products. These newer machines are all computer controlled. The company also made some high-technology smaller investments.

United Biscuits made its first large investment in capital equipment in the biscuit factory in 1994. An entirely new line which is capable of making hard and semi-hard cookies was purchased from The Netherlands. Unfortunately, there have been problems with installation, and this machine has not produced satisfactory test runs. There were also detailed plans for development of the wafer plant, to be completed in 1995. However, these have been shelved because of the recession in the Hungarian economy and the increase in competition in the wafer market.

Some differences remain between the technology in operation in the UK and that in Györi Keksz, notably that the quality of the product is more stable in the UK. The biscuit technology will need to be intensively upgraded if McVitie's carries out its plans to introduce some of its own products.

The snacks factory

United Biscuits' main technological contribution to Györi Keksz came via the snacks plant. The company has built three lines: one for peanuts, one for crisps and one for extruded products (which are maize-based products that are moulded into different shapes). The technology employed was defined by the products that the company wanted to produce. Methods are not high-technology but the machines are of the highest quality. The technology is equivalent to that of United Biscuits in the UK.

Quality

United Biscuits introduced new processes to improve quality management. Györi Keksz did not have facilities to monitor quality and consistency of ingredients, mixing and baking processes or final products. Occasionally it would test final products but, by the time the tests were received, the products had often already been sold. McVitie's sent in the International Production Service unit to work with the production team in Györ to ensure consistency of product and to organize reliable supply chains.

In fact, the uniformity of quality became the most important issue for United Biscuits in the early years of the investment. The priority was to ensure that equipment for quality control was available in all three plants (i.e. biscuits, wafers and confectionery). A quality assurance system was introduced which involved close collaboration between many departments in the company, including raw materials, purchasing, and specification of ingredients and quality control. Now every stage of the production process is rigorously checked. Purchasing of raw materials was done in the past through the central authorities, and the company did not have much control over the choice or quality of the supplier. Now there are new company technical specifications for raw material purchases which have to be met to ensure that the best inputs are received. Tests are carried out on raw materials, and new suppliers are vetted to determine whether adequate hygiene requirements are met and whether supplies meet production needs.

Similar specifications have been introduced at the production level. Controls have been introduced at every step of production; fact sheets explain everything from the mixing of raw ingredients to the temperature for baking. Wastage has decreased and incentives have been introduced to try and reduce wastage further. The use of modern equipment has reduced energy consumption, though with the price increases in the energy sector, total costs have increased greatly.

Packaging was also upgraded to ensure that products had a longer shelf-life. Simultaneously, the logo was redesigned and, instead of using Györi Keksz, which means 'biscuits from Györ', Györi was emphasized. The products were relaunched using a national television campaign to advertise a range of the core products.

Prices and packaging

The design of the packaging and upgrade in the quality of materials used was a cost that McVitie's had to pass on to the consumer. Prices were increased prior to relaunch to try and disassociate the two, and the company absorbed some of the additional cost. Prices were increased again in line with inflation five months later. The new package design was well received by the customers and in the trade.

Marketing

McVitie's employed an expatriate commercial director, an Anglo-Hungarian marketing manager for the biscuits market and an expatriate manager for the marketing of snacks. Given skills shortages, the company felt that it had no choice but to go down the expensive route of employing expatriates.

Györi Keksz has tried to adjust Western marketing techniques for selling biscuits to suit the Hungarian environment. Initially, after the take-over, advertising concentrated on the use of television commercials. This is now proving more expensive and the marketing focus is on promotions, offers and competitions, though television commercials are still used. Competitions have proven particularly successful. For example, there have been promotions to win surf boards and mountain bikes that had a phenomenally high number of participants. Children are particularly targeted for prizes.

The strategy applied for the marketing of snacks uses the same techniques as in the UK and the rest of Europe, though snacks are new to Hungary. Although KP is the United Biscuits snack producer, in central and eastern Europe McVitie's is producing snacks.

Sales

McVitie's expanded the internal sales force and introduced an external sales force. The internal sales organization was based on the McVitie's Dutch sales department, which was considered the one best suited to the Hungarian market in terms of size of population. McVitie's sent a Györi Keksz employee to The Netherlands to analyse the Dutch internal system. He then returned to Hungary and implemented an internal and external sales network following the same principles.

Demand and the market

The biggest problem for McVitie's in the Hungarian market has been the declining purchasing power of the population. Average wages have fallen very sharply in the recession which began in 1991, and are even in the late 1990s only beginning to recover slowly. The biscuit factory is only working at 70 per cent capacity, and there is insufficient demand to justify increasing production levels, though at peak times it is not possible to produce enough for the market.

The company's performance in terms of revenues despite sluggish market conditions has been good. The customer base has been rationalized so that Györi Keksz now deals with wholesalers and national chains only. However, in total, the number of customers has decreased, mainly due to poor market conditions and increased competition; nevertheless, Györi Keksz has been able to maintain its position as market leader.

Employment and training

There were no big redundancies at the biscuit factory itself after the take-over and nearly all the managers stayed. Around 70–80 people took early retirement and some people were moved from maintenance to production. The ratio of blue-collar to white-collar workers has changed. Five years ago there were less than 13 per cent white-collar workers; the average for the food industry in Hungary was 20 per cent. Now, Györi Keksz has a greater than average percentage of white-collar workers, mainly because of the creation of the commercial team. Györi Keksz used to own a plant in Jánossomorja producing ground chicory, a coffee substitute, and employing 350 people. This plant was sold and not all the people were taken on at the biscuit factory; 80 were made redundant by Györi Keksz.

On the commercial side there are still three expatriates, two in marketing and the commercial director. The company operates a system of 'one in, one out', and three Hungarians are working in other branches of McVitie's. This emphasis on expatriate managers for key functions within the organization illustrates the perceived skills gaps, especially in the provincial towns.

Pay and conditions

In 1994 a system was introduced that categorized workers by the importance of their job in the company. Györi Keksz are considered to be average payers in the region. This probably means that the annual increase is average for the region, though the actual income for the majority of the workers in the company is probably below average for the area, since the majority of employees are manual workers.

Wages have increased in line with inflation since take-over, and 200 white-collar workers have a bonus system which is 10 per cent of their base wage. They receive this if the company is doing well, and the bonus is judged on their individual contributions to projects. The only incentives for blue-collar workers cover those working at the snacks factory, where the wages are already significantly higher than at the biscuit factory. Their bonus is based on quantity, quality and cost.

Absenteeism

Absenteeism in the biscuit factory is around 14–17 per cent per year, and the company has introduced incentives to try and reduce this level. Employees typically do not have secondary jobs, but they have plots of land on which they work. In the snack factory, a strategy to deal with absenteeism has reduced it to only 3–4 per cent. The company created a strong disincentive for the workers to call in sick by only issuing one-year renewable contracts contingent on attendance.

Training

United Biscuits has improved training levels, especially for the white-collar workers. For this group of employees, needs are assessed by the line managers, and an appraisal system, introduced in December 1993, highlights the strengths and weaknesses of individual employees. Learning English is mandatory. Employees have been provided with computer training courses, presentational skills training, management training, time management training, and an array of other training schemes. Blue-collar training has not been much greater than the legal minimum, which includes training for driving forklift trucks, for operating lifts and ovens and other equipment, and the minimum required to ensure that United Biscuits' standards of quality and hygiene are met.

Selecting the workforce for the snacks factory

The snacks factory was United Biscuits' first greenfield investment in eastern Europe. The most important factor in the selection of workers was that they should be skilled in more than one area, since there was only a relatively small number of workers. The company interviewed typically younger employees from the biscuit factory and chose only those with good attendance records. The new employees arrived in the new plant before the machines, and were involved in their installation. The skills have been found to be adequate and, since the plant was opened, the company has only had to dismiss two people for misconduct.

Industrial relations

There is a long tradition of trade unions in the Hungarian food industry, and 70 per cent of the workers in Györi Keksz are trade union members. The Györi Keksz management has good relations with the union. Since the 1992 Labour Law, the importance of trade unions has lessened and their aim is to ensure that the employers' actions are in accordance with the law in terms of health and safety conditions, wages etc. The most important right that the trade union has is to be present when the collective contracts are signed. With the exception of the managers, these contracts apply to everyone in Györi Keksz. The trade union's rights have been reduced for wage discussions, and the final decision is the employer's.

A new feature of the company is the works council, which participates in management. It was set up in 1992 and the second elections were due to be held in May 1995. The Labour Law does not prohibit the amalgamation of the trade union and the works council, and in Györi Keksz the two work in parallel, with the same head.

Performance

Overall, United Biscuits achieved its objectives in Hungary. In biscuits, wafers and confectionery, sales have fallen in line with the market, but the company has succeeded in maintaining its market share despite fierce competition. In snacks, however, McVitie's forwent first mover advantage because of delays in entering the market. Exporting has proved difficult, as Györi Keksz's products are not included in any inter-country export agreement.

12

British Vita plc

Overview

This case outlines the experience of a UK chemical company, British Vita plc, in establishing a Polish wholly owned subsidiary, Vita Polymers Poland (VPP). The company was already highly international in 1990; around 60 per cent of turnover derived from continental Europe, and Vita sought further expansion into central and eastern Europe (CEE). As a manufacturer of semi-finished products, primarily polyurethane foam, the company also sought to follow its mainly German customers in the automobile, furniture, bedding and packaging industries who moved eastwards in search of lower labour costs. The factory was built in Poland to fit the perceived market, in terms of both technology and product. Though there were problems in striking the deal, the company has achieved a remarkable degree of cost control in the investment, primarily by using Polish inputs. Output targets were easily met 1995 and the operation in Poland is already profitable.

Overall, the experience has been extremely successful, with Vita establishing itself as Poland's second largest supplier of foam within a year, taking a 30 per cent market share. Moreover, the company has been able to concentrate its sales in the growing part of the market – 80 per cent of output is ultimately finished goods, mainly furniture. Another important element in the success story was Vita's ability to manage the greenfield investment operation, in terms of keeping costs down while attaining both quality and production targets.

History of British Vita

British Vita plc is a medium-sized UK chemicals company based in Manchester. It is an international leader in polymer, fibre and fabric materials technology, with 9,500 employees. Sales in 1994 were £770 million, with a further £300 million in associated companies. British Vita is capitalized on the London Stock Exchange at a value of around £500 million.

Products and markets

The company was founded in 1949–50 by Norman Grimshaw, to make latex foam. The most important product that Vita makes now is cellular polymers, comprising 62 per cent of sales in 1994. One of the production processes for the product was patented by Unifoam, a Netherlands-based manufacturer acquired by Vita, which now holds the patent rights. In the production process, liquid chemicals are mixed under pressure and the foam rises a few seconds after the reaction.

The company's staple product in the cellular polymers division is polyurethane foam, the major markets for which are the automotive, furniture, bedding and packaging industries. The company also has an extremely diversified product range, and does not compete with anyone in all areas. Vita also makes fabrics and fibres, on its own account making up 15 per cent of total revenue, as well as bedding, automotive upholstery and latex.

On a worldwide basis, British Vita is the third largest foam manufacturer, after Foamex and Carpenter in the United States, and it is the largest supplier in Europe. The company has a 4–5 per cent share in the United States, however. It claims to be market leader in the UK, Germany and the Benelux countries, and number two in France and now Poland. There are associated firms in the United States and some African countries.

Multinational activities

British Vita was always internationalist in outlook, in part because the founder attempted to manufacture locally for each market. Early expansions were to the Commonwealth, e.g. Canada, Rhodesia, Nigeria and Zambia, usually via joint ventures. By the 1970s, Europe was becoming an important market for the company, which gradually shifted its focus of activity, until now almost 60 per cent of sales go to continental Europe, with a further 33 per cent to the UK and the remainder around the world.

The company has expanded in Europe, mainly through acquisition. Some £60 million was spent on European acquisitions in the 1980s and early 1990s. In addition to the 35 factories in the UK, Vita has 17 factories in Germany and 35–40 in total on the continent. There are also companies in the United States, Canada, Australia and Africa, though the US company was purchased only recently.

An important reason for this diversity of production base is that the core product – foam – is very bulky, comprising primarily blocks of more than 1 metre in thickness. As a result, transport costs are relatively high and the industry view is that it is not competitive to transport the foam long distances. Maximum ranges of 300–500 kilometres were mentioned in the interviews. Hence factories have to be quite near the final users, i.e. automobile, furniture or bedding manufacturers. This assessment of the relative advantage of multiple sites is strengthened when the technology is taken into account. Foam plants appear to have approximately constant returns to scale, so there are only limited cost advantages to manufacturing at a single large plant. Factories comprise a large mixing tank, a line to allow the foam to dry, and a cutting/curing area. It takes around 14 minutes for the foam to go down the manufacturing track; then it is cut and cured. If we take the technology used in Poland as an example, the foam can be stored for around four weeks. Fixed costs are relatively high, variable costs are mainly raw materials, and transport costs are high.

Performance

After rapid continental expansion during the 1980s, British Vita was hit by the recession, first in the UK, and then in Germany. Demand-side pressures have come from all markets, but especially automobile and furniture customers. Operating profits in 1990 were £53.4 million, slightly higher than in 1994. The main falls in profit were in 1991 and 1993, and press reports in 1993 primarily blamed declines in volumes in continental Europe. Profits in 1993 were squeezed not only by declining volumes but also by increasing raw materials prices: margins were 7.3 per cent in 1991, and 5.9 per cent in 1994. Margins have also been under long-term downward pressure in British Vita's business because the firm's customers, especially those in the automobile industry, have been seeking to cut costs throughout the 1990s.

Despite the resulting weaker cash flow, the company was still in a position by 1993 to make further acquisitions, because there had been a rights issue in 1992 which raised £73 million. Indeed, there was some pressure on management to spend the money: press reports commented negatively in 1993 on the firm's failure to find a use for the funds generated by the rights issue. Just prior to the Polish investment, the chief executive Rod Sellers is reported to have said 'we could get ourselves in a gearing position, move from a net cash position of nearly £40 million to a quite heavily geared position if we wanted to'. He noted acquisition possibilities in eastern Europe. 'If you look into Poland and eastern Europe, there are lots of opportunities there', he said, 'but it is a bit more venture capital there, you have got to take it carefully rather than rushing into it quickly'.

Company structure and strategy

British Vita plc is managed by a main board, which formulates corporate strategy and approves investment and acquisition/disposal decisions as well as treasury policy. The main board consists of a non-executive chairman and five executive and three non-executive directors. Operational issues are addressed by a management board comprising the three executive directors and the senior chairman of the major UK and European subsidiaries. The membership of executive directors on both boards is intended to ensure a close link between strategy and its operational implementation.

Strategy and objectives

The company's main objective, stressed in its publicity material and by management, is to earn profits for its shareholders. This is seen as most likely to be achieved by continuous expansion, initially into Europe but now to the United States and the Far East. The competitive strengths of the company to be exploited by expansion are:

- its technology;
- its understanding of the markets for cellular polymers;
- its relationships with customers and its suppliers.

An important aspect of the firm's technology in the marketplace is the ability to produce at high quality, and to produce a wide product range, so as to meet the particular demands of a wide variety of customers. The 1994 Annual Report, for example, notes both the role of quality, with the widespread use of total quality management, and the firm's ability to control costs, especially of inputs.

The decision to invest in eastern Europe

It must be remembered that British Vita was already a multinational firm in 1991, operating from more than 80 plants worldwide. Moreover, around one-quarter of the factories were in Germany, selling primarily to the automobile and furniture industries. Though decisions were ultimately taken in the UK head office in Manchester, from where the investment process was also managed, there is little doubt that it was signals from the company's German plants which helped to bring home to senior management the profitable opportunities opened up by the fall of the Berlin Wall and the opening up of central Europe. As we have seen, the earlier rights issue and low gearing meant that Vita had ample finance to undertake an eastern European venture.

There seem to have been a number of pressures operating simultaneously to influence the company's decision to move eastwards:

1. Vita was determined to follow its customers, especially German automotive and furniture manufacturers, who were entering the region in large numbers. This lay behind management's prediction that the eastern European market was likely to grow very rapidly. It also indicates how they formed their judgment about the particular products that they could successfully supply to the Polish market. However, Vita did not organize the operation through German subsidiaries, because management did not feel that it was appropriate to attempt to replicate the technology or the outputs from its German factories in eastern Europe.
2. Lower labour costs also played a key role in Vita's decision. The costs of construction were expected to be much lower than, for example, in the UK, because of cheaper labour. Labour savings on the production side were expected to be modest, however, because 60–80 per cent of Vita's operating costs are material inputs. Low labour costs were also seen as a significant driver to moving eastwards, because they were expected to encourage more and more of Vita's customers to shift their own production to central and eastern Europe, and the company wanted to be established when they arrived. In the company's view, the low labour costs in the region will continue to determine the pattern of its own demand for a further 15 years.
3. Vita felt that it had the experience to operate successfully in central and eastern Europe, because it had built and run profitably foam factories all over the world, including in Africa.

4. Management concluded that it could not expect to satisfy the growing eastern European demand from German factories. There were several factors at work here:
   (a) Because foam is bulky, transport costs are relatively high, and the firm would find it hard to compete with German firms which were already planning to manufacture over the border.
   (b) Tariffs seemed likely to place major difficulties in the way of competing via exports. For example, imports to the Polish market from Germany faced high tariffs and border delays. In 1993, there were 15 per cent import tariffs and 6 per cent border duty on foam, probably enough to wipe out any cost advantage that British Vita might have gained from superior technology or cost control over its competitors. In addition, it was noted that trucks would have had to stand at the borders for days, so Vita would not have been able to ensure just-in-time delivery (JIT), which is its standard supply method. In western Europe, customers receive 24-hour delivery as a matter of course; this would have been impossible to achieve from Germany. But JIT is a key element in the firm's competitive advantage over its rivals, being closely linked to both the superior quality and intimate relations with customers stressed by Vita management as core competencies. It was expected that JIT would prove even more important as a vehicle for successful entry into eastern Europe. According to Keith Bradshaw, divisional director for eastern Europe, Polish firms, for example, are still not able to achieve JIT; he claims that the delivery time from the main Polish supplier was two months when Vita was exploring the market in 1992.
   (c) Raw material costs were to some extent a countervailing factor. These represented a high proportion of operating costs, and it was expected that prices paid would on average be higher than in western Europe. This was because by 1993 eastern European chemical firms already offered only a very slight discount to western European prices. Moreover, Vita calculated that it would not be able to meet the company's demand once production was fully established. Hence Vita would need to import and pay duties amounting to 10.4 per cent, with 5 per cent border tax (in 1994). In practice, this proved to be the case with Vita's Polish operation, where it ended up importing around one-third of raw material inputs.

In short, the company saw prospects for very rapid growth in Poland, to offset the recession still dominating in most of its other markets, and believed that it could enter the market rapidly and profitably. To quote Bradshaw, 'I thought we should look east; there is a big market with lots of people in it.'

The decision to invest in Poland

Once the decision to invest somewhere in central and eastern Europe was made at board level in 1991, its chief proponent – Keith Bradshaw – was given a roving brief to explore the situation and bring proposals back to the board. There were three initial choices to be made: the choice of country; acquisition versus greenfield investment; and the exact location of the new facility.

Why Poland?

As we have seen, Vita's ambition was to service what it expected to be a growing market in Poland/Czech Republic/Hungary, especially from its customers moving over the border from Germany, as well perhaps as to obtain for itself the lower labour costs to satisfy some of the demand in Germany. The company's search seems to have narrowed itself down to Poland quite early. The main reasons appear to have been as follows:

1. The population in Poland was large, so the market was likely to be large and the potential for growth was good. Margins in the foam business are narrow and under constant pressure from customers, so volumes are critical to success.
2. Several of Vita's major German customers were moving their furniture manufacturing sites to Poland to exploit the cheaper labour. Some 30 companies had moved over to southwest Poland, which was the old Germanic part of the country, by 1995. This suggested some clustering effect, which Vita was keen to exploit. Given the transport cost factor, Vita decided to stick close to this important element of its customer base.
3. It was a significant part of the decision that Vita was able to purchase the two main raw material inputs – TDI and Polyol – from chemical companies in Poland; indeed, one company was located next to what became Vita's manufacturing facility.

4. Though it was never explicitly discussed, both Vita and its customers must have had some confidence in the irreversibility of the reform process in Poland. The choice of region in Poland was straightforward. Vita chose western Poland to be near its customers, who typically had not moved far over the border. It also wanted to be close to the Czech and Slovak republics, into which it felt it might expand next. The southwest of Poland was also felt to have better infrastructure, especially in terms of communications. For example, managers were able to fly directly to Wrocław via Frankfurt or Düsseldorf. Even so, the roads were not yet good, though developments were planned.

Why greenfield?

The choice between acquisition and greenfield site was difficult. The company had been expanding steadily through acquisition for more than thirty years; its last greenfield site had been in Africa more than twenty years previously. But the decision to go greenfield was made within six months of deciding to enter eastern Europe; Bradshaw first went to Poland in the middle of 1991 and the choice was made by the end of the year.

The reason was Vita's desire for 100 per cent control in acquired companies. In almost every one of its subsidiaries, Vita owned all the shares. Its experience of joint ventures in Africa and Canada had not always been easy. The partners in the venture had wanted close involvement in making decisions, and in how the business was run, which Vita did not wish to give. The company had developed its own way of doing things – its own technologies, information systems, corporate culture, based on its core competencies – and it sought to introduce these from the start in the new subsidiaries. Indeed, a large part of the company's competitive advantage, as we have seen, is felt by management to derive from its own technologies and its way of approaching new markets. It was felt that these would be compromised in a joint venture.

However, outright acquisition proved to be impossible in the Polish context. The problem was that the Ministry of Privatization insisted that significant shareholdings had to be retained in the hands of other Polish groups, so that it was impossible for Vita to get a 100 per cent stake. For example, in some firms local managers wanted to keep 40 per cent, while in another the workers had wanted to keep 40 per cent. In fact, Vita entered serious negotiations for an acquisition, but in this case the Ministry of Privatization sought to give the workers a 40 per cent stake. There was no room for compromise. Vita would not accept a minority shareholding but, from the Polish side, the authorities felt that the workers needed to be persuaded to accept the privatization, with a 40 per cent stake being their minimum price.

A secondary problem was the condition of the firms that were investigated with a mind to acquisition. To quote Bradshaw: 'in general, we found the companies were overmanned and the equipment old. For example, we currently employ 38 people in production to manufacture 8–9,000 tonnes per year; a company we looked at in Łódź produced 4,000 tonnes per year using 350 people'. Bradshaw felt that much more capital expenditure would be needed in those firms than in a greenfield plant, and even these expenditures ignored costs resulting from the social problems associated with the required reduction in the labour force.

Vita went on to look for a further three months at possible joint ventures, and examined existing factories in which to put its own machines. However, it could not find any plants that were suitable for its production requirements: it calculated that running costs would be too high and found insufficient facilities for storage. The facilities that it saw also offered only limited prospects for expansion if the market were to grow in the way that it had hoped. Vita gradually convinced itself that, despite the recent corporate emphasis on growth by acquisition, this was not the right strategy for it in Poland. However, this did not lead it to drop out of the Polish project, because management felt that it still retained sufficient expertise to attempt a greenfield development once again.

Which site?

The search for an appropriate site was conducted very carefully. Vita managers visited about 30 potential sites, and looked in detail at several. The key elements in the choice concerned utilities, especially electricity, raw material sources, sewage and space for expansion. The site they finally chose was opposite an established Polish chemical company – Rokita – which provided polyol for the foam production process. Rokita was a large firm, with 2,500 employees, which had been privatized and was already a chemical supplier to Vita's German operations. The presence of such a major chemicals employer in the area meant that there were sound engineering skills in the locality, and, of course, raw materials were on tap. The existence of a large chemical complex meant there were also good services, such as steam from a central generator for heating and mains sewage. A lot of land was available, and Vita bought 20 hectares, at a price which was very reasonable. The attractions of the region have not been lost on other foreign investors, many of them British. There is now a cluster of UK firms in the Brzeg Dolny region, including Cadbury, BOC and Cussons.

Negotiations

The negotiations with both Rokita and the local authorities, who were very helpful in finding the site, were fairly straightforward. However, the deal still took eight months to close. Vita managers signed a protocol at the end of April 1992, but it took until Christmas to get all the agreements from Warsaw, e.g. from the Ministries of Privatization, Finance, Industry and Foreign Affairs. Vita had planned to start building in August 1992. However, it did not commence until March 1993 because of the bureaucracy. This delayed its entry into the market by eight months. Among the main problems encountered were those concerning land registration and ownership. There were also negotiation problems concerning the electrical supply. Vita wanted to buy it from Rokita; the authorities tried to force Vita to put in a line to the grid. This was only resolved in the end by a threat on Vita's part to pull out from the deal.

The greenfield investment

An important element in Vita's plans was its particular approach to developing the site. It did not wish to replicate its production process or its products from Germany, or to use the same highly sophisticated technologies. From its preliminary dealings in Poland, it had become convinced that the Polish market could be developed around 12.4-metre foam blocks. These were more basic than those manufactured in western Europe, but more sophisticated and of higher quality than blocks currently available in Poland. Indeed, it was planned that the simplicity of the new product would not detract from its quality. To produce this block, Vita developed its own technology from a Spanish factory in Valencia, with expanded storage space.

The core technology was relatively unsophisticated in terms of control systems and output capacities, but it would produce a small product range to a high quality, and, most significantly from Vita's point of view, the factory could be built within Poland, drawing on the region's own large construction facilities and strong engineering traditions. Unlike, for example, its German competitor, Vita wanted to avoid purchasing expensive, sophisticated equipment (e.g. cutting equipment, conveyors) which would have to be imported. This meant that it could not manufacture short foam blocks, because these have to be cut hot, or much longer blocks. An important element in Vita's later success proved to be its initial evaluation of the appropriate product for the market, and the choice of appropriate (and relatively low-cost) technology to manufacture it.

The concept of sourcing almost all the investment and construction in Poland was also a considerable success. The UK engineer from headquarters given total responsibility for the construction process was Jack Tetlow, operating within financial constraints set by the board. His approach was to determine the final building costs as a fixed price in ECU. The original contract was in fact at a 'keen' price because, according to him, 'the Poles wanted to show what they could do'. Tetlow supervised the construction process personally. He employed a local privatized building company, Ideco, which was very motivated to get the contract. It guided the plans through the local authority. Tetlow decided to operate at arm's length, via a detailed tender for the construction itself. There were only a few tenders and he chose the company which he felt would be the best, though it was not the cheapest. He also hired a consultant to keep a check on developments on site during the construction.

Everything for the new factory was manufactured in Poland except for the fire doors and sprinkler system. Much of the machinery was also built within Poland, e.g. the lifting equipment, built to Vita's specification by a crane company. Only a few items of machinery were imported from the West. Vita also showed considerable concern for the environment, a point stressed in its Annual Report. The Polish plant was built to the highest environmental specifications (UK requirements, not Polish) and emissions are negligible. Once again, the environmental equipment was constructed in Poland, at around half the cost that would have pertained in the UK. Management felt that it was important to get the environmental issues right, because the authorities were felt to scrutinize foreign investors closely on this matter.

Overall, the construction phase was a great success. The production plant was completed on time and satisfied Vita's quality requirements, and the cost was only 7 per cent above the (low) ECU denominated contract price. Costs of construction per square metre were £5.00, some 40 per cent below equivalent UK prices. Moreover, the factory was constructed not to be too specialized, so that, if the whole project proved to be a failure, the building could be more easily sold. This would not have been possible if more sophisticated manufacturing technologies had been used. The plant was also designed to facilitate relatively low-cost expansion if the market proved to warrant it. The foam plant runs for two hours per day at the moment, with one shift. The bottleneck is in the curing hall, where the foam dries, and in the storage facilities. There is space for these to be expanded. The plant was built to manufacture 9,000 tonnes per annum, at a cost of £7 million, including all equipment. For a further £1 million, in building curing sheds and further storage, it could be expanded to a capacity of 16,000 tonnes.

Setting up operations

Management

Vita's entry to the Polish market was two-pronged. While the manufacturing plant was being constructed and staff recruited, a small conversion factory was set up to cut and sell foam to customers, in order for Vita to become established in the Polish market. The manager was recruited through advertisements in the paper; there were 130 applicants and 12 interviews. The site now employs 40 people.

In France and Germany, Vita's approach has been to let local people manage the subsidiaries, while monitoring progress centrally. Its approach has been similar in Poland. Bradshaw hired four people himself, and left it to them to recruit the rest of the staff. The man who was appointed general manager of the new factory had been the local project manager and site agent, a former employee of Rokita with some international experience. The three other appointments were the commercial, technical and finance managers, all of whom were English-speaking. There were irresolvable problems in recruiting an accountant, so Bradshaw recruited a British woman from the Manchester office who had Polish parents, and spoke the language fluently.

The Polish company is run by a board comprising the top management team along with two British members, Bradshaw and another Manchester-based executive. The board meets monthly, primarily to agree major expenditures, plan strategies and discuss operations. The Polish managers have autonomy over day-to-day decisions.

Links to head office

Interviews with senior management in Poland suggest that the Polish subsidiary is run at arm's length. The subsidiary is managed by the managing director, along with the technical and commercial people whom he recruited when the factory was being built. There are discussions with Bradshaw and Bowling (the other British board member) about strategy, and all investments need to be approved centrally; for example, at the time of the interviews the Polish team sought to purchase more computers. The production process is run by the manager, who is responsible for quality control and all technological aspects of the business. The local company checks the polyol, for example, taking laboratory samples for every production run. There is no local research and development (R&D), though the Polish laboratory does have the capacity to test new materials and to check quality as new grades of foam are introduced. Marketing is similarly decentralized; Vita's approach in Poland, as elsewhere, is based on the view that local sales managers will understand the market better than will head office.

Labour

Many of the remaining staff were hired from Rokita, one of the most important aspects of the shrewd choice of site. Recruits are usually young (around 25 years old) and well educated (degree level). Salaries are around 10 per cent higher than in Rokita, and people are generally keen to move, because the Polish company is overmanned and its future is uncertain. However, Vita offers no social facilities and the company is not unionized (Vita is not opposed in principle to unionization; its German, French and UK plants are unionized).

Training

On the training side, UK and Dutch operatives went to Poland to help the new Polish workers prior to the commencement of production, while the technical director and two main operators were sent to Germany for two to three weeks. The financial staff was trained by the expatriate accountant. However, now she has left (to have a baby), there are serious recruitment problems once again and existing staff are not yet felt to be capable of running the financial side undirected.

Inputs

The main foam machine was bought from Norway, and the cutting machines are from Denmark. All the other equipment was built to specification in Poland, e.g. the curing racks and the chemical tanks. Raw materials are bought primarily from Rokita (polyol) and from Zachem (TDI), which is also Vita's major competitor in foam manufacture. This peculiar relationship with Zachem as main supplier and main competitor has meant that Vita has carefully avoided trying to take away Zachem's customers. Rather, the company's very rapid expansion has been based on selling to new customers in Poland entering from Germany. However, this uneasy truce with Zachem in product markets may not hold, because Vita produces higher-quality products, and offers better supply facilities (e.g. JIT delivery) at broadly the same price as Zachem. The relationship works for the moment because Zachem cannot afford to restrict input supplies; Vita pays for its inputs on time, while its competitors do not have equivalent financial resources. Nonetheless, Vita may be preparing for the worst: it already buys around one-third of raw material needs from outside Poland, as we noted above at higher cost, primarily because of tariffs. This may in part be for strategic reasons.

Quality

Vita has managed to achieve very good quality for the Polish market, indicated by hardness, density and consistency of the foam. Its technology yields flat tops on foam blocks, which reduces waste. Vita commenced production in Poland in July 1994 with two grades of foam, and this number has now risen to eight.

Marketing

The marketing director is a chemical engineer (like the managing and technical directors) and, after some training in the West, was left to devise the strategy by himself. The sales approach to industrial users stresses the better quality and service that Vita provides, noting that it sells at the market price. The bulk of its sales (80 per cent) are in the form of blocks; in the UK the proportion is much lower but in Poland labour is cheap enough for firms to cut the blocks themselves. Vita hopes to raise the proportion of cut blocks, because value added is higher in that market segment. The service dimension to its competitiveness comes from JIT delivery. Vita delivers within 24 hours of a phoned order, a speed not yet matched in the market. The company believes that its entry has changed the market for its product.

Sales objectives

Vita planned to sell most of its output within Poland, though a small amount of foam is now being targeted to the Czech Republic and Lithuania, probably as the first stage in the planned expansion of production. Prior to Vita opening up its new factory, there were five domestic Polish manufacturers. Three used Vita's patent (Maxfoam), though on less sophisticated machines. The process Vita has introduced to Poland, however, is more advanced and produces to a higher quality. The biggest Polish manufacturer is, of course, Zachem, which is a privatized, state-owned firm. An eastern German firm which supplies primarily to Poland is also an important competitor, because, according to Vita managers, German furniture manufacturers are often directed to buy from it by their head offices, and a German supplier is introducing a new sophisticated plant elsewhere in Poland. A local businessman also set up a foam line near Brzeg Dolny about eight months before Vita opened up; he is now bankrupt.

Zachem had more than 50 per cent of the Polish market prior to Vita's entry. An indication of Vita's success is that Zachem's share is now down below 35 per cent, with Vita itself having jumped to more than 30 per cent over a year. As of 1995, Vita sold around 95 per cent of its output to furniture and bedding manufacturers in Poland. It has about 250–300 customers; up to 70 of these are large and medium-sized customers. Turnover in 1995 will be about £20 million, and the average small customer will spend £1,000 per month. Most customers are located within 300 kilometres of the factory.

Performance

Vita did have a few problems in Poland. In addition to the delays in construction, since Vita has entered the market raw materials prices worldwide have been increasing. According to Keith Bradshaw, the reason was very fast economic growth in the Pacific Rim, diverting chemical supplies from Europe and North America. TDI in particular became in very short supply, and prices for imports went up by 30 per cent. It has been very difficult for Vita to pass these increases on in western Europe, but because inflation is higher in Poland, it has been easier to do so there. Even so, margins have been hit everywhere, including in Poland.

The Polish investment has nonetheless been very successful, perhaps even more successful than Vita had originally hoped. The plant was built to exacting technical and environmental standards very cheaply, and has proved able to produce so efficiently in terms of waste that margins are higher than elsewhere in the company. The combination of quality and service has allowed Vita to establish itself very quickly in the market: a market share of around 30 per cent in about a year. Turnover has already reached target; the firm is supplying to capacity and expansion is planned.

In this, Vita has been assisted by the large upswing in demand from foreign-owned furniture suppliers – an upswing which Vita carefully foresaw and upon which its plans were originally predicated. The market increased from about 20,000 tonnes per year in 1992 to more than 30,000 in 1995; Vita calculates that around 80 per cent of its output is sold to foreign-owned companies in Poland. According to Bradshaw, the Polish subsidiary is already profitable and the payback period, originally planned to be three years, will probably be shorter. Future investment seems likely, both within Poland and elsewhere in central and eastern Europe.

13

General Bottlers

Overview

This case tells the story of a US production and distribution company, PepsiCo Cola General Bottlers, entering into Poland to produce, distribute and market PepsiCo Cola and other soft drink products and bottled water. General Bottlers is a subsidiary of a large Chicago-based holding company, Whitman Corporation.

While Whitman's other businesses operate internationally, General Bottlers had no prior foreign experiences, but was the largest franchised bottler of the PepsiCo Cola company (PepsiCo) in the United States. Strategically, the Polish market offered an opportunity to meet the growth objectives of General Bottlers, Whitman and PepsiCo.

The case illustrates the application of US capital, managerial skills, technology and know-how in the transitional economy environment. Key elements in the company's apparent success so far, which contrast sharply with PepsiCo's previous weakness in the Polish carbonated drinks market, include a large cash commitment, the choice of greenfield operations, and an emphasis on marketing and labour recruitment as well as training.

Background

PepsiCo and Coca-Cola in eastern Europe

This case is part of the story of the expansion of the two global competitors in carbonated soft drinks (CSDs) to central and eastern Europe (CEE). In most countries in the region, there are a variety of secondary domestic brands (known as 'b' brands) as well as Coca-Cola and PepsiCo. Both companies see emerging markets as an important way to establish their brands in areas of expected current and future growth. PepsiCo in particular has been attempting to expand international sales since its 'Vision 2000' mission in 1990, calling for rapid growth outside the domestic US market, promising a $1 billion investment in soft drinks up to 1995. The amount has since been doubled. The objective of 'Vision 2000' was to raise PepsiCo's non-North American sales from around $900 million in 1990 to $5 billion in 1995. Growth has since been particularly rapid in the Asia-Pacific region, northeast Europe and central and eastern Europe.

Within central and eastern Europe, PepsiCo's strategy was to build on previous links established from the 1970s. It had established itself as market leader in several countries, with, for example, a market share in Hungary of 25.3 per cent in July 1993, compared with 18.6 per cent for Coca-Cola. Hence through the whole region, Coca-Cola's sales in 1993 slightly lagged behind PepsiCo's. Poland was an especially important market for PepsiCo, the second largest in the region after the former Soviet Union (with around 17 per cent of regional soft drinks sales). The initial levels of carbonated drink sales were also low – CSD consumption, which was at 435 annual servings per capita in Germany, was only 202 in Hungary and 107 in Poland. Moreover, the fact that 'b' brands still held some 70 per cent of the market in 1992 offered another potential source of rapid sales growth.

PepsiCo in Poland

However, PepsiCo's early lead in Poland was rapidly eroded by Coca-Cola between 1991 and 1994. One reason may have been that PepsiCo was seeking to expand its restaurant, snack food and carbonated drink activities simultaneously, rather than focusing on any one area. PepsiCo invested some $500 million into Poland in 1993, but largely into '3 in 1' restaurants (TacoBell, KFC and Pizza Hut). It had also purchased a majority stake in the Polish chocolate and confectionery firm, SA Wedel, in 1991, and a new snack food facility had been built under the auspices of this joint venture.

A second reason for PepsiCo losing its initial advantage in Poland was that, having been the market leader in CSDs since a bottling plant had been opened in 1972, PepsiCo was probably overconfident about its first mover advantage. It was therefore slow to respond to Coca-Cola's challenge when it came, post-reform. Finally, there were problems with PepsiCo's marketing and distribution network. PepsiCo's approach in the communist period had been to work with Polish state-owned bottling companies. By 1993, there were nine of these, in addition to the company's own bottling plant. According to PepsiCo's reports, these companies were neither efficient enough, nor sufficiently skilled in Western marketing, to see off Coca-Cola's rising market challenge. This led PepsiCo not to renew these contracts. Rather, it decided to try to involve one of its other distributors in its Polish venture.

PepsiCo's decision to seek the involvement of a Western distributor in Poland was consistent with a general strategy which had recently emerged for both PepsiCo and Coca-Cola. In the past, both companies had entered emerging markets by linking with existing local businesses – brewers or mineral water companies – and giving them five-year contracts to develop a soft drinks business. However, there were serious drawbacks to this approach. Most notably, the distributors were found to be short-termist and often failed to make the investments required to build a long-term distribution business. In addition, they had no concept of marketing or promotion. Moreover, many partners did not survive the large economic fluctuations which tend to characterize these more volatile markets.

Hence both PepsiCo and Coca-Cola developed the new strategy of seeking to involve the bottlers and distributors from their mature markets in ventures abroad. Coca-Cola now has 20 ventures with Coca-Cola Amatil, an Australian bottler around the world, and PepsiCo has done the same in Latin America with Baesa, an Argentinian company. The strategy seemed to offer an answer in 1993 to PepsiCo's difficulties in Poland.

Whitman Corporation

Whitman Corporation is a large holding company based outside Chicago which owns the PepsiCo distribution company, General Bottlers (GB). Sales of Whitman in 1994 were $2.7 billion, up from $2.39 billion in 1992, while earnings in 1994 were almost $122 million, with a return on equity of 23.5 per cent. Earnings per share have been increasing by more than 12 per cent for three years, and debt is being gradually reduced, from 55 per cent of capital in 1992 to 48.8 per cent in 1994. The chief executive officer of the holding company is Bruce Chelberg, who heads an organization of around 15,000 employees.

Core businesses

Whitman has three core businesses, and there are no obvious synergies between them. Hussmann is a commercial refrigeration company, producing, for example, refrigerated display cases and storage coolers for supermarkets and convenience stores. It has sales of about $860 million, and an operating income of $82.5 million. Midas provides automotive, brake and suspension services from a network of retail outlets, which are primarily franchised. It had sales in 1994 of about $540 million, with an operating income of $75 million. Both Hussmann and Midas have experience operating outside the United States. For example, Midas is active in 14 countries, notably France, while Mexico represents Hussmann's second largest profit centre. Taken together, sales in these two operating companies were around $1.4 billion in 1994, of which around $470 million were earned outside North America. The third core business, GB, generated about half the holding company's total revenue – nearly $1.3 billion – in 1994. It had not operated outside the United States prior to the Polish venture.

History of Whitman

Whitman Corporation has only recently become established in its current form. The company began life as the Illinois Central Railroad Company in the 1850s, employing Abraham Lincoln as its lawyer. The company owned the Chicago–Florida railway route, and remained primarily concentrated in the railroad business until the 1960s, when it expanded into a variety of other activities, including food, defence, textiles and manufacturing. Management strategy during the 1970s and 1980s was to use the strong cash flow from the railway to buy other companies. This was because management recognized the increasing competition to the core business, from trucks and barges on the Mississippi river, and the resulting need to diversify revenue sources. At one time, the company owned more than 100 businesses. However, management decided to divest itself of most of these during the 1980s. The smaller ones were sold for cash, as was an aerospace company, while the railroad itself was spun off.

By 1989, the holding was down to four businesses, with a turnover of around $4 billion, half of which was in the food industry and the remainder in the current three groups. Debt was high, at $1.8 billion, and holdings were not popular in the stock markets. Moreover, the value of the stock had fallen sharply (from $35 to $17). Management decided to cut the business in half, and spun the food company off to shareholders, along with half the debt. Whitman stock rose sharply in reaction, to $30, indicating that the markets continued to seek a more focused company. The spin-off process was managed by an interim chairman between 1989 and 1991, after which Bruce Chelberg took over as chief executive officer.

Whitman corporate structure

One of Chelberg's first tasks was to reorganize the relationship between head office and the three core businesses. The corporate office was dramatically reduced – from 260 people in 1989 to 38 in 1992. Corporate aircraft were sold and the offices relocated to less expensive quarters. Savings amounted to $42 million after tax. The corporate office acts as the bank for the operating companies, and controls financing and tax as well as providing an umbrella supervision of employee benefits, such as pensions.

However, operationally, the three companies run themselves independently, according to their separate plans. The corporate office neither seeks to, nor has the capability to, interfere in day-to-day operations, though it can get involved if a particular company gets into trouble. As Chelberg puts it of Whitman, 'in some ways, we are a closed end mutual fund'. For most employees, Whitman stands rather in the background. Only at a very senior level in the operating companies, for example, do people get stock options in Whitman. For almost all employees, the point of reference is their local operating company.

However, a key role of the corporate office remains to devise long-term strategies for the group as a whole; to act as catalyst for, and to allocate the resources to back, change. According to Chelberg, 'we need to find the people in the organization as a whole who are "looking for adventure" and to encourage them to take the risk'. The corporate office participates in the negotiation of the larger of these ventures, to provide support, continuity and motivation. For example, Chelberg has been closely involved personally in the Polish development. The project here has been to turn the GB division from a successful US company to a successful global company.

Whitman's strategy

The three Whitman core businesses are all very profitable, producing a return of about 20 per cent on capital and with considerable cash generation. The strategic problem for Whitman was that, as of 1993, the United States accounted for 80 per cent of group turnover and the prospects for sales growth were probably at best 5 per cent per annum. Productivity improvements could perhaps raise that to 8–9 per cent operating income growth. However, the company had in fact been able to achieve net 12–15 per cent income growth since 1991, when it took its current form. This was because it had taken on a lot of high-priced debt in the 1980s ($1 billion at an average interest rate of 10 per cent) and, with declining interest rates, had been able to refinance this to an average rate in 1995 of about 7.5 per cent and, with its excess cash, to reduce total debt to around $850 million.

Options for maintaining income growth

The company target, noted in the 1994 Annual Report, is to achieve income growth of 12–15 per cent per year: 'Our most important long term goal ... is to provide superior returns to our shareholders'. From Chelberg's point of view, with the exhaustion of interest cost savings by 1994, this left Whitman with only four options:

1. Accept modest growth and the resulting low market valuation.
2. Sell one of its businesses.
3. Spin off one or more of its businesses.
4. Invest in high-return activities within its businesses. This probably implied increasing their international exposure, because, as we have noted, the US businesses already provided very high returns in relatively slow-growth markets.

We can consider these options in turn. Accepting a low market valuation did nothing for the shareholders. Selling a business would generate cash, but the company is cash-rich already. The fundamental problem would remain of how to generate 12–15 per cent per annum on the money raised by the sale.

The third option seems to be popular amongst fund managers. This is because they believe that shareholders prefer to pick their own portfolio of business, rather than have the choice made for them by investing in a holding company. However, there is a big problem with spinning activities off. It puts the business in question into limbo for a long period, and, in Chelberg's judgment, the operating subsidiaries need a long-term development strategy at this stage rather than increased uncertainty. Since spin-offs are tax-free under special tax rules, there are also major tax risks from this option, if the tax rules are not followed precisely. This left the fourth option.

Of the three Whitman businesses, Hussmann and Midas were already actively involved abroad, notably in Mexico and France respectively. However, GB, which generated half of total Whitman sales, was entirely US-based. It was also closely linked to PepsiCo (which, as we have seen, was expanding internationally), being by far their largest US bottler. GB sales represented some 12 per cent of the total PepsiCo market in the United States – some $1.3 billion, mainly concentrated in the Midwest. The next largest US bottler had about 1 per cent of US sales. There was also a close financial relationship, in that PepsiCo owned 20 per cent of the shares of GB.

To quote Chelberg, Whitman's immediate task became to convince PepsiCo that GB could provide the assets – finance and people – to meet PepsiCo's requirements in waging their 'world war' with Coca-Cola. At the same time, Whitman had to try to convince the financial markets that the advantages of its international links with PepsiCo were real, and that it could handle the risks in less developed areas. Poland offered both sides a testing ground for their new strategies.

Whitman's long-term objective from all this was to realize a market valuation at around a normal multiple of earnings. Whitman, like most conglomerates, sells at a discount of around 20 per cent below this. Establishing GB's potential to earn high returns in high-growth areas would make a major contribution to that objective.

General Bottlers' 'core competencies'

The competitive strength of GB in moving outside the United States to emerging markets is viewed internally as having three dimensions. The first is financial muscle. According to Chelberg, the company generates 'free cash flow' (e.g. cash flow after all commitments such as dividends, normal capital expenditures and working capital requirements) of between $80 million and $100 million per year. This implies that over the next five years it can spend about $1 billion on its strategy of international expansion, and keep the debt/equity ratio constant at its current acceptable level of 50 per cent. As we shall see below, this has meant that the company has been able to act quickly and effectively in Poland, which is crucial to its aim of establishing in the minds of current and potential shareholders (primarily institutions) its capacity successfully to expand in these new markets.

Second, GB emphasizes its close relationship with PepsiCo, which is internationally known. One could not imagine Whitman following the same strategy with a less well-known brand name. The relationship has allowed it to build up a unique know-how in production and distribution in the United States, which it sought to reproduce in Poland. The key is the capacity to run a highly efficient and cost-effective distribution organization. In the United States, GB earns $1.10 per case of PepsiCo, while the largest Coca-Cola bottler earns 85 cents.

Another important element in the long-standing relationship between PepsiCo and GB is the way in which contracts have been constructed. PepsiCo runs its business by making high margins on the sales of its concentrates, but returns a proportion of this money to franchisees via the advertising and promotion budget. In this way, PepsiCo induces the bottler to undertake distribution and marketing activities in conformity with PepsiCo's broader strategy, e.g. to cover the range of volumes or all the regions of a franchise, rather than merely the profitable parts. As we will see, the Polish deal was in large part constructed on the basis of the two companies' close relationship in the United States, and a key element to its success has been the keen understanding on both sides of how franchising arrangements of this sort work.

The decision-making process

Why Poland?

Whitman had been discussing for several years opportunities outside the United States with PepsiCo. As noted above, this was consistent with both PepsiCo's and Whitman's long-term strategies. The initial approach for a relationship in Poland came from PepsiCo. Whitman agreed to go along for the following reasons.

Opportunities

The market is large. In the deal, Whitman was allocated distribution in about half the country (the north and west; PepsiCo will cover the rest of the country, including Warsaw itself). Whitman forecasts that it could generate sales in such an area of $200 million with $30 million operating income over a five-year horizon, deriving from an investment of $80–100 million.

Risks

On the political side, it was noted that there are virtually no ethnic divisions in Poland. Moreover, the currency is convertible; inflation is coming under control, 60 per cent of Poland's gross domestic product (GDP) is generated by the private sector and the country is clearly Western-oriented. Politically, US policy is to support Polish independence, and Whitman saw little risk on that score from Germany or Russia. Moreover, as far as it could see, the legal and tax environment was being put in place. There was plenty of evidence from other foreign companies active in Poland, and their presence seemed to be accepted.

Poland represented a particularly attractive option for international expansion to Whitman because its GB operation could be built from scratch, and this was felt to be a major part of the company's 'core competence'. If GB had taken up equivalent options in Spain or Germany, the company would have had to pay a high price for the 'goodwill' in the previous franchise; possibly up to 80 per cent of the price. But then, according to Chelberg, the company would 'inherit other people's mistakes'. In Poland, GB was able to build its own distribution structure in its own way; all of its commitment was to new investment.

A second problem with investing in existing markets derives from PepsiCo's market position. Coca-Cola tends to dominate in western European markets, so GB would have had to pay a premium for a franchise, and then compete from a position of weakness. This was not true in eastern Europe. Thus in Poland, according to Chelberg, 'the fight is on a level playing field'.

The contract

Eventually, Whitman went along with a particular, and to their minds attractive, deal offered by PepsiCo in Poland. The deal gave GB the franchise rights for 15 years with renewal options (rather than the standard five years) to distribute the basket of PepsiCo products, with 100 per cent ownership of distribution rights covering approximately 50 per cent of the population of Poland, in the north and west. The remainder was in PepsiCo's hands. There is a jointly owned company for the production side, which is operated on a break-even basis. Capital is put in on the basis of production taken, readjusted each quarter. PepsiCo bought the plant, which is outside Warsaw, from a French company, at a cost of around $40 million, with GB contributing its share. Both PepsiCo and GB maintain administrative headquarters in Warsaw and develop a common marketing programme for the country as a whole. According to the publicized agreement, the objective of the venture was to 'boost the PepsiCo share throughout Poland by three-fold by the year 2000'. Press coverage discussed investments of the order of $100 million in western and northern Poland, creating about 1,000 new jobs. The investment programme was to include 'development and introduction of new products, packaging, and the establishment of an extensive sales and distribution network'.

General Bottlers in Poland

GB expanded extremely quickly in Poland. 'Negotiations with PepsiCo began in winter 1993, an agreement was signed in June 1994 and the operation was up and running by August 1994', according to the expatriate Polish company president, Robert Murray. The view from corporate headquarters is that things have gone extremely well. To quote Bruce Chelberg: 'From an overall operational perspective, they had no significant problems. Everything went faster than expected.'

Investment

Initially, GB spent some $20 million in purchasing fleet, trucks, access vehicles and cars, and around $6 million on real estate. It bought 215 Volvo trucks, 113 cars, and uniforms, etc. The equipment was largely imported, because it was felt that Polish equipment was not up to the job e.g. forklifts and trucks. However, high prices were paid for capital equipment by US standards.

The two surprises for the local company president concerning the early experience in Poland were the degree of bureaucracy, especially dealing with land rights, and finding reliable suppliers. The latter problem has been solved by absorbing higher than expected costs. Despite the former problem, GB managed to open 10 distribution centres in 9.5 months, when the operating plan had estimated that it would take three years to do so. According to the expatriate sales director, Larry Young: 'We saw there was so much opportunity and so had to do it quickly. It is very different from the US.'

The distribution system

The process of developing a distribution system started in Poznań, which was GB's largest market, and was followed in Bydgoszcz. The operations director, another expatriate, preselected locations, teamed with a UK real estate agency which claimed to know Poland well. Management first had to learn how to negotiate real estate deals in Poland – there were numerous problems in finding suitable sites, in establishing clear ownership and in getting agreement amongst the variety of different owners. Initially there were problems in negotiations with Polish landowners, who, according to GB managers, did not regard verbal agreements as binding and who kept on changing their minds about deals.

GB approached each site differently, using local advice and its real estate firm; eventually it would seem that its own employees found as many sites as the real estate company. In Poznań it leased a warehouse. Purchasing would have been very time-consuming because the Ministries of Interior and Defence were involved. The Bydgoszcz site was purchased; this took six months to arrange. In Wrocław, a greenfield site was leased to build warehousing etc. Of the other seven sites, only one has been purchased, though in two others purchase is an option in the lease.

Strategy

One reason behind the haste in setting up was the seasonality of Polish soft drinks sales. Consumption of CSDs in Poland is traditionally very low in winter, rising in May through August; 60 per cent of sales occur in these four months. GB wanted to get adequate sales levels in 1994, and certainly by 1995. Another aim was to reduce the payback period set by corporate headquarters: though Whitman was willing to provide the capital expenditure, the Polish company seems to have been keen to repay quickly.

Coca-Cola had had a three-year head start in the territory given to GB, and had already established a powerful market base. For example, in Poznań, PepsiCo had a 7 per cent market share, Coca-Cola 33 per cent and 'b' brands 60 per cent in 1993. To counter this, PepsiCo agreed to spearhead a combined marketing strategy, which has included bringing in dubbed commercials from the United States. However, GB has had reservations about this; commercials do not always translate well. GB seems to believe that the transfer of themes in marketing needs to be studied more closely in the longer term, and may want to be involved in developing the national marketing campaigns. Elsewhere, PepsiCo has not shown itself to be keen on collaboration in this area. PepsiCo spends less on advertising than

Coca-Cola everywhere; by a ratio of 2 or 3 to 1 in the United States and probably by 3 to 1 in Poland.

Coca-Cola uses pre-sale as its marketing device; salesmen come round first and delivery follows later. GB has introduced direct store delivery (DSD) into Poland; under this system, the truck becomes a mobile warehouse and drivers become salesmen. It was felt in the industry that this would not work in Poland because the staff would not understand DSD, and because the stores would not accept it. In fact, GB believes that it has worked very well and is an important element in GB's success. However, GB's difficulties in introducing the new system were initially compounded by the fact that its part of the Polish market comprises mainly very small shops (50 square metres or less), so it has numerous accounts with which to deal. Larry Young from sales argues that 'there is usually a 90-day window before customers realize that GB is good and reliable, and then they start giving them space'.

Technology

Given GB's approach to the Polish market, two issues of paramount importance in implementing their plans have been technology and human resource management. The company plans to introduce the most recent technology into Poland, providing truck drivers/salespeople with handheld computers to invoice customers directly. The intention is that within six months there will be no paperwork in the validation process. At present, Kuba Keszynski, the management information systems director, estimates that 25 per cent of salespeople's time is spent writing.

Human resource management

The introduction of such advanced technology will bring even more to the fore the question of labour and training for Polish staff. As we saw earlier, GB's initial involvement in the region was based on the selection of key personnel by corporate headquarters, which sees its role as being to motivate managers to take the risks abroad. GB started with five expatriates in Poland in operations, finance, marketing and sales. However, it is intended to place almost everything in Polish hands once appropriate staff become available. Hence the expatriates have three- or four-year contracts only. The regional directors who run the distribution network locally are all Polish, as are their staff. They were recruited one to two months before their location in the distribution system was ready, and trained, often in part outside Poland. Recruitment relied on paying higher salaries, and regional managers were also guaranteed a considerable local independence. Staff numbers have now reached more than 600, and will continue to grow as the number of routes from each regional headquarters increases.

Training is taken very seriously at GB in Poland, with a full-time training manager and three people working for him, as well as a training centre in Poznań. Technology training is linked to the information systems department. According to the (Polish) human resources manager, the main problems in recruitment and training are rather non-specific: developing staff willingness to take decisions, to understand markets and to manage people. Staff were usually technically skilled and educated, often with MA degrees.

However, despite the sense of dynamism and purpose at the top, there remain a number of problems on the human resources side. GB is being sued by some former employees, who claim that the company should pay overtime. The traditional approach in the distribution sector in Poland had been to pay a high base salary with low commission, and include overtime. GB decided to rely on a lower base salary, a higher-rate commission plus bonuses for good work, but no overtime. The Labour Inspector was very unhappy about this decision, regarding it as a breach of Polish law. Moreover, absenteeism in the company apparently remains high, with high sick leave rates as well. At a deeper level, several senior managers expressed concerns about the experience and skills of the Polish staff, in particular in their decision-making and in financial control. But most also stressed their enthusiasm and willingness to work, attributes strongly rewarded by pay and promotions (there have been 53 promotions from internal staff in the first year of operations).

Relations between the small expatriate group at the top and the regional manager and staff appear to be good. For example, in the sales division headed by an expatriate, meetings are conducted in Polish, 'so managers can express themselves freely'. The promise to send only five expatriates to Poland, and to send some back soon, seems accepted as real, and indicates the company's intentions.

Performance

GB seems to have achieved a lot in Poland in a short period of time, though perhaps its achievements were bought at a higher cost than would have been paid by a more experienced company. It started with a market share in its regions of about 10 per cent or less: this has now grown to 15 per cent, compared with Coca-Cola's 25%. 'Coke is defending, Pepsi is growing' says Mike Hill, marketing manager. In its first regional centre, Poznań, it entered with a 7 per cent share against Coca-Cola's 33 per cent. By the end of the first year, the market share had already risen to 12 per cent and GB believes that it is now getting close to parity.

General Bottlers has now also begun to turn its attention more to the financial side. An important element of its approach in the United States is that it has been successful in collecting receivables in less than 30 days. After a weak initial performance, it is now focusing more effectively on this in Poland as well. It is improving margins and is managing to improve inventory turnover rates.

The pace of expansion has been very rapid; so much so that, according to several local managers, they have not always done things in the best way. We have seen this with respect to the cost of capital equipment, locations, staffing and training. However, once the network is established, GB intends to address these issues, and cut the costs of operations.

14

Volkswagen Bordnetze GmbH

This is a case study of Volkswagen Bordnetze and its investment in a subsidiary in Poland – Volkswagen Elektro-Systemy Sp. z o.o. Volkswagen Bordnetze is an automotive components firm which produces electrical cables and electrical wiring circuits which connect electrical and electronic components in cars.

Overview

Volkswagen Bordnetze is a wholly owned subsidiary of Volkswagen AG and Siemens AG. All of its output goes directly to Volkswagen AG. This is a case of a medium-sized firm facing, on the one hand, opportunities for expansion and growth, and on the other hand, increasing intensity of national and international competition leading to pressures to reduce costs. A strategy of international expansion to low-cost sites is a logical strategic reaction to these pressures, and the investment in Poland can be understood in this context. The industry also operates under other pressures, notably the need to guarantee both the quality of products and the speed and time of delivery – just-in-time (JIT) production period. The choice of low-cost foreign investment sites has also, therefore, to pay close attention to the questions of quality, logistics and speed and reliability of delivery. The Polish investment had strong locational advantages in terms of supply links. Volkswagen Bordnetze also has a subsidiary in Turkey, and is now looking to expand further, probably in another central and eastern European (CEE) location. Overall, the investment in Poland is seen as successful and has contributed to a dramatic reduction in costs for Volkswagen Bordnetze.

The automotive components sector

The intensity of competition in this sector is increasing strongly, both nationally and internationally – competition is now essentially worldwide, reflecting the increased internationalization of car producers. In general, there are pressures to produce more rapidly, with higher quality and lower costs. This has led to new forms of organization and management of production to complement new production methods. Methods such as JIT have increased, and, together with a growing emphasis on quality control, have reduced production times and resulted in higher cost-effectiveness.

In the automotive components sector, there are a large number of small and medium-sized enterprises (SMEs). However, some concentration is likely to develop, as vehicle manufacturers are increasingly forming tighter links with their suppliers. Vehicle manufacturers are tending to focus on their core activities and on so-called 'lean production' techniques. Vehicle manufacturers are increasingly outsourcing and are passing on the responsibility for product development, manufacturing and quality assurance functions to their suppliers. At the same time, they see an increasing need to coordinate design and production processes in order to achieve global competitiveness. Together, the above facts imply a restructuring of the automotive supply chain. It is now common for there to be cooperation between manufacturers and suppliers, including product development of complete sub-systems and assemblies, and for their supply to be on a JIT basis. Vehicle manufacturers are also looking for continuous improvement in the cost structure of component suppliers and for flexibility of supply in changing market conditions. There are, therefore, competitive pressures on costs, prices, quality and delivery.

Ownership and structure of Volkswagen Bordnetze

Volkswagen Bordnetze was founded in 1987. Its sole customer is Volkswagen AG. Its ownership is shared – 50 per cent by Volkswagen AG and 50 per cent by Siemens AG. It was established with an initial capital of DM 4 million; it employed 266 workers and had a turnover of DM 26 million. By 1992, sales had increased to about DM 280 million. Two subsidiaries were established – one in Turkey and one in Poland – and employees total about 2,600, of whom about 300 are in Berlin.

There were a number of reasons for the initial establishment of Volkswagen Bordnetze. Volkswagen itself had previously manufactured most of its electrical wiring components and still employs about 700 employees on this, although it is reducing this number. As the importance and complexity of electrical wiring circuits increased, Volkswagen wanted to limit the number of employees in this area of production and out-source the increased production needs. It also wanted – in common with industry trends – to concentrate on its core business areas. Volkswagen Bordnetze is located in Berlin, which is an area where Volkswagen itself was under-represented, and it was seen as an advantage to have a production site in Berlin at that time. Furthermore, production in the subsidiary could be cheaper, as it was possible to set lower wages. This was because the main Volkswagen wage rate was higher than the trade union agreement with the electrical engineering industry, which is what applies in Volkswagen Bordnetze. There was also the opportunity for additional cost savings through using the know-how that Siemens has in electrical wiring manufacture. As an owner and purchaser of electrical wiring circuits, Volkswagen was also able to acquire a clear knowledge about cost structures in the electrical wiring subsector which could assist it in its talks and negotiations with other electrical wiring circuit suppliers.

The Siemens motivation to be a joint owner of Volkswagen Bordnetze was relatively clear – it had substantial know-how and experience of manufacturing electrical cables and wiring circuits but was not a major supplier to Volkswagen. Through this joint subsidiary, Siemens could develop stronger links to Volkswagen.

Volkswagen Bordnetze supplies about 50 per cent of Volkswagen's demand for electrical wires and cables and in some models it supplies 100 per cent. Although Volkswagen Bordnetze supplies all of its output to Volkswagen and is 50 per cent owned by Volkswagen, it is in competition with all the other actual and potential suppliers of electrical wiring circuits and cables. If it does not match worldwide competitive standards, it will not remain a supplier to Volkswagen. Thus, although the close links and strong vertical coordination between vehicle manufacturers and component suppliers mean that there are barriers to entry into the sector, competition within the sector is nonetheless intense.

Volkswagen Bordnetze has two main categories of competitors – large, international firms, and SMEs. In terms of size, Volkswagen Bordnetze actually lies between these two categories of competitors, as it is a fairly substantial medium-sized firm, with Volkswagen and Siemens as the parent companies. This competition includes Volkswagen itself, as it continues to produce some electrical cables and wiring circuits, Packard (a GM affiliate), Yrasake (a Japanese concern), Siemens, which also has wholly owned firms which produce for Opel and other manufacturers, and a number of other medium-sized and smaller firms.

An investment in Turkey was established in 1990 and production started there in 1991. In Turkey, the commercial director is German but all the other managers are Turkish. The Polish investment was made in 1992 and production there started in 1993. Production is still undertaken in Berlin but at a lower level than before. Key central functions are located in Berlin, including senior managers in the areas of: technology, logistics, manufacture, development, quality assurance, personnel, commerce, purchasing, and accounts. Product development is located only in Volkswagen Bordnetze in Berlin and not in the two foreign subsidiaries. The managing directors of the Turkish and Polish subsidiaries report directly to the Volkswagen Bordnetze directors. The senior managers in the subsidiaries report directly to the subsidiary managing directors but they also have a line of communication to their respective director in the Volkswagen Bordnetze head office. Thus, for example, the logistics, quality assurance and accounts managers all have lines of communication to the Volkswagen Bordnetze logistics, quality assurance and accounting managers.

The product and the production process

Volkswagen Bordnetze produces electrical cables and electrical wiring circuits which connect electronic and electric components within a car. They are not easy to standardize, and product specifications and technology are changing rapidly. The share of electrical and electronic parts in vehicles is increasing rapidly. The share of electrical and electronic parts in total car production costs went up from less than 8 per cent in 1965 to over 20 per cent and rising in 1995.

Electrical cables and connections are a crucial to the operation of a car. Relevant issues here include the aim to develop better technology for both economic and ecological reasons, the need to increase safety, the need to increase comfort, such as heating and electric windows, and the need to increase information to the driver. All these aims and changes mean that the product itself changes rapidly and the production processes can be quite complex.

In Volkswagen Bordnetze, about 80 per cent of the work is done by unskilled, female labour. The manufacturing processes are mainly learnt on the job through learning-by-doing. Male labour is used particularly for the wire-cutting processes, which involves skilled machine-tool operation. The labour force is mostly female, in part because this is a low-wage sector, and also, from the management perspective, because female labour is superior for this work, as it requires manual dexterity and reliability. The company supplies Volkswagen with wiring products for the Golf, the Vento, the Passat, the Polo, and the new model Audi A4. Volkswagen Bordnetze expects to achieve the ISO 9000-4 certification in 1996. Volkswagen AG is already certified. It also employs other standards, including the VDA Band 6 Audit procedure. These certifications and standards act as entry barriers to other suppliers, including other suppliers in central and eastern Europe making it extremely difficult to enter this market from outside.

Volkswagen Bordnetze is jointly developing with Volkswagen a new product for the new model generation Audi A4. It won this contract through a process of international competition. This new product is a platform product that can also be used for different car models of Volkswagen such as Skoda, Seat and the Golf successor.

Overall strategy

There are three key success factors for electrical cables and wiring circuits production: quality and reliability; low-cost production, and customer-oriented logistics. The Volkswagen Bordnetze strategy aims for improvement and development in all these three areas, and to maintain or to improve competitiveness. In this sector, it is relatively hard to differentiate a firm from competitors, but Volkswagen Bordnetze aims to do this via both its product development strategy and its logistics strategy. Foreign investment is a necessary part of this strategy to cope with the twin pressures of increasing demand – and so a need to expand production – and increasing pressures to reduce costs. Firms that have not gone to central and eastern Europe or other low-cost locations will not have survived in this sector. The move to central and eastern Europe is seen as comparable to Japanese firms moving into Southeast Asia and US firms moving first into southern states of the United States and then into Mexico. Competition also depends on quality and accuracy of information flows, and Volkswagen Bordnetze aims to be, if possible, better informed than its competitors.

Despite the investments in Turkey and Poland, there is still some manufacturing in Berlin. There are a number of reasons for this. It was seen as important to keep some production in Berlin, in part to ensure adequate control and development of the technology. The Berlin location also guarantees fast response, supply and service times to the customer. To some extent, some of the particularly complex and higher-quality and more recent technological work is also carried out in Berlin. Berlin essentially gives the company greater flexibility with regard to both new products and logistics. Flexibility is one of its biggest success criteria – it must be able to turn round products extremely fast, and there are many changes in demand, technology and the product during the year. On average, there are usually about three – small or large – jumps in technology and product composition every year. As Berlin is closer to the customer, the firm can respond more rapidly there. However, the labour force in Berlin was reduced substantially – with the agreement of the works council – from 1,000 to 300 workers during 1994 and 1995. This was accepted by the works council, as it was realized that without such a reduction the firm could not continue to compete and therefore to operate.

The decision to invest in Poland

The decision to invest in Poland was determined by two broad factors: first, the pressures of competition leading to the need to reduce costs, and second, the need to expand production. Before the opening of the Iron Curtain, production tended to go to southeast Europe, Ireland and Turkey when firms in this sector were looking for low-cost locations. For German firms, central and eastern Europe now offers a location that is both closer and lower cost. Subsequent to the Volkswagen Bordnetze investment in Turkey, sales trends meant that the firm needed to double its capacity and, given the new opportunities in central and eastern Europe, it decided to search for a location there. Furthermore, it was particularly concerned to ensure security of supply and, therefore, would not have considered having two plants in one country.

The choice of location for the new investment had to be made relatively fast, given the pressure to expand output. Having decided to go to central and eastern Europe, they first did an initial study of all the CEE countries and looked at issues including the political environment, legal framework and also how many geographical and political borders would have to be crossed to get to and from Germany. It narrowed the choice down to five CEE countries: the Czech Republic, Hungary, Slovakia, Slovenia and Poland. The main location search criteria in this process were: transport and logistics; investment climate; expected productivity; labour potential; and labour costs. Labour costs comprised the decisive search criterion and had the major weight in the decision, while the other factors were of approximately equal weight. Hungary was seen as having too high labour costs, while the Czechoslovakian 'divorce' had raised fears about stability and risks. Poland not only had low costs but it had very strong potential locational advantages and a good potential labour supply.

Within Poland, the firm looked at four regions: Szczecin, Poznań, Warsaw and Upper Silesia. The region of Poznań ranked first in terms of cost level, while Szczecin and Warsaw had cost levels that were 110–120 per cent of the national average. The town of Gorzów in Poznań had costs that were about 80 per cent of the national average and a good potential labour supply. After identification of the Poznań region, an in-depth study of the region was undertaken and 10 potential sites evaluated. The four main advantages of the Gorzów location were: the existence of a suitable site (a large – 10,000 square metre – one-storey production area was needed); low labour costs; acceptable levels of political stability; and favourable logistics (only 130 kilometres from Berlin and 400 kilometres from Wolfsburg, the Volkswagen headquarters).

The site that was finally chosen was a storage building, which was leased from a firm called Stilon, the Polish successor of the former IG Farben. This is a large chemicals company which used to have 15,000 employees and in 1995 had about 4,000. Volkswagen Bordnetze is now the second largest employer in the area. It did initially negotiate to buy a piece of land so that it could build its own production site. However, while these negotiations were continuing the option of renting a building came up and so – although it also bought a piece of land – it actually started production in the rented building, as this was also faster. A question remains as to what it will do with the piece of land it owns in the future.

Negotiations took about nine months and were not always without difficulty – for example, there were questions about who actually owned the piece of land that the firm wanted to buy. It also had to make various enquiries before it was clear how it could go about renting a building. However, a major advantage in the negotiations was the local Polish spokesman or representative of the local regional authorities. He was very welcoming and positive to the Volkswagen Bordnetze negotiators and dealt with both the regional and national governments to try to assist the deal. It was seen as a particular advantage to the region to get such a well-known and large concern as Volkswagen in the area and so the local authority was prepared to make more efforts to assist in negotiating with relevant national ministries than they might have in other cases.

The number of foreign investments in the Gorzów area have increased rapidly over the last three to four years. The majority of these are German. In mid-1995, there were 440 joint ventures, of which about 320 were German.

Organization and experience in Poland

The subsidiary in Poland was established and built up relatively rapidly, as indicated in Table 14.1. Both sales and employment expanded quickly. The recent fall in employment reflects restructuring and increased efficiency. The largest size of plant has about 1,100 employees. The subsidiary is not in a position to expand much further in its current building, although the company continues to own the adjacent piece of land. However, future expansion plans appear likely to focus on another central or eastern European location, possibly Slovakia.

Most of the plant and equipment is new, although some machines were brought from Berlin. Sunk costs are relatively low. Production is organized by product and split into four main groups or areas, within which production is organized on a series of islands. The four groups are: the Polo and cables; motors and ABS; the Golf, Passat and others; and the new A4 Audi. Main inputs are wires, contact systems and miscellaneous small parts. The quality of inputs is as important as the quality of the firm's own production process. It does not as yet use CEE suppliers, as the quality is considered to be too low. To some extent, its suppliers are also moving to central and eastern Europe, though not to the same extent, as the advantages at that point in the supply chain are not so great. The firm produces 100 per cent for re-export to Germany, and so its production avoids import tariffs, although import of investment goods into Poland does attract tariffs – not an incentive to foreign direct investment. There are four people from the Polish Customs Office working directly in the subsidiary to check the import and re-export of products and their tariff status.

Table 14.1 Sales and employment in the Polish subsidiary

	Sales (DM million)	Employment
1993	17.7	483
1994	46.6	1223
June 1995	62	1091

Logistics

Logistics are very important in this sector, in particular given the importance of JIT methods of production and delivering products in the appropriate sequence. Logistics were one important factor taken into account in choosing the location of the Polish subsidiary, as it is only 130 kilometres from Berlin and 400 kilometres from the Volkswagen headquarters in Wolfsburg. Furthermore, there is only one border to cross.

However, even with only one border there are potential problems of slow border crossings and busy motorways. Such problems cannot be allowed to interrupt deliveries to Volkswagen, which must be reliable. Volkswagen Elektro-Systemy, therefore, has contingency plans such as putting output into smaller vans rather than large lorries; these can then use different and less congested border crossings and motorways.

Management

There are two joint chairmen of the Polish subsidiary Volkswagen Elektro-Systemy – one from Volkswagen and one from Siemens. One is responsible for overall commercial management and the other is responsible for technology and detailed production management. The subsidiary reports directly to Berlin and there is an annual visit to Poland from a supervisory/management committee from Germany. There is frequent communication between Wolfsburg, Berlin and Poland – daily telephone and fax and frequent visits, including informal monthly meetings.

Six of the senior managers in Poland are German and four are Polish. Some of the German managers may be described as German/Polish, as they were originally from or have links to Poland and have some Polish language skills. It is intended over the next three years or so to increase the number of Polish senior management, with the ultimate aim of having only a German chairman.

There are a number of difficulties and challenges in developing both senior and middle Polish management. The location of the Polish subsidiary in Gorzów contributes to the difficulties of finding good local managers. The region is in western Poland – distant from Warsaw – and provincial. In general, there are better prospects for people in the big Polish cities or even in Berlin, and so it is difficult to find and to attract suitably qualified people. If there were an adequate supply of Polish management, they would already have been put into all senior positions other than that of managing director. These problems in personnel management are seen as fairly typical of operations in central and eastern Europe.

In training and developing local middle management, more time has been required than originally expected – this is related to the need for middle managers to adopt and develop new ways of thinking, including taking a more global perspective and seeing the wider/more general context of an issue. In general, they are perceived to work well in hierarchies but to have more difficulties in working in teams. However, there is also a recognition on the German side that learning processes are required for both sides and that there are alternative ways of organizing some activities.

Finance

The Volkswagen Bordnetze subsidiaries are financed through a mixture of equity financing, in-country financing and hard currency financing. Each year an overall budget is agreed with each subsidiary – the overall amount and credit lines are determined by Volkswagen Bordnetze. A consolidated balance sheet is established with the two subsidiaries on an annual basis. Both German and Polish banks are used. The main financial accounting is done in Polish, but Polish and German accounting methods are considered to be similar.

Initially, the subsidiaries bought the inputs – cables, wires etc. – and sold the output. However, the current strategy is to keep the subsidiaries' assets as small as possible and charge only for the manufacturing process, i.e. the cables and circuits remain the property of the Berlin headquarters. There are some problems with some potential relationships between the Polish subsidiary and the headquarters. For example, inter-country leasing is not used because it is not possible to subtract the lease rate from taxable profits. A similar problem occurs with import duties on investment goods/fixed assets.

The legal situation in Poland is also not seen as being either entirely stable or transparent. There can be unclear allocations of competencies and responsibilities across different authorities who do not necessarily recognize each others' authority. Other problems include continuing communication problems such as reliable telephone connections.

Costs

The cost structure of production of Volkswagen Bordnetze has changed dramatically due to its investment in Poland. Wage costs per hour in 1995 were DM 3.5 in Poland, DM 5 in Turkey and DM 45 in Berlin. The ratio of labour to material costs in Volkswagen Bordnetze used to be about 1 to 1 but in 1995 was about 1 to 10. The result of this change is a cut of 50 per cent in the price of electrical cables and wiring circuits. Any firm that did not manage to make this change in cost structure would not survive in the current competitive environment. Such a change in cost structure could only be achieved by investment in a low-cost location. There are technical possibilities to substitute capital for labour in the production of the products. However, this is more costly and if the costs of these products go up too much the vehicle manufacturers will look for ways of reducing the proportion of cables and wiring that they use in cars and manufacture.

Labour force

At the start of the operation of the subsidiary, Volkswagen advertised for 400 employees and about 5,000 applied. It aimed to select the best people but, especially at the start, there were problems with attitudes to work, in particular the expectation that the work would not be particularly intensive or even that they would not have to work all the time. Initially, some of the workforce were taken to Berlin for training; when they returned to Poland, they then assisted in training the others. In general, however, training is on the job and largely learning-by-doing. When a worker is first taken on, she will be trained for one week and then given the simplest type of cable to work on. If an acceptable standard of work is achieved then a 10-day contract will be given, and subsequently a three-week contract, and then a three-month contract, and so on. The best workers can be given an unlimited contract – this is a particular advantage for them not only in terms of greater job security, but also because it makes them eligible for bank credit, for example.

Productivity levels in the subsidiary match those in Berlin. This is due both to the fact that the plant is new and to the fact that most of the work in Poland is on the simpler cables; more complex work is done in Berlin. The machinery used is, in general, the same in all three production locations – Berlin, Turkey and Poland. Although Poland is cheaper in terms of labour costs than Turkey, management and workforce learning and experience are greater in Turkey.

As discussed above, quality is a critical aspect of production. Quality levels are acceptable in the Polish subsidiary but substantial work has been required to make the workforce understand the importance and meaning of quality and their individual responsibility for, and contribution to, this. There is a system of 100 per cent quality control. Quality checking and testing is done at each stage of the production process, as to go back and do reworking at a later stage is very expensive.

Although productivity and quality, together with costs, are competitive, there are still thought to be some problems with workforce attitude. Management would like to see a greater commitment to work matched by a recognition that rewards for such a commitment – such as longer contracts – are forthcoming. They have tried to teach the workforce the importance of quality, concern with performance and other concepts such as the dominant importance of the customer, and communication and interaction within an organization.

In all these areas, the workforce is seen to lag behind that in Germany. One of the lessons of the subsidiary's experience is seen to be that it is best to start with relatively simple production, as this aids learning, productivity and motivation. Learning and the transfer of management systems would also be easier where production was built up more slowly if market conditions allowed this. There have been concerns about absenteeism, in particular excessive use and possibly abuse of sick leave. It is considered that it is better to have younger workers, as there is more chance of changing their mentality and attitude to work, whereas this is seen as unlikely with older workers.

Despite some of these difficulties experienced with the labour force, there are advantages in addition to the low costs and reasonable – though behind German – education levels. In particular, although the plant normally works on a two-shift system, it can if necessary work on a three-shift system, including a night shift. There are, inevitably, some concerns about future wage levels, given Poland's future entry into the EU and the location of the subsidiary near the German border. However, these are not of immediate concern. Wages are expected to rise at some point in the future in Poland but not to the same extent as in the Czech Republic, and current cost structures are expected to continue for the next few years.

In the Polish subsidiary, no trade unions are as yet established. Wage negotiations take place at the level of the subsidiary. A works council may be established but this has also not yet occurred. Wage negotiations in Germany are at national level and this is seen as being simpler by management. However, a more informal and personal approach to industrial relations in Poland is seen as the most flexible structure in the early period of establishing and developing a new plant.

Conclusion

This is a case of a medium-sized company investing in Poland to improve its cost competitiveness. Poland was also chosen for locational reasons. Through this investment the company has succeeded in maintaining its position in a highly competitive market and in expanding its sales.

Part III

15

Lessons from the Cases

Introduction

We noted in Chapter 3 the significant literature enumerating the scale of Western direct investment into the transitional economics of central and eastern Europe and discussing its determinants and impact (see, for example, Meyer, 1996; Organization for Economic Cooperation and Development, 1995). However, most of this analysis is at the sectoral or aggregate level. As a result, it has little to say about the issues raised in the second chapter of this book; namely, the effects of foreign direct investment into the transitional economies on enterprise restructuring and the broader spillover effects on the development of a market economy. We have sought to address these questions through cases, using a small number of carefully chosen examples to understand more about the relationship between FDI and transition. The advantage of such an approach is the provision of a wealth of details about how Western firms have gone about restructuring existing state-owned firms, or constructing entirely new ones, in the uncertain and bureaucratic environment of central and eastern Europe. The disadvantage of the method is, of course, that it is extremely difficult to generalize from such cases to the transition process as a whole. Nonetheless, in this chapter we seek to provide an overview of the findings across the entire project, by comparing results for a number of the crucial areas highlighted in Chapter 2 across the 10 cases together.

As discussed above, the study involved 10 case studies of UK, German and US firms entering the Czech Republic, Hungary and Poland. Following the conceptual framework of Chapter 2, we first analyse in this chapter the motivation of firms entering the region, distinguishing between the three basic motives for entry: to cut production costs, to increase market share and for strategic motives. In practice, several of the cases display multiple entry motives, and these are also discussed below. We go on to compare and contrast the behaviour and experience of our case firms, assessing the implications for the investing firms themselves as well as (where relevant) for the firms being restructured. To assess the wider implications for the transition process, attention is also paid to the spillovers for the host countries. Of particular interest in the first part of the chapter are the questions of why firms chose to enter the market, the entry vehicle used, and the relationship between these and performance of the investment thus far, from the perspective of the investor. The third section is devoted to the impact of the investment on the 10 firms involved – in the source and host country – while the fourth considers the implications for the transition process more generally.

The characteristics of the cases

In this section, we first consider the array of enterprises covered in the cases in terms of sectors, host country and donor country. We go on to analyse how well the investments have performed, and seek to link this with our perception of the motives for market entry, as well as the chosen entry vehicles.

Sectors and countries

The 10 cases are made up of four UK, three German and three US multinational enterprises (MNEs) as follows.

- UK: British Vita, Glaxo, Lycett, United Biscuits (UB).
- German: Pyramid, Schöller, Volkswagen Bordnetze (VW-B).
- US: General Bottlers (GB), Guardian, Otis.

Their investments into central and eastern Europe by sector and host country are set out once again in Table 15.1. It can be seen that the distribution of cases across countries and sectors provides a good basis for a comparative study of this sort. There is at least one case from each of the three Western countries in each of the three CEE countries. This facilitates the comparison across the Western investors as well as across the three host countries.

We noted in Chapter 3 that the United States is home to the largest, and greatest number of, MNEs and that its investment in the region has been concentrated in a relatively small number of large investments. All the cases concerning US firms are of large

Table 15.1 Distribution of cases by sector and host country

Sector	Host Country Czech Republic	 Hungary	 Poland
Food and Drink (low technology)		Schöller (Germany) United Biscuits (UK)	General Bottlers (US)
Pharmaceuticals (high technology)	Glaxo (UK)		
Engineering (medium technology)	Otis (USA) Pyramid (Germany)	Lycett (UK)	Volkswagen Bordnetze (Germany)
Bulk Intermediates Glass (low technology)		Guardian (US)	
Chemicals (medium technology)			British Vita (UK)

multinationals expanding their activities in central and eastern Europe. Given the distances involved, it is unusual for a US firm to make its first foreign investment in central and eastern Europe, though this does apply to one of our cases (GB). Two of the three German investments are very small MNEs, which reflects Germany's locational advantage, as seen in the relatively large number of investments in the region by small German (and Austrian) firms. Three of the four UK investments are by large, established MNEs, and, the small, first-time British MNE was not successful in its investment, in part due to locational problems.

Sectors for the case studies were chosen to reflect the competitive advantage of CEE economies, as well as the sectoral composition of FDI into the region described in Chapter 3. We therefore concentrate on food-processing, intermediate manufactured goods and various branches of engineering. In the original formulation of the project, the objective was comparison by sector across all three transitional economies, or at a minimum pairwise comparisons across countries, and this was largely achieved. Thus we have three cases of food-processing (two in Hungary and one in Poland), four of engineering (Czech Republic, Hungary and Poland) and two bulk intermediates (Hungary and Poland). Our attempts to provide a pair for the pharmaceuticals firm in the Czech Republic were ultimately unsuccessful, however. As can be seen, the sectors represent a spread across high, medium and low technologies, with more emphasis towards the middle- and low-technology activities. They also cover both intermediate and final goods, including sectors that are both sectors of high multinational activity and that are important sectors for central and eastern Europe in terms of size and likely comparative advantage (see Hare and Hughes, 1992).

Characteristics of the investing multinationals

The cases were also chosen to cover several different types of multinational firms, as set out in Table 15.2. Although most of the MNEs are large firms with a considerable variety of multinational operations, two of the cases concern firms which were not previously multinational – one UK and one German – and one is of a medium-sized firm with only one subsidiary prior to its CEE investment, also German.

The 10 MNEs in the study also vary in their organizational structures. We find rather differing degrees of centralization and decentralization. In the interviews for the cases, managers in several of the headquarters expressed the view that their companies were fairly decentralized. In our judgment, this sometimes reflected the fact that they had moved to flatter management structures but did not in all cases appear to imply genuine decentralization of control, particularly over key issues such as marketing, investment or research and development (R&D). Differences in organizational structure did, however, appear to affect where the decision to invest was made within the company and where overall strategic responsibility for setting up and managing new subsidiaries rests, and this clearly influenced the making of decisions. For example, in several of the more centralized companies, the investment project itself, and its initial execution, originated at or near the level of the main board. In more decentralized firms, the development and execution of strategy for the region was carried out at a lower level, often (for US and UK firms) via continental European subsidiaries.

One might have expected more decentralized MNEs to be more flexible and experimental in their approach to investments in a new and volatile environment. However, in our cases the fact that a MNE is decentralized does not necessarily mean that its CEE subsidiary is initially given the same degree of autonomy as other subsidiaries. The most centralized of the 10 cases were the two smaller German companies – reflecting both the cross-border nature of these investments and the lack of multinational experience leading to an

Table 15.2 Types of multinational enterprise

Home country	Not previously MNE	'Small' MNE (one or two subsidiaries)	International/ global MNE
Germany	Pyramid	Volkswagen Bordnetze	Schöller
UK	Lycett		Glaxo British Vita United Biscuits
United States			General Bottlers Guardian Otis

objectivc of ensuring clear control of the subsidiary. The small new British MNE – Lycett – in contrast, did not exert such clear control.

Performance of the investments

Case studies can be self-selecting, in that firms with unsuccessful investments are unlikely to agree to act as case studies. However, the situation was more complex in our study because our approach involved interviews in both head office and in the operating companies in the region. The cases threw up some clear differences in the motives of different managers for participating in the project,[1] as well as in perceptions of performance. In general, head office was more optimistic than the local interviewees about performance, perhaps because it tended to take a longer-term perspective and was able to relate outcomes to pre-project plans. It is difficult to assess success of an investment, since companies are not necessarily expecting short payback periods. However, we attempted a subjective evaluation of our cases into high, medium and low success categories. The evaluations were based on whether the firms appear to have achieved their main investment aims, whether of sales, market share or lower costs. This was supplemented where possible with an assessment of profit and financial information, and with an assessment of performance relative to main competitors.

On this basis we have made a classification as set out in Table 15.3. It is striking that almost every case is at least moderately successful; we identify six MNEs as high success cases, three as medium

Table 15.3 Assessment of the outcome of the investment for the multinational enterprise

	Overall success		
	High	Medium	Low
Home country			
Germany	Pyramid Volkswagen Bordnetze	Schöller	
UK	Glaxo British Vita	United Biscuits	Lycett
United States	General Bottlers Otis	Guardian	
Host country			
Czech Republic	Glaxo Otis Pyramid		
Hungary		Guardian Schöller United Biscuits	Lycett
Poland	British Vita General Bottlers Volkswagen Bordnetze		

success and one as a low success. Though, as we noted above, the case study method biases selection in favour of successful examples, our study provides evidence that some very important Western firms are already achieving a strong and positive performance, including in several cases a significant contribution to profit, considerable market shares and rapid sales growth, in central and eastern Europe.

All three Western home countries include high and medium success cases. However, it is striking that the three medium success cases and one low success case are all based in Hungary. As discussed below, this is probably not directly related to problems of investing in Hungary – this would, *a priori*, seem unlikely, given, as we saw in Chapter 3, that Hungary has been the main host country in the region. Rather, the performance of these four firms appears to be related to the form of entry – acquisition – to their sector's market structure (in three cases), and to the challenges of being the first mover in a market, notably establishing brand identification. In one of the four cases – Guardian – difficulties were primarily due to external causes, notably the fact that the investment was planned prior to the reforms in 1989, so the investment was intended to secure the COMECON market and located accordingly. There were also problems because of the nature of the privatization programme, which has led to investments via acquisitions in manufacturing being a dominant form of entry (see Estrin, 1994), and due to the lacklustre Hungarian macro-economic performance, which has led to a belated turnaround in gross domestic product (GDP) and only very modest growth rates in recent years (see European Bank for Reconstruction and Development, 1995).

Motivations for investment

In Chapter 2, we classified potential motivation for FDI into three categories: markets (sales), market share ('strategic' motives) and cost reductions from any source. These categories broadly accord with the main groups identified in the literature (see, for example, Meyer, 1996, for survey). In the majority of our cases, motives for investment were evaluated to be a mixture of two or even all three of these motivations, as set out in Table 15.4. Motivations also have to be understood in the context of the companies' overall global structure, performance and strategy. Thus, for example, the size of CEE markets may be a motivation in its own right or the CEE investment may also be strongly motivated by weak demand growth in the company's home or existing markets.

Table 15.4 confirms a common result in much of the literature (see, for example, Organization for Economic Cooperation and Development, 1995; National Economic Research Associates, 1991), namely that the most common motivation for investment is a mixed market/ market share motivation (four cases, plus one including costs). One case was driven purely by market and one by market together with costs. Three cases were primarily cost driven – one in each of the three CEE countries. Of the two cases with a market but no market share motivation, both were in Poland, probably reflecting the substantially larger size of the Polish market. Of the six cases that include a market/ market share motivation, we have classified three as of medium success. An implication may be that investments motivated by the strategic oligopoly can be relatively more difficult to bring to successful fruition in the transitional economies, in comparison with investments for more straightforward reasons such as factor costs or market shares. We return to this issue below.

Table 15.4 Motivations for FDI

	Market	Market/ market share	Market and costs	Market, market share and costs	Costs
Home country					
Germany		Schöller			Pyramid Volkswagen Bordnetze
UK		Glaxo United Biscuits	British Vita		Lycett
United States	General Bottlers	Guardian		Otis	
Host country					
Czech Republic		Glaxo		Otis	Pyramid
Hungary		Schöller United Biscuits Guardian			Lycett
Poland	General Bottlers		British Vita		Volkswagen Bordnetze

Table 15.4 suggests that among our cases cost motivation is particularly important for German firms, while for the US firms, markets and market share dominate. This probably reflects the greater ability of German firms to benefit from lower costs in central and eastern Europe – both due to Germany's high costs and due to the advantage of locational proximity in managerial and logistical control. The cases thus provide some evidence that at least for the high-cost manufacturers of continental Europe, the bordering low-cost economies of central and eastern Europe may be a source of improved competitiveness and flexibility. In contrast, US firms looking for a combination of low costs and locational proximity would be more likely to choose Mexico and other central American countries, or, if costs alone are the priority, other locations worldwide. The key motive for entry into eastern Europe by US multinationals is therefore market access and potential growth. Interestingly, the UK is in an intermediate position between the United States and Germany in this

respect. The CEE locations are closer than other similar low-cost possibilities but historical and cultural links suggest that transactions costs may be higher than, for example, in Southeast Asia. Furthermore, the transitional economies are probably still too far away to allow the benefits of close managerial control. Moreover, UK labour costs are lower than German and the industrial manufacturing base smaller, so the benefits of shifting production are less compelling.

Forms of entry

The two basic choices for entry into the transitional economies are greenfield investment or acquisition, whether through 100 per cent ownership or joint venture. Since the sorts of firms of interest to Western multinationals in central and eastern Europe typically lag technologically and in product quality, and often face severe financial difficulties as well, joint ventures without 100 per cent acquisition are perhaps less common than one might expect for Western entry into new and risky markets. In our cases, the post-communist partner usually brings either market share or brand names or both to the partnership rather than management skills, know-how, technology or finances. The Western partner usually seeks to acquire 100 per cent ownership if the remaining shares become available.

In some cases, however, companies have used a mixture of both forms of entry, and we also observe what we term 'brownfield' entry. This we defined in Chapter 2 as being where Western companies acquire a firm but almost completely replace plant and equipment, labour and product line. The acquisition yields brand name or market share, and perhaps valuable supply or customer relations, but the production processes and organizational structures are effectively reconstructed from scratch.

Table 15.5 relates these various forms of entry to motivation for entry. About half the cases are pure greenfield investments and the other half are a mixture of greenfield/acquisition, brownfield, and acquisition. It is notable that only one case – Otis – involves an acquisition where there is restructuring without a complete brownfield operation and without any additional greenfield investment on a separate/nearby site. United Biscuits is the only other case where the acquisition did not entail a brownfield operation, but it also involved a new investment in an adjacent site for a related product.

The cases taken together offer no clear relationship between motivation for investment and the investment vehicle chosen.

Table 15.5 Form of entry and motivations for FDI

	Form of entry			
Motivations	Greenfield	Greenfield and acquisition	Brownfield	Acquisition/ Joint venture
Markets	General Bottlers (P)			
Market/ market share	Glaxo (CR)	United Biscuits (H)	Schöller (H) Guardian (H)	
Markets/ costs	British Vita (P)			
Market/ market share/costs				Otis (CR)
Costs	Pyramid (CR) Volkswagen Bordnetze (CR)		Lycett (H)	

Note: P = Poland; CR = Czech Republic; H = Hungary.

Investments to save costs and to obtain market share took both greenfield and acquisition forms. However, the cases do suggest that performance of the investment is related to its form. In particular, the more successful cases are those involving greenfield entry. More difficulties appear to have been encountered by firms entering through acquisition. The cases also suggest that the reason why Western firms chose to acquire rather than develop a greenfield site is to acquire existing brand names and, possibly, associated customer and distribution networks. This is, of course, especially true of 'brownfield' operations. Thus, any difficulties and worse performance involved in entry through acquisition may reflect the unexpectedly serious problems faced in restructuring former socialist enterprises and the problems of taking over and developing brand identity in a transition economy.

The Polish cases are all greenfield, reflecting the slow Polish privatization process with the result of initially restricting the role of foreign capital. The Hungarian cases are all initially acquisitions, though the Western firms all went on either to add greenfield capacity or to adopt a brownfield modest development. The Czech mass privatization also restricted Western involvement in the early phase to a small number of enterprises, which is reflected in the fact that the bulk of our Czech cases are greenfield.

The impact of foreign investments on enterprises in the transitional economies

In this section, we first consider the impact of foreign investments on the transition country firms, in the cases of acquisitions, or on the new enterprises created by the project. Key areas concern technology, management and labour. We also consider the relevance of national and sectoral characteristics of investing firms to the motives, performance and impact of the investments.

Technology and products

The technology used in the CEE subsidiaries of our case firms is, in almost all cases, at the same level as in donor firms' Western plants. Indeed, new investment in the subsidiary may mean that the eastern European plant has the newest state-of-the-art technology. In one or two cases, older machines were physically transferred from Western plants to eastern European subsidiaries but this reflected relocation of production rather than any relative downgrading of CEE technology, and there was often new investment as well. State-of-the-art management strategies and logistics were also introduced, including the widespread use of just-in-time production. This is an extremely important finding across the cases, and suggests that FDI may be a major way for the transitional economies of central and eastern Europe to close the productivity gap with western Europe.

The technological level of production is, therefore, only generally lower in the CEE subsidiaries in the case of joint ventures and acquisitions, where some of the existing plant and equipment was retained. However, all of the cases that involved joint ventures with existing firms or acquisitions did involve at least some new investment, and in three of these cases – Guardian, Lycett, Schöller – virtually all existing plant was scrapped. In one case, United Biscuits, there was a mixture of greenfield and acquisition, and Otis is the only case where there was pure acquisition without a brownfield strategy, though even in this case there was substantial new investment and some scrapping. This confirms that foreign investors are making very limited use of the existing technological resources of subsidiaries in the host countries, relying on high levels of fixed investment, usually financed internally, to upgrade the technological capacity of the subsidiary.

None of the cases involved the establishment or development of

R&D facilities in the subsidiary, though in one – British Vita – some local testing capacity was established, and in another – Glaxo – medical trials were being implemented. This may reflect the tendency of multinational enterprises to centralize their R&D, though in fact only one of the cases is from a high-technology sector – pharmaceuticals.

While technology of the same level as the parent company is being applied, nonetheless in a number of cases the full technological range of production processes – and of related products – was not immediately introduced. This appeared primarily to be related to the complexity of products and production processes – firms would first introduce simpler processes and products and then, as learning progressed, begin to introduce more complex ones. In some cases, such as British Vita, the decision to introduce only part of a product range was closely linked to the analysis of market opportunities. In one case – Guardian – the subsidiary had a higher share of high-quality glass production than was typical for other subsidiaries.

The cases also varied with regard to the product range that the foreign company chose to introduce to the new market. In some, it was the same as in Western markets, while in others the range was significantly narrower. For the cases which were acquisitions, some or all of the subsidiary's previous product ranges were, at least in the short run, retained. This variety of experience reflects the range of sectors and products in the cases as well as whether existing firms and product ranges were being acquired. In the latter firms, the cases suggest that existing brands were retained (or sometimes withdrawn and then reintroduced) to build on existing consumer goodwill and to cater for low-income consumers.

Management

The nature of the relationship between Western headquarters and the subsidiary offices varied across the cases. As we noted above, the strongest degree of centralized control from the Western headquarters (or Western subsidiary responsible for the CEE investment) was in the case of the smaller firms such as Pyramid and Volkswagen Bordnetze. In the other cases, subsidiaries were given more autonomy, although strategic decision-making remained ultimately with the headquarters. Nonetheless, there was variety in the extent of local autonomy. The parent companies were in general aiming to establish similar relationships with their CEE subsidiaries, as with their other subsidiaries, though often in the initial phase of the investment this was not viewed as being possible, and more Western managerial time was needed to assist the subsidiary. In terms of functions, day-to-day operational decisions were generally taken at the level of the subsidiary, while investment and strategic decisions were made at headquarters. The location of control over finance and marketing varied from case to case.

The relatively tight control of the central European operations by head offices in our cases may relate both to the particular difficulties of operating in transition economies and to difficulties experienced in the availability and quality of host country managerial skills. In many cases, the costs of setting up the projects proved to be greater than expected, and headquarters needed to be closely involved in agreements to finance the over-runs. Headquarters also sometimes needed to be involved to ensure that the new subsidiary integrated effectively into the company's global network. This could include, for example, bringing new products from the West onto the market, integrating the new subsidiary into international marketing campaigns, developing sophisticated new distribution systems, including just-in-time delivery, and ensuring a supply of material inputs of suitable quality. All of these examples relate to the special difficulties of operating in a transitional economy.

The tight control structures also in part reflect deficiencies in the local managerial market. The most common comments in our cases about managerial expertise were that local staff had problems in decision-making, in learning to devolve decisions, in taking responsibility, in understanding markets and in using constructive leadership and teamwork rather than operating hierarchically. The use of expatriate management, including twinning and other training, was surprisingly widespread in our case studies, and, together with on-the-job learning by local managers, they had often improved and augmented local management skills considerably.

Expatriate management played an important role in all the cases – most commonly as general managers, and in finance and marketing. It was the norm for Western multinationals to aim to reduce dependence on expatriates and to increase use of local management as soon as possible, in line with companies' normal practice in their other subsidiaries. Some of the case firms had already succeeded in reducing local management dependence on expatriates, while others were aiming so to do in the future. In one case, however, that of Lycett, the use of expatriates had needed to be increased, a case of serious management problems and ultimate failure of the investment. The relatively slow shift to local management does reflect some of the specific characteristics and problems of the transition economies together with a learning process that is beginning to remedy these problems. Another common view was that management learning and training was substantially more successful with younger staff.

There appears to be no simple relationship between motives or mode of entry and the managerial process in our sample of firms. The cases suggest that there is some tendency for a subsidiary formed by acquisition, and taking the form of a joint venture, to be more likely to use a local general manager. It is not clear whether this is because, in such cases, the local partner brings skills and local knowledge of importance to the success of the venture, or whether it is simply a part of the deal (indeed, one which is a factor in the apparently relatively less successful performance of some of these arrangements). In several cases, the quality of particular local managers was highly praised, though the appropriateness of fully transferring Western management strategies rapidly, as well as the problems in finding and training suitable local managers, is also a consistent theme.

Labour

As we have seen, low wage costs form an important part of the motivation for investment in several of the cases. However, the wages paid in subsidiaries tend to be either average or above for their area and sector (paying the average wage rather than above it is more common in these cases). Because unemployment, actual or hidden, tends to be high and because jobs in Western-owned firms are seen as secure, the subsidiaries in many cases are able to pick the best workers from the region, even though neither pay nor conditions are exceptional. In almost all cases, Western managers express satisfaction with the quality and technical skills of their central and eastern European labour forces. In the cases where we have information, it would appear that the rapid introduction of Western management practices and more advanced machinery and equipment is associated with significant increases in productivity, near Western standards in some cases. This may in part reflect the focus in the CEE subsidiaries on simpler production processes. Even in Lycett, where managerial factors exacerbated inherent problems of high labour turnover and weak motivation, the skill level of the labour force was praised by the UK management and Western productivity levels were apparently attained. It seems likely that the apparent success of the MNEs in establishing Western work practices and productivity levels in such a short period was greatly influenced by their ability to hand-pick an appropriate labour force in a very slack labour market. However, training was also an important factor. Most companies provided training which varied in scope and intensity from relatively simple on-the-job training to more in-depth training, including periods in Western subsidiaries. Particular areas where training was important included sales and marketing. In some cases, employee attitudes to work were seen as a potential problem, and training in this area was more patchy.

Only two of the cases – United Biscuits and Otis – had trade unions operating in their subsidiaries, even though the majority had trade unions in their Western plants. United Biscuits and Otis reported no problems with having trade union representation and both paid only average wages. The other subsidiaries all had more informal means of wage determination – usually negotiation and/or communication with their workforces. In some cases there were also works councils, though these never had the decision-making powers common in the early 1990s, e.g. in Poland. Some of the companies admitted to discouraging the presence of trade unions, despite having unions in their parent companies. Interestingly, we could discern no difference between UK, German and US multinationals in this respect, or any differences with respect to host countries. This lack of trade union representation may reflect, on the one hand, a general preference of the companies, when in a position to choose, and on the other hand a particular concern with the legacy of trade unions and employee protection in the planned economies.

There were mixed attitudes among the Western managers in the cases regarding overall work attitudes in the subsidiaries. Views ranged from workforce attitudes being assessed as good through satisfactory to noting problems of lack of commitment. As with managerial staff, workforces were perceived in the Western head offices as needing to develop teamwork skills and the ability to take responsibility and decisions. Training and learning was also felt to be necessary for staff to understand the importance of quality and their responsibility for it. In at least four of the cases, the subsidiaries had experienced problems of relatively high levels of absenteeism; this happened in Polish and Hungarian but not Czech cases, though this is an area where generalizations are unconvincing. Some steps had been taken to deal with this in terms of payment systems and bonuses, but absenteeism and labour turnover remained a problem.

Language was mostly not a problem in our cases, with senior

management levels in the subsidiary being expected and able to communicate in the language of the parent company. Serious communication problems arose in one case – Lycett – mainly due to the workforce coming from a variety of countries.

Market structures and first mover advantages

The challenges facing companies investing in the transition economies and the strategies they adopt are likely to be influenced by the nature of competition in the market. Table 15.6 sets out our evaluation of the main elements of competition in the 10 cases. Six of our cases operate in essentially oligopolistic markets and four in competitive markets. In general, it would appear that investments motivated for cost reasons pose less of a threat to competition.

Table 15.6 Market structure and competitive strategy and marketing

	Nature of competition/Competitive strategy				
Market structure	Price/ costs	Quality	Product differentiation/ marketing	Innovation	User/ supplier relations
Oligopolistic					
Glaxo			√	√	
Guardian	√	√			(√)
Otis	(√)	(√)			√
Schöller	(√)	(√)	√		
United Biscuits	(√)	(√)	√		
General Bottlers	√				√
Competitive					
British Vita	√	(√)			√
Lycett	√				(√)
Pyramid	√	(√)			
Volkswagen Bordnetze	√	(√)			

√ = dominant importance.

(√) = important.

Table 15.7 Motives – firm-specific

Motives	Organizational changes		Management skills		Technology transfer/upgrading	
	High	Low	High	Low	High	Low
Markets			General Bottlers		General Bottlers	
Markets/market share	Schöller United Biscuits Guardian		Schöller Glaxo United Biscuits Guardian		Schöller United Biscuits Glaxo Guardian	
Markets and costs			British Vita		British Vita	
Markets, market share and costs	Otis		Otis		Otis	
Costs	Lycett		Lycett Volkswagen Bordnetze		Pyramid Volkswagen Bordnetze Lycett	

In the four cases in competitive markets, price and costs are the key competitive factors, with quality also playing an important role, together with some role for supply and customer relations. In the case of the six firms operating in oligopolistic markets, the nature of competition is more varied. Price and quality matter but are not the dominant factors, except in the case of Guardian. Product differentiation and marketing are key aspects of competition for four cases – innovation is also important for one of these. In the case of Otis, supply relations – establishing a network of maintenance and repair staff – are central.

Four of the six oligopolistic cases were first movers in their markets – Guardian, Otis, Schöller, United Biscuits. Of these, our categorization in Table 15.3 suggests that all except Otis were only moderately successful. Both Schöller and United Biscuits faced problems in establishing brand identity and this was the key to their entry strategy. In contrast, Glaxo depended on innovation as well as brand identity in its competitive strategy. Companies coming later into the transition markets could learn from the first movers what some of the key issues and characteristics of the market were in relation to brands and marketing. Guardian suffered as a first mover for different reasons – it invested before the transition had begun and was then constrained by its location. One might deduce that, taken together, the cases suggest that being first mover into the transitional economies is more of a disadvantage than an advantage.

Enterprise restructuring, performance and motives: a summary

In this section we attempt to bring together our findings on the effects of motives, performance and impact of FDI on enterprise restructuring. We then go on to consider what lessons can be learned from the cases for firms in host countries, donor countries and with respect to sectors. In doing this, we return to the criteria, outlined in Chapter 4, by which sectors and countries for the cases were selected, and to our attempts to achieve at least pairwise comparison by sector, host country and donor country.

The comparison of motives and performance in areas of firm-specific restructuring can be summarized with reference to Table 15.7. We focus on the three aspects of enterprise adjustment in transition – organizational firm changes, the development of managerial skills and the transfer or upgrading of technology. For simplicity, changes in each area are put into two categories – high and low. Clearly, some of these changes do not apply to certain firms; for example, the greenfield entrants General Bottlers, Glaxo, British Vita, Pyramid and Volkswagen Bordnetze do not need to undertake organizational changes. Moreover, in our judgment, the Pyramid subsidiary is too small and too subject to direct external control to permit a sensible evaluation of the development of managerial skills.

Table 15.7 clearly confirms the hypothesis proposed in Chapter 2 that FDI can have a major impact on the particular firms and sectors into which it goes, in the key areas required for successful transition, including technology transfer. We categorize none of our cases as being 'low' in any of the three areas of specific restructuring, and this is regardless of motives for entry and entry mode, from acquisition to greenfield development. Of course, the effect on existing firms is by definition greater with acquisition or brownfield development, though the effect on industry-level supply is probably similar in the two situations. This important result holds for all three donor countries, and in all three host countries.

Turning to the sectoral comparison, consider first the food and drink sector, where there is an intra-country comparison in Hungary, and a cross-country comparison with General Bottlers in Poland. United Biscuits and Schöller are both large Western food manufacturers who entered the Hungarian market for market and market share reasons as first movers. The similarities between the two firms do not end there; both chose to enter through acquisition, though in Table 15.5 we classify Schöller as brownfield, while United Biscuits added a greenfield manufacturing capacity in snack foods to its initial acquisition. Both firms, as noted in Table 15.6, compete primarily on product differentiation and marketing. There seems, therefore, to be little of analytical interest in the Anglo-German comparison in these cases. More significantly however, both firms were classified in Table 15.3 as being only moderately successful, and for similar reasons, related to their motives and mode of entry. Both firms ran into similar initial problems in maintaining market share, in pricing strategies and in managing the development of new products, which only further investment of managerial time, money and effort began to resolve. In this, the two companies can be contrasted with Glaxo, another oligopolistic company motivated by markets and market share, and deeply concerned with product differentiation. However, Glaxo entered as a greenfield investment and appears to have achieved greater initial success, perhaps because the brand was easier to establish, since the customer group (doctors and hospitals) is much more focused.

The two food sector companies in Hungary can then be compared with General Bottlers, the drink company in Poland. The differences are striking. The drink company used price competition as well as product differentiation and marketing, and focused more closely on supplier relations. It was motivated primarily by markets rather than market share (though its partner company in Poland, PepsiCo, was probably motivated by both). The company followed a greenfield entry strategy and, according to Table 15.3, can be classified as a successful investment.

The project also studied four engineering and electrical engineering firms; Otis, Lycett, Volkswagen Bordnetze and Pyramid. Of these, the Western company was a small or middle-sized enterprise (SME) in two cases, and the subsidiary was also relatively small in three cases. It is notable that it is these SMEs which represent the cost-motivated entrants in our sample, while Otis is unlike all the other cases in being motivated by markets, market share and costs simultaneously. Otis entered by acquisition and joint venture, Lycett via acquisition and brownfield development, while the two German SMEs entered by greenfields, but all operate in competitive markets and compete on price. Again, Otis is unusual in competing primarily though the development and exploitation of supplier and customer networks, though price and quality are also important elements in the strategy for the region. With the exception of Lycett, which in many ways is a special case, the engineering firms are all classified in Table 15.3 as being highly successful. In summary, the engineering firms in our sample belong to a medium-technology sector with few or no marketing or brand problems to tackle; hence it proved easier for them to enter this sector than for firms to enter final product sectors like food, and entry was also typically more successful. Host country does not appear to be an important factor in this story, though it is suggestive that small-scale German entry into the engineering sector was more successful than UK entry, for reasons associated with higher transaction costs of logistical management over long distances.

Finally, we turn to the pair of intermediate suppliers we have grouped together as 'bulk intermediates' – Guardian and British Vita. These are both firms in sectors supplying intermediate products, where scale economies and transport costs are very significant factors in investment decisions. Their motivations were slightly different – in Table 15.4 we classify Guardian as being motivated by markets and market share, but British Vita by markets and costs. This may in part be explained by the fact that the glass industry in Europe is oligopolistic, while the chemical foam industry is not. However, with high transport costs and large economies of scale, location becomes a crucial element in the entry decision, and here Guardian suffered from being a first mover, while British Vita judged the time and place of entry well. Both firms needed to develop entirely new plant and equipment; British Vita by greenfield development, and Guardian, in Hungary pre-reform, by joint venture/acquisition and brownfield development. The initial problems that Guardian faced, given its entry method and location, are enough to explain its relatively weaker performance compared with British Vita.

Spillovers from foreign direct investment to the transition process

In this section, we consider the externalities from the foreign investments analysed in our cases for the broader transition process. Our main concerns are the development of donor country supply networks and of labour (including managerial) skills, and the consequences of the investments for market structure. At the end of the section we consider the role of host country governments in these foreign investments.

Positive and negative externalities

The cases represent a mixture of experiences in their use and development of local supply networks relative to dependence on imports. Tariff barriers are one important reason for firms to source locally – and local sourcing also influenced exact location decisions – but firms in many cases were also importing substantially primarily for quality and reliability reasons. In addition, two cases involved outward processing and so the subsidiaries were being supplied from the parent firm and re-exporting back to it, thus avoiding custom duties. There are some examples, however, of firms trying to work with local suppliers to improve quality.

Another key element in the transition process is the development of local capital markets, which can be influenced by how Western firms finance their investments and subsidiaries. As we noted above, there is a pronounced trend in the cases for firms to establish 100 per cent ownership of their subsidiaries. A number of the joint ventures and acquisitions started off with much lower levels of ownership (Guardian being the lowest, with an initial 49 per cent) but in all but two cases eventually moved to 100 per cent ownership. United Biscuits has 96.5 per cent, with the remainder being employee shares; the only case significantly under 100 per cent is Otis at 51 per cent. This pattern of ownership reflects a desire by companies for complete control in the transition environment, not wishing either to allow the state to retain any influence or to allow continuing influence to initial joint venture partners. Thus though there has been a lot of capital investment, this has not engendered much local financial participation, and finance has typically relied on internal or Western sources.

Speedy restructuring is expected to lead to major declines in employment, and therefore to rapidly increasing unemployment, and one might expect foreign multinationals to be particularly ruthless in this area. In our cases of joint ventures and acquisition, restructuring has indeed led to job losses and these have sometimes been substantial. However, Western firms have been keen where possible to dissociate themselves from the job losses and rather to stress their role in the creation of new, long-term employment; this was part of the reasoning behind brownfield investments where the joint venture partners were left with the bloated labour forces in old factories, while the MNE subsidiary cherry-picked a handful of workers for its virtually new plant. Job losses were also sometimes outweighed by new job creation, e.g. when a reduction in production staff was offset by speedy expansion in the sales department.

Several of the cases also displayed elements of unbundling, which Earle and Estrin (1995) have stressed as an important element of long-term restructuring in transition, particularly given the highly integrated character of socialist firms under planning. The Western investors in our study which acquired enterprises in central and eastern Europe frequently chose to sell off parts of the companies they had bought in order to focus on the core activities. The cases therefore confirm that this important element of restructuring is accelerated by foreign ownership.

The impact of FDI on the balance of trade is not very clear from our cases. Most of the cases motivated for cost reasons exported most of their output: Guardian, Lycett, Pyramid and Volkswagen Bordnetze. However, because of their concerns for quality in supplying Western, primarily western European, markets, these were for the most part the same companies that put particular stress on the use of imported material inputs. Hence, though the balance of trade effects were probably positive (since these were positive value-added activities), the net effects were probably less substantial than would be implied by the export figures alone. Companies whose investments were motivated

Table 15.8 Spillovers

Motives	Supply networks: High	Supply networks: Low	Skills: High	Skills: Low	Market structure: Oligopolistic	Market structure: Pro-competitive
Market		General Bottlers	General Bottlers		General Bottlers	
Markets/market share	United Biscuits Guardian	Schöller Glaxo	Schöller Glaxo United Biscuits Guardian		Schöller United Biscuits Glaxo Guardian	
Markets and costs	British Vita		British Vita			British Vita(?)
Markets, market share and costs	Otis		Otis		Otis	
Costs	Lycett	Pyramid Volkswagen Bordnetze		Pyramid Volkswagen Bordnetze Lycett		Lycett

by the desire to capture new markets or to establish market share were clearly less concerned with exporting – United Biscuits, Schöller, General Bottlers and Glaxo. To the extent that initially capital, and some of the material supplies, were imported, these investments probably acted to worsen the balance of trade slightly.

Entrants and host governments

Our sample companies' main interactions with government were when they made their initial investments. Negotiations were frequently considered to have been lengthy and bureaucratic, with ministries often perceived to have unclear and overlapping responsibilities. In Poland, local authorities were usually felt to be of more positive assistance than central government, however. The most common problems in negotiating initial market entry appear to have related to land regulations and land ownership, and these seemed to be particularly serious in Poland. Tax incentives were not seen as important in our cases in general, although exemptions from tariff payments on imported machinery were important in some. In one case – Schöller – the government and the company disagreed on what had been negotiated over tax exemption, and subsequent discussions and a further compromise were necessary to resolve a situation which could otherwise have been damaging for the company. Otis also experienced difficulties in the Czech government's refusal to give tax exemption to its write-off of a major building. Other incentives were less clear. In some cases, for example, the payments notionally for acquisition appeared not to be for ownership rights at all; rather, the funds were then made available for investment in the company.

Motives, mode of entry and spillovers

We can bring together these points with reference to Table 15.8, which considers three crucial areas of spillover: the development of supply networks; the development of the labour force, especially managerial skills; and the evolution of market structure as a consequence of the foreign firms' entry. These are cross-classified with the motives for entry into the market, and we also in our discussion consider mode of entry as a determining factor. As in Table 15.7, we classify each of three types of spillover effects into two categories – high and low for supply networks and skills, and pro-competitive versus oligopolistic in character for market structure external effects.

Commencing with the cost-motivated entrants – Lycett, Volkswagen Bordnetze and Pyramid – it is striking that these firms provide at best limited spillover effects from raising the skills of their labour forces and managers, though they do transfer some knowledge about quality control, and some management capacity. There are two reasons for this: first, the firms are all relatively small, both in the source and host countries, so the complexity of the skills required to organize them may be more modest, and second, because they are anyway in relatively low-skill sectors.

The two German SMEs also provide few externalities in their supply chains; they receive most of their inputs from their parent companies, to whom they supply 100 per cent of their output. For this reason, they also have no impact on competition in the donor countries – they are assemblers and outward processors but do not make their host country's market structure more or less competitive.

Lycett, however, perhaps because of the greater distance involved, was actively involved in developing new supply chains and in raising supplier quality. Moreover, as a new small-scale entrant in metal processing, its investment probably acted in a pro-competitive way. The somewhat more positive spillover effects from Lycett may in part derive from the fact that the entry took a brownfield form, evolving from a joint venture, so that the new subsidiary was forced to address issues of existing supply quality and distribution chains.

The firms motivated by both markets and costs – Otis and British Vita – provide significantly greater spillover effects in terms of supply chains and skills. To some extent, both firms were, like Lycett, entering to obtain cheaper materials, and hence sought to develop local suppliers in terms of quality, deficiency system and reliability. Moreover, both were motivated in part by lower labour costs and therefore generated spillovers via training. Both firms are much larger and more sophisticated operations than our examples of purely cost-based entry, so the required transfer of managerial know-how and skills was greater.

However, the implications for market structure are less clear. In the short term, British Vita is a greenfield entrant reducing concentration in the Polish polymer sector. Moreover, the company is market rather than market share oriented, and focused on exports and world markets. However, since it is technologically more sophisticated, manufacturing at higher quality and lower cost than its competitors, it seems likely that the company may expand further, to the detriment of Polish incumbents and competition. There were already signs of this; a local Polish entrepreneurial entrant to the market was rapidly driven out once British Vita started to manufacture. Even here, however, the European scale of the polymer market suggests that this is not necessarily anti-competitive. However, we have placed a question mark against British Vita's spillover impact as being pro-competitive in Table 15.8. Otis entered the Czech market by acquisition to buy market share, position and service contracts. The industry in Europe is already oligopolistic, and the entry has done little to change that situation for the Czech Republic.

The remainder of the cases were motivated by markets and market share; there were five of them. For firms operating in final product markets or competing on product differentiation and quality, the perceived deficiencies of central and eastern European firms as input suppliers have led to considerable reliance on imported materials and therefore often a low spillover effect through the value chain. Schöller is an important example of this. However, this is not a completely general result – both United Biscuits and Guardian appear to have invested somewhat more in developing local supplier links, perhaps because, for both transactions, costs in maintaining traditional suppliers were much higher for reasons of distance.

Whether entrants by greenfield development or acquisition, the market-motivated firms all have considerable effects on host country skill levels, and have put great emphasis on training and the development of managerial, accounting and control systems. There are a number of reasons for this. The five firms, by their very motivation, are seeking to fill vacuums in the post-communist economic structures. Most of them seek to provide consumers with new, differentiated goods, and success in these markets requires all employees in the subsidiaries – from unskilled workers to top managers – to learn new skills, methods and motives. Also, the donor firms are large, and operating in high-skill industries, and so have developed an understanding of appropriate training and education systems. In short, in order to succeed in their home countries, and in international competition with their rivals, these firms have to invest in high-level skill development and training for all their labour force, and this provides strong spillover benefits from such investments in transitional economies. These effects appear from our cases to apply in all reforming economies studied, and to be independent of the country of origin of the investing multinational.

Finally, we consider the impact of these five firms on the evolving market structures of the transitional economies. Whether the entry is by acquisition or greenfield development, it seems unlikely that any of these entrants will in the long term act to enhance competition. All of them come from sectors which are oligopolistic and global, and most were motivated to enter in part for strategic reasons. In the short term, the greenfield entrants may have acted in a pro-competitive manner, but, as noted above in the case of British Vita, it seems likely for reasons of quality and cost that even these new entrants could drive out existing manufacturers – e.g. General Bottlers against incumbent Polish soft drinks suppliers.

Summary

FDI into the transitional economies appears to provide the greatest spillovers when the entry is by large multinationals motivated by markets or market share. These companies invest considerably in developing technology, labour training, managerial know-how and an orientation to the market and to customers – critical areas for success in transition. These skills also seem to spill over to the broader economy through labour turnover, and up and down the value chain. However, some companies, because of their reliance on imported products, have less impact in the latter area. But there is another side to this coin. These significant positive externalities may be matched by the dangers of increased concentration and anti-competitive behaviour in the future arising from the fact that these entrants have lower costs than incumbents and are very large. Policy-makers in transitional economies need to be aware of these potential difficulties ahead.

The situation is very different for firms motivated primarily by costs. While their entry is for the most part pro-competitive, or has no obvious effect on domestic market structure in the host countries, the positive spillover effects from these investments are much more modest. This is because these entrants are usually operating in low-skill sectors, and are often very small firms, with activity focused on outward processing. For reasons noted in Chapter 3, such investments are much more likely to come from Germany than the UK or, especially, the United States. Indeed, the cases suggest that, because transaction costs are higher for cost-driven investments from the UK and the United States, investors from these countries find themselves more involved in the host countries than their German counterparts, and hence providing larger spillovers. This may act to the benefit of the host country, but, as we saw in the case of Lycett, the effects may be damaging for the Western partner.

Conclusions

It has been argued that FDI could play a particularly important role in transition, because it simultaneously establishes private ownership, effective corporate governance, access to capital funds for restructuring and investment and access to managerial know-how (see, for example, Blanchard *et al.*, 1990). In the light of our cases, does FDI live up to these high expectations, and has the experience been sufficiently positive for Western firms to ensure a continued and growing flow?

Commencing with the experience from the MNEs' perspective, the cases do suggest that Western partners have for the most part been able to attain their profit, sales and other objectives in central and eastern Europe. These successes have usually been fairly rapid, though the picture is not entirely rosy; bringing operations up to Western standards has often been more difficult and costly than expected. Though it is hard to generalize from such a small sample, we find that greenfield operations seem easier to bring to fruition than acquisitions or joint ventures.

The picture of progress in transition at the enterprise level in our CEE subsidiaries parallels the success story from the perspective of the MNEs. The investments have successfully introduced or upgraded products, management systems and technology to Western levels. Unsurprisingly, this has been harder to achieve in acquired firms than in greenfield sites, though brownfield investments have proved an intelligent halfway solution. There is only one case of failure – Lycett – though, of course, the sample itself is self-selected. Perhaps more interesting is the uniformity of progress in the key aspects of transition – product quality, production method, information and control systems, applications of Western technology, management training, labour productivity – across a variety of sectors and countries.

The broader benefits of FDI for the transition appear from our cases to be somewhat more mixed, however. The very speed of restructuring in foreign-owned firms may have exacerbated unemployment problems, and as yet has not resolved the deep shortages of managerial skills and talents; reliance on expatriates in key managerial functions remains uncomfortably high. Western firms in our sample have also tended to displace local suppliers by imports from their home countries, thus weakening industrial supply networks in the host country and perhaps leading to a deterioration in the balance of trade. Though capital investments in the new subsidiaries have been large, these have always been financed internally and therefore have done nothing to develop fledgling local capital markets. Finally, Western entrants, notably in final goods sectors, have tended to replicate their global oligopolistic structures, increasing the chances of monopolistic abuses in these areas.

Note

1. It is certainly correct that it was often difficult to obtain agreement to participate, especially from German firms. However, this may in part reflect the commercial sensitivity of the investments, as well as less experience with the case study approach.

16

Conclusions

We have analysed foreign direct investment into central and eastern Europe on the basis of a conceptual framework which informed both aggregate data analysis and the comparative case study. In this final chapter, we review some of the main themes and arguments, before briefly discussing some policy issues.

Conceptual framework

Our conceptual framework for the study brought together the analysis of FDI and the analysis of transition in the post-communist countries of central and eastern Europe in order to assess both how FDI may impact on transition and how transition may affect multinationals' motivations, behaviour and experience. In particular, the conceptual framework focused on three broad areas: motivation for investment into transition economies, likely impact on enterprises in central and eastern Europe, and possible broader consequences for transition economies. A three-fold set of motives for FDI was set out, together with an assessment of how these might be affected by transition. The three broad motives were markets, market share and costs. With respect to markets, the transition economies were seen as highly attractive, as they offered a large number of potential new consumers with low pre-existing levels of consumption of many products and with substantial prospects for future growth. These markets could be served by exports or FDI, but exporting and investment are often complementary, not competitive strategies and the specific nature of the transition economies meant that local knowledge could be particularly valuable in accessing markets. In terms of the related motivation of acquiring and building market share, the low existing consumption levels also offered Western firms the prospect of building brand and product loyalty in a new and growing market. This suggests possible strong first mover advantages, reinforced by prospects of being the first to develop distribution systems. The transition economies also had high pre-existing levels of monopoly, offering strategic advantages through acquisition. However, disadvantages may also attach to being first in these markets, due to the potentially steep learning curves faced. Finally, low costs in the region, especially low labour costs combined with high skills in many sectors, have also been seen as an important motivation for some FDI into the region. However, again these advantages have associated disadvantages: for example, there is a notable lack of managerial skills in the transition economies, and among both management and labour there is a lack of experience of working in relatively flat organizations, of teamwork, and of taking responsibility and of making decisions.

Other aspects of the transition affecting these motives to invest included levels of political and economic stability, levels of risk and uncertainty, development or otherwise of legal systems, institutional and physical infrastructure, and scope and quality of local supply networks. The policy environment, including macro policy, trade policy, and inward investment policies, could also influence in a number of ways the investment decision. Transition may have specific effects on multinationals' entry strategies, some of which may encourage greenfield investment, while others encourage acquisition. Where local knowledge is important in a risky environment, acquisition may be appropriate. Privatization bargains may also have stimulated some acquisition entry strategies. However, transition poses particular problems for acquisition where firms in central and eastern Europe have excessively high employment levels, low environmental standards, inappropriate mix of plant and technology and high levels of social assets connected to firms. These problems may encourage firms to enter by greenfield investment but they may also motivate 'brownfield' investment whereby a multinational acquires a firm for brand/market share reasons but then effectively scraps almost all or all of the existing plant.

In assessing the impact of FDI in transition economies, we were concerned in our conceptual framework to consider the likely effects on multinationals' behaviour and performance, the consequence for the host country firms (in the case of acquisitions and joint ventures) and the broader results of spillovers. In the case of the investing firm, a variety of decisions and actions would be taken in establishing a subsidiary, most of which could be affected by the specifics of transition. These decisions include the ownership structure of the subsidiary, financing, the place of the subsidiary in the global organizational structure, wages and training strategy and the strategy with respect to supply chains and marketing strategy. Multinationals' aims and performance cannot usefully be evaluated only in terms of short-term profitability; rather, one should focus on longer-term cost and market share objectives. From the point of view of the acquired firm or joint venture partner, the incoming multinational could be expected to have a substantial impact on the subsidiary, both in developing clear profit orientations and in restructuring the firm. Multinationals may also have a major effect on unbundling the subsidiary's assets, and in creating new organizational structures and new functional departments, including product and sales, marketing and human resources. More generally, multinationals may be important through the transfer of capital, technology and management skills. The very strength of likely restructuring by multinationals may itself pose a problem, especially where there are strong employment effects. Finally, FDI may also have wider – positive and negative – spillover effects in product, capital, management and labour markets. We have argued that multinationals may be expected to have positive effects on skills and training, especially managerial skills and through technology transfer. However, they may have anti-competitive effects and their impact on local supplier networks could be positive or negative. Equally, while multinationals may have positive effects at a wider level – e.g. encouraging clarification of legal frameworks – spillovers may also be less than expected if, for example, multinationals use their own domestic finance networks. In general, many of the spillovers from FDI for transitional economies parallel those for less developed economies – effects on balance of payments, domestic market structure and existing supply networks. To counter these, benefits would come from enhancing local supply capacity via improvements in the quality of the human and physical capital stock. We hypothesized that these effects might depend on the character of the investing Western company, the motives for the investment, the mode of entry and the performance of the investment. We returned to these themes in Chapter 15.

FDI flows

To investigate many of the detailed questions and hypotheses set out required the in-depth case studies set out in Chapters 5 to 14, but prior to undertaking the analysis of these cases we brought together and assessed the available data on FDI flows to transition economies, focusing on the Czech Republic, Hungary and Poland and tracing in particular the nationality of investing companies. Our analysis demonstrated that of the top five countries in terms of global FDI stocks – United States, UK, Japan, Germany and France – only two play a large role in central and eastern Europe. The United States and Germany are the two largest investors in the region, while Germany is the dominant trader. France's investments in the region are comparable to its proportion of global capital stocks, while the UK's investments are relatively and absolutely low and Japan's negligible. The Czech Republic, Hungary and Poland are the three main host countries, with Hungary receiving the largest absolute amounts of inward investment. The attractiveness of these countries appears to be related to the success of their economic and political transitions, the pace of privatization, attitudes to FDI and market size. FDI flows per capita into these countries are comparable to those in most of the EU cohesion countries and higher than into most of the top FDI-receiving developing countries. Contrary to other commentators, we argue that FDI flows have not been disappointing and the prospects are for higher growth, especially in countries with larger markets (determined by population and income) and where transition is relatively advanced.

We put forward a number of reasons for the low investment performance of the UK compared to Germany and the United States. We argue that the main explanations lie in scale, costs and location, though factors including attitudes to risk and patterns of global investment are likely also to be part of the story. The large German investment flows appear to relate to the importance of geographical location and to the knowledge and logistical advantages that this confers. Furthermore, the cost advantages to German firms are greater, with relative wages in the Czech Republic being about one-tenth of German wages but only about one-fifth of UK wages. US firms investing into the region are typically much larger, and entering for reasons of markets and global market share. Scale economies are particularly important to these firms, which appear more prepared to take on the risks of the central and eastern European environment.

Comparative analysis through the case studies

Our case studies analysed firms from three Western countries – the UK, Germany and the United States – investing into three of the leading transition economies – the Czech Republic, Hungary and

Poland. Our 10 cases were selected to ensure at least one case from each source country in each host country. As explained in Chapter 4, we also selected cases according to specific sector characteristics and to the size of multinational, ensuring that some of our cases were of small and medium-sized enterprises – an important phenomenon in FDI flows into central and eastern Europe.

The detailed analysis of the comparative lessons from the cases is set out in Chapter 15. In terms of motivations, we found that the foreign investors in our sample were often driven by a mixture of two or even all three of the motivations that we proposed. The majority of the investments were in fact motivated by markets and market share – a view confirmed in the broader empirical literature (see, for example, Meyer, 1996). Two of our three German cases were motivated by costs, reflecting our earlier argument that such considerations may be more compelling for German firms. In terms of entry modes, greenfield and acquisition were of approximately equal significance in our sample. However, the desire of Western firms to purchase market share and brands but to avoid massive restructuring costs led to a considerable amount of 'brownfield' development in firms acquired for markets and market share. Indeed, brownfield development was more common in our cases than acquisition or joint ventures without a brownfield approach. Furthermore, to the extent that joint ventures are more problematic to manage in transition economies, the multinationals in our sample mostly aimed to achieve 100 per cent ownership even if initially this was not possible.

Our cases suggest that most Western investments into the region have been at least relatively successful, and even in the less successful ones, Western multinationals experienced setbacks which were costly, but did not lead to total failure. The one case of bankruptcy – Lycett – illustrated, in part, the difficulties of running a small, cost-motivated investment from the UK. From the perspective of the multinationals, therefore, most investments were evaluated rather positively. The sectoral dimension is important here, however. In general, firms supplying final consumers – typically motivated by markets and market share – found it harder to establish their brands, their distribution networks and their quality standards than they had at first expected. Being a first mover does not appear to be particularly advantageous, especially in the early years of transition and of investment to transition economies. Enterprise development was much simpler and more effective in firms motivated by costs, which manufactured for the most part in less highly skilled sectors. Restructuring and performance was also simpler in sectors such as engineering, where issues of brand and product differentiation were less compelling or absent.

From the viewpoint of host companies, or in the case of greenfield entrants, for industries in host countries, the inward investment was generally highly positive in its direct impact. The investments for the most part achieved productivity, quality, technology and know-how transfer objectives. The Western multinationals, in general, transferred state-of-the-art technology, modernized organizational structures and transferred managerial skills – although in the latter case, often with more difficulty than initially anticipated.

Interestingly, spillover effects appear to have been weaker than may have been originally anticipated by host governments. There may be potential negative externalities, e.g. in the development of capital markets, the strengthening of pre-existing domestic supply chains and via balance of payments effects. However, in some cases positive supply network effects were observed. There may also be adverse competitive effects or at least an absence in many cases of pro-competitive effects with the transposition of oligopolistic market structures into host countries. However, it is the firms motivated by market and market share which appear to have the greatest potential positive spillover in terms of labour skills and supply chains. The firms motivated by cost may, as we have seen, find it easier to restructure or to bring new production methods to the country, but they offer fewer external benefits for the transition process. Overall, training and improved skill levels is one key positive externality influencing host country skill levels in the medium term. Accelerating long-term restructuring through unbundling of assets appears to represent another positive consequence of some investments.

Policy issues

During the early years of the transition, there was probably more variety in the attitudes of governments in different central and eastern European countries to FDI. However, over time, policy stances have tended to converge, reflecting in particular the influence of international agreements and organizations, notably the EU. Most CEE countries consequently now have a generally open policy stance towards FDI, but without providing substantial incentives to foreign relative to domestic investors – Hungary, for example, amended its previous incentives to multinationals to ensure balanced treatment of foreign and domestic firms.

There is no evidence from the cases presented in this study that tax incentives are of general importance in investment decisions into central and eastern Europe. However, the cases did identify investments where tariff exemptions were important and where tax treatment concerning write-offs was important. What seems of most importance, however, is accurate and easily accessible information for firms on the tax environment, together with clarity in negotiating conditions surrounding individual investments. The transition economies are not in a position to offer substantial investment subsidies as incentives to multinationals and so cannot compete in this way with subsidies offered by Western countries. The main role of inward investment agencies in these economies, therefore, may be in providing and effectively disseminating information about their respective economies and the opportunities and advantages that the transition environment can provide. They can also set out information on progress in transition, in particular to reassure investors that negative features of transition are weak and declining.

As this study has argued, success in transition, and the markets and low costs that these economies offer, are important determinants of investment. Overall policies towards transition are consequently more important in establishing an environment that will be attractive to foreign investors than specific FDI policies. However, policy-makers may need to give more careful attention to some of the spillover effects of foreign investment. Where FDI may not be pro-competitive, this should be adequately dealt with through competition policies rather than requiring additional FDI-specific policies. Other potential negative spillovers, or absence of positive spillovers (such as failing to develop local supply networks), may require a more active regional/industrial policy both to assess what is inhibiting the existence or quality of local supply networks and to ensure that there is adequate information and communication between relevant actors – local firms, regional government and multinationals. Where multinationals are generating positive spillover effects such as improving the stock of human capital, governments may wish to assess how this affects their wider policies, such as with respect to training.

Appendix: Questionnaires

FDI Questionnaire 1 HEAD OFFICE

SUBJECT AREAS: I. Markets; II. Organizational structure; III. Corporate strategy; IV. FDI – General; V. FDI – Specifics; VI. FDI – Central and eastern Europe.

I. MARKETS

[In this group of questions, we want to discover the key characteristics of and the major trends in the sectors in which the firm is active, and especially why the firm is investing in CEE.]

1. Product Lines

   The question is about the firm's product lines (e.g. what are your main product lines?).

   What we are interested in is:

   – the diversity of the company in terms of products produced.

   Dimensions of this diversity include:

   – extent of vertical integration up or downstream.
   – the range of sectors in which the firm is active. In particular, are they product complementary (e.g. biscuits and cakes), input complementary (e.g. sulphuric acid and fertilizers), or totally diverse (e.g. biscuits and tractors)?
   – the variety of products produced (e.g. number of brands within particular sectors).

2. Structure of Sector (in which there has been FDI in CEE).

   We need to find out about:

(i) How many firms are in the market globally – who are the market leaders – what is the market position of this firm?

(ii) What has been the pattern of demand growth?

- fast/slow
- highly cyclical/stable
- even growth worldwide/growth concentrated in particular regions.

(iii) What is the structure of costs – labour-intensive, capital-intensive, costs rising quickly? Are costs cyclical?

(iv) What have been the major technical innovations in the sector? How have they affected profitability, market position, competitive structure?

(v) What are the main global drivers in the sector over the next five years and why?

II. ORGANIZATIONAL STRUCTURE

1. Can you tell us about the global distribution in 1994 of:

   - sales
   - employment
   - investment
   - R&D expenditures?

   [divide the globe into large regions, e.g. USA, Europe, Asia]

2. Does your firm have any major individual shareholders, holding say more than 10 per cent? Please name them, or tell us whether they are:

   - banks
   - other financial institutions (e.g. pension funds)
   - other manufacturing firms: domestic, international

3. Can you give us an organizational plan of your company and explain it to us?

4. If the organizational plan does not cover it, give an account of the division of responsibilities between the head office and the subsidiaries.

   Please make sure that your discussion covers:

- the logic of central functions
- intra-firm trade
- allocation of functions:

  (i) corporate strategy
  (ii) finance
  (iii) marketing
  (iv) R&D
  (v) investment
  (vi) mergers and acquisitions

To what extent do subsidiaries have decision-making powers in these areas?

5. Describe the communication structures within the firm. How is information gathered and processed?

6. What are the major functions undertaken by the subsidiaries. Does this differ by region? By sector? Why?

7. How would you describe your company's approach to industrial relations? Does it differ from country to country? Are the firm or subsidiaries unionized? Do the firm or subsidiaries have works councils?

III. CORPORATE STRATEGY

1a. Can you tell us your firm's overall business strategy?

1b. What are the main aims of your business strategy in the following areas?

- in terms of expansion, do you seek greater market share in existing product markets, vertical integration upstream or downstream and/or greater diversity of production?
- in terms of market share, do you seek to target market shares globally, or in particular regions?
- in terms of profits, do you require speedy returns from foreign investments, or can you take a longer view in developing markets?
- in terms of human resource management, do you seek to promote a unified corporate image? How would you describe the firm as a place to work to potential employees?

2. Taking your global business strategy into account, how has this affected:
   - your global investment strategy
   - your global research and development strategy
   - your global trade/production strategy
   - your global production sourcing strategy
   - your human resource management strategy
   - your organizational structure?
3. How has your business strategy developed over the previous decade? Explain the reasons for the changes.
4. How do you see your business strategy evolving over the next five years? Why?
5. How do you evaluate achievements in the firm, relative to business strategy?
6. What do you consider to be your main competitive strengths, e.g. brands, product innovation, design, cost control?
7. What is the process whereby business strategy is developed or changed?
8. Who is responsible for developing business strategy? Who is responsible for carrying out the strategy?

IV. FDI – GENERAL

Objectives in Foreign Direct Investment

1a. What are your main motives in FDI?

1b. Are your motives in investment concerned with establishing or maintaining a global market share? Do you enter new international markets in order to obtain market share?

2. Alternatively, are your motives in FDI concerned with reducing manufacturing or transport costs?
3. Alternatively, are your motives concerned with the nature of your global competition with your major international rivals, e.g. pre-empting them in new markets or following them?
4. Do your motives in FDI vary according to the products/brands which you seek to sell in different countries?

5. Do your motives in FDI depend on the region or country in question, e.g. in Europe versus Southeast Asia?

6. Is the level of your foreign investment to particular regions influenced by trade barriers and tariff regimes? If so, how? Can you give significant examples?

7. Is your investment to particular regions significantly influenced by:

   - your knowledge of the market?
   - your firm's traditional association with the country or region?
   - political and economic factors in the region, e.g. general risk factors?
   - infrastructure?
   - difficulties of doing business – language, traditions, bureaucracy, etc.?

8. Do you regard exports to a country and region and FDI as complementary? Does this apply globally (e.g. across all your products taken together) or for each particular product?

9. In general, what do you think that the host countries to your foreign investment believe that you are providing? Why do they welcome your investment?

10. How important are other forms of internationalization e.g. joint ventures in R&D?

Decision-making Process

11. What methods are used to gather information about FDI opportunities?

    - globally
    - by 'region', e.g. Southeast Asia
    - within a region or country

12. What is the procedure whereby this information was collated and evaluated, and decisions made? If necessary, refer back to the organizational chart.

13. What factors influenced the choice of FDI form, e.g. between:

    - joint venture
    - licence
    - acquisition
    - greenfield site
    - brownfield investment?

14. How were such decisions made, and by whom?

V. FDI – SPECIFICS

1. In your foreign subsidiaries, do you use local managers? Does it depend on the region and/or the production process/nature of subsidiary? Can you give an outline of the company strategy with regard to the use of local managers versus expatriates?

2. Are any special roles in your foreign subsidiaries kept for expatriates, e.g. finance, accounts, human resource management? Does your answer depend on the form of the collaboration, e.g. joint venture, acquisition, greenfield site?

3a. What procedures and processes do you use in your company to transfer skills from head office to foreign subsidiaries?

   - for management
   - for professionals

   Do these differ by region, and by form of relationship (joint ventures, greenfield, etc.)?

3b. What procedures do you use for training blue-collar workers?

4a. Do you attempt to implement a global human resources management policy, or are human resources management policies at the discretion of local managers?

4b. If the former, what are the key elements of the policy? What have been the main problems in implementing it in foreign subsidiaries?

4c. If the latter, do you have any policies which advise local managers, e.g. covering unionization, bonus schemes, etc.?

5. Do you have a global strategy on setting wages, e.g. high paying, paying what markets will bear?

6. How do you finance your foreign investments?

   - stock market
   - debt
   - retained earnings

   Do you have different methods for different forms of investment, or for different regions?

7. How do you approach the issue of transferring technologies and know-how to foreign subsidiaries? What determines which technologies you transfer, and which you do not?
8. What difficulties have you encountered in transferring technology and know-how to foreign subsidiaries? Do they vary by region?
9. How have you sought to resolve these difficulties?
10. Have your investments been encouraged or deterred by the policies of:
    - domestic government
    - the host governments?

    Can you give some specific examples?

VI. FDI – CENTRAL AND EASTERN EUROPE

1. Did you have any trade, investment or other links in CEE prior to this investment? Did these influence the decision to invest?

The Investment Decision

2a. When did you first consider investing in CEE? Who was involved in the decision?

2b. What were the main reasons for making the investment?

3. Were the main reasons primarily the opportunities presented by the transition in CEE, or was the investment driven by existing global strategy?
4. How important were competitors' actions in your decision to invest? Were you either following or aiming to pre-empt competitors?
5. How important were resources available in the country? – firms available for privatization, natural resources?
6. Was the location of the country important? Why?
7. How important were actual and potential markets?
8. How important were labour, costs and skill factors?
9. When making the decision to invest, what were the main

uncertainties, and what did you expect to be the biggest difficulties? Were these similar to uncertainties when investing in other parts of the world?

Choice of Location

10. When evaluating the investment decision in CEE, did you consider other regions too? Which? What were the main advantages and disadvantages of the other region(s)?

11. Within CEE, which countries did you consider? How did you assess these different countries? What were your main information sources? Where did you obtain more detailed sector information?

12a. How important were domestic or host country policies in the decision to invest? (General policies, specific FDI policies?)

12b. Who was responsible for the final decision? What was the basis for it?

Nature of Investment

13. What factors influenced the choice of form of investment – greenfield, acquisition, joint venture (majority/minority holding)? Was this a similar choice to investing in other, non-transition economies?

14a. What is the ownership structure of the subsidiary?

14b. What were the main procedures involved in making a greenfield investment? What problems did you encounter in implementing the investment decision? Were these problems similar to those you might experience in non-transition economies?

14c. What was the ownership structure of the firm you acquired/ entered into a joint venture with? Was this part of the privatization process? What were the main procedures involved? What problems or difficulties did you encounter? Did you negotiate specific conditions or requirements with the government (e.g. employment levels (from government); market share, tariffs (from firm))?

15. What were the main funding sources for the original investment? Is this similar to funding for other investments in new subsidiaries?

Role in Global Company Structure

16. What role does the subsidiary play in the company's overall global structure? What is its position in the value chain and/or in the product range?
17. Does the FDI represent an expansion of total global production or is it (in whole or in part) a transfer of production that would have occurred elsewhere?
18. Does output from the subsidiary substitute for exports to the market, or are the two complementary?
19. What degree of autonomy in decision-making does the subsidiary have? Does this differ from other subsidiaries? Lower finance, innovation, etc.
20. Could you describe the main communication and information structures between the parent and the subsidiary? Do these differ from those between other subsidiaries?

Experience of Operating in CEE

21. What is the overall business strategy of the subsidiary?
22. What were the major changes and developments that have had to take place in the subsidiary? (Changes in organizational structure, restructuring, rationalization, investment etc.)
23. Are there major differences in consumer behaviour in your market in CEE relative to other, more established, markets? How has this influenced/what has been your advertising and product differentiation strategy? Do you expect greater or less brand loyalty?
24. Are there major differences in inter-firm relationships? Do you use local suppliers? Are there difficulties?
25. Who are your main competitors in the country? What are they doing (or are they located in other CEE countries)?
26. What is the current market structure in the sector?
27. How did you select the expatriate managers for the subsidiary? What use do you make of local managers? Are expatriate managers responsible for particular areas (e.g. finance, marketing)?
28. How have you trained and selected local managers?

29. What management problems have you experienced?

30. What is your overall assessment of the local labour force in the subsidiary? Skill levels, work ethic, flexibility etc.

31. What training do you provide? Does this differ from that in other subsidiaries? What methods do you use?

32. How are wages and conditions decided? What is the industrial relations climate? What is the role of trade unions? Are wages above average for the country and sectors? How were they decided?

33. What is your overall assessment of the initial technology level of the subsidiary?

34. What technology have you transferred? Is it state-of-the-art? What problems were there in transferring it? How does this compare to experience in other subsidiaries?

35. Does the subsidiary carry out any R&D activities?

36. How does the subsidiary access finance for investment, restructuring and development? Are local and internal financing sources used? Who takes financing decisions?

37. How has the subsidiary performed overall up to the present – profits, productivity, quality, reliability, sales, exports and imports etc.? If you have other CEE plants, how does this compare? Is performance better or worse than you expected?

38. What contribution is the subsidiary currently making to your global competitiveness?

39. What problems in practice have you found are specific to operating in transitional economies:

    - governments/bureaucracy
    - infrastructure – physical, institutional
    - capital
    - management
    - skills/labour force
    - market environment
    - recession?

    To what extent have these been resolved?

40. Would you assess your overall experience as positive or negative?

41. What do you think is the attitude to foreign investment of: host government, local firms, labour force, population? Does this affect your behaviour?
42. What benefits do you think your investment is providing to the country?
43. What are your future plans in CEE?
44. Do you have any views as to why UK FDI is relatively low in CEE?

FDI Questionnaire 2 EAST EUROPEAN SUBSIDIARY

1. History of Firm

1. Can you give a brief history of the firm?
2. When was the firm privatized/taken over/set up?
3. Who is your foreign partner? How was the relationship established?
4. Has the company always produced in the same sector? Has it always produced in the same region?

2. Organizational Structure of Firm (Subsidiary)

1. What are your responsibilities in the firm, and what is the chain of reporting?
2. Can you provide me with an organizational plan of the firm?
3. In what ways has the organizational structure altered since the foreign owner became involved? Please cover:
   - extension of functions (e.g. new marketing, finance, human resources management directors)
   - change of personnel (hirings/firings)
   - backgrounds of new managers; how recruited etc.
   - (new) board structure – supervisory/advisory board where relevant. How does the foreign owner actually control and monitor the subsidiary – via the board, via reporting requirements etc.?
   - change of accounting procedures and information technologies

4. What is the division of decision-making responsibilities between head office/regional headquarters and the subsidiary in your functional area, e.g. finance, marketing etc.? (For managing director, in general what is the division of responsibility in the company?) How has this been changing in the years since the joint venture subsidiary was formed?
5. What is the business strategy of the subsidiary? How does it relate to the global strategy of the company? In what ways has your strategy been evolving since the subsidiary was formed? Why?
6. In your view, what was the original strategy behind the take-over/formation of the subsidiary? Did it represent a major break with the previous strategy?
7. What is the current ownership structure of the subsidiary? How has it evolved since the foreign partner became involved?

3. Sector and Markets

1. Describe your position in the market relative to your competitors; in terms of price, quality, product mix (differentiation), reliability.
2. What is your domestic market share? Give an approximate idea of your main competitors and their domestic market share.
3. How has the structure of the market been evolving since 1990? In what ways is the nature of competition changing?
4. How has the country pattern of sales altered over the past five years (e.g. between domestic, CMEA, EU, other) and why?
5. What are your marketing objectives? Is your marketing strategy to build a domestic market share, or to seek to export? If the latter, which are your target countries and why?
6. What are your marketing strategies to achieve your marketing objectives? How long will it take? What about the competitors?
7. In what ways have your marketing objectives changed since the foreign involvement? How have the changes been implemented organizationally?

8. How has the situation concerning your input supplies altered since:

   - 1990
   - the involvement of the foreign partner?

   Has the quality of inputs, reliability etc. improved?

4. Decision to Invest

1. What were the key motives behind the decision by the foreign firm to invest in this company, e.g. markets, costs, location, brand?
2. Were you involved in the decision-making process? Can you describe the process?
3. How was information obtained about the possible investment opportunities? How were they assessed and by whom?
4. Why was this particular location/faculty/company chosen? What special characteristics did the market have – local labour quality, location, traditions, transport costs etc.?
5. What factors influenced the choice of FDI form – joint venture, acquisition, greenfield site?
6. How important were competitors' actions in your decision?
7. What was the role of government policies and local attitudes in your choice?
8. To what extent have changes in the firm been a consequence of the transition process in general rather than caused directly by the foreign investor?

5. Expectations and Experience

Except for the managing director, this must be covered in detail for all the functional areas separately by interview. The managing director can in principle address all the areas, though (s)he should probably only look at the key ones.

A. *Overall*

1. What was the firm's situation in 1990?

2. What did you do about the situation in 1990?
3. What happened in terms of production, sales, profits, exports, cash flow, labour skills etc.?

B. *Management Structure; Organizational Structure*

1. How did the firm used to be run? How has it been changed organisationally – e.g. development of new functions, structures, decision-making etc.? Have they been successful? If not, why not?

2. What were the proposed arrangements for dividing decisions between the head office and the subsidiary? How was the subsidiary's performance to be monitored? What were intended to be the mechanisms for intervention?

3. Were these expectations right? How do you now divide responsibilities with head office? How is monitoring done? Have there been any cases of headquarters intervention? Why? Can you explain them?

4. Would you describe your subsidiary as centralized/decentralized in its decision-making?

5. Are your subsidiary's operational arrangements with head office the same as those for other subsidiaries? Are there any special arrangements because of the transition problems?

6. How do your reporting arrangements to head office work? Have they changed since the take-over/formation? If so, why?

C. *Production*

1. Has capacity been reduced or increased since the foreign partner became involved?

2. Has the firm been successful in obtaining inputs at the deserved quality?

3. What are your links to head office in terms of production? Does it advise/intervene/help? Do you report to it, etc.?

4. Has productivity increased since the involvement of the foreign partner? If so, why? If not, why not?

5. Was the wastage rate very high before the foreign partner's involvement? Has it now been reduced? If so, how?

6. Have there been major energy savings since the foreign partner became involved? Are levels now comparable with those of Western firms?

7. What are the environmental implications of the new production programme since the foreign partner became involved?

D. *Sales and Marketing*

1. How much did you plan to sell and to whom (domestic, EU, CMEA)? Have these plans been fulfilled? If not, why not?

2. Are there differences between your domestic and other markets, e.g. in marketing, production differentiation, outlets?

3. What is your marketing strategy? How is it evolving? Have you introduced new techniques? Why?

4. How much are you spending on advertising? Is the amount increasing substantially? What are you spending on?

5. What is the relationship between your own marketing and that of your head office? How are they integrated? How is the relationship developing?

6. How do you see the market structure for your product developing over the next five years? Who will be the main competitors – domestic firms or importers?

7. Do marketing techniques differ from those used in the UK?

E. *Employment, Wages, Training*

1. Are there any expatriate managers in the subsidiary? How were they selected? Is this a permanent arrangement?

2. What proportion of managers are local? How were they recruited? Were they previously in the company? or the sector? What are your plans for senior recruitment in the future?

3. How were local managers trained? What are the outside opportunities for managers in the sector or region?
4. What management problems have you experienced? Were they expected? How have they been resolved?
5. What is your assessment of the local labour force:
   - skills
   - work ethic
   - flexibility, etc.?

6a. What has been happening to employment levels in the past five years, e.g. layoffs, part-timers?

6b. If employment has been falling, have the declines been achieved by natural wastage or redundancy? If the latter, outline the arrangements made. How do you evaluate the downsizing? Has it been a success? Has it been expensive or damaging to morale in the firm, or damaging to morale in the region? What has been the impact of local government? Were there any agreements on this at the time of purchase of the company?

6c. If employment has stayed roughly constant, is this because employment levels are about right? If not, why has it not been reduced?

7. Do you think employment levels are now about right? If not, what do you intend to do about it?
8. What training does the labour force require to meet your company plan? How is this being provided? What training methods do you use? Why?
9. How are wages and conditions decided? What is the role of trade unions nationally and locally? Do you regard yourselves as 'good payers'? What is the company strategy towards pay and conditions?
10. What is the industrial relations climate in the firm? Is it what you had expected? How has it evolved since the acquisition/take-over, etc.?
11. Do you plan to introduce, or have you introduced, bonus or incentive payments – for managers and for workers? How do these schemes work? Have they been a success?

12. Is labour productivity high enough in your plant? Is it as high as you expected? How do you plan to raise it?

F. *Finance*

1. How does the subsidiary assess finance for investment, restructuring, development? Are local and internal sources used?

2. Who takes the financing decision, local managers or headquarters? What is the division of responsibilities? How does it work out in practice? Can you give examples?

3. What was the financial plan for the firm at the time of acquisition/opening, e.g. in terms of investment, cash flow, profits?

4. Has the plan been achieved? If not, why not?

5. How closely does head office monitor financial developments in the firm? In what situations does it react and how? Give examples.

6. What are the relationships between the subsidiary and local banks? Does it borrow in the short term, or in the long term? Who makes such decisions?

7. What were expectations about payables, receivables, and inter-firm debt? Have they been proved right? If not, in what ways? How has the subsidiary reacted?

8. Does the subsidiary apply the same accounting procedures as other subsidiaries? If so, when were the changes introduced? What was the effect? Have the changes been successful? If not, why not? In what ways do they differ? What are the implications?

9. Does the subsidiary sell its an own commercial paper? If so, on which markets? Who decides etc.?

10. How has the subsidiaries' balance sheet been developing over the past few years?

G. *Ownership*

1. Is the firm a wholly owned subsidiary? If not, who are the other owners? In what proportions? Why was this structure chosen?

2. How do you plan to develop the ownership structure, e.g. will you buy out outside holders etc.?

3. What benefits do the current ownership structure bring, and what problems?

4. Do you propose to increase your equity in the firm? When and why?

H. *Dealing with Governments*

1. What were your experiences dealing with *local* and *central* government in:

   - the planning phase of the project
   - the early operational phase
   - now?

   Give examples of key problems or when the relationship went well.

2. From your experience, what are the main problems posed for FDI by Hungary's legal and political system? Are they more serious than you originally envisaged?

3. What have you done which is special to the transitional situation to deal with the institutional, political and legal weaknesses? What do you plan to do?

I. *Technology*

1. What was the level of the technology in the plant before the involvement of the foreign partner? How has it developed?

2. What technology has been transferred to the subsidiary? How has this been achieved? What were the problems and why?

3. What is the level of the technology used in this plant compared with the parent company?

4. Does the subsidiary undertake its own R&D? How do these activities relate to head office and other subsidiaries? How is R&D managed? How is it disseminated?

5. What are the local links between R&D and marketing?

6. How important is technology to productivity, growth and competition?

7. In what ways have the functions of the R&D department changed since the involvement of the foreign partner?

8. Do local technological capabilities exist and are they complementary to those brought in by the foreign partner?

J. *Unbundling and Social Assets*

1. Did the firm have significant social assets or distant plants before the foreign involvement?

2. Did you unbundle any parts of the firm, e.g. distant plants, social assets, housing etc.?

3. Do you need to do more unbundling? If so, how much? How do you plan to do it?

4. Does the firm still have too many diverse assets, or social assets? What are the main constraints on changing things? How do you plan to achieve change?

6. *Performance*

1. What have been your main successes in the subsidiary? Were they planned from the outset?

2. If relevant, what have been the main successes in:

   - production restructuring
   - financial restructuring
   - rising productivity
   - sales and marketing
   - organizational changes?

   Why have you been successful in these areas?

3. What have been your main failings in these areas? What do you intend to do about them?

4. What have been your main successes in long-term restructuring – investment, R&D, technology transfer, managerial training? What have been your main failings and why?

5. What problems have there been with infrastructure, language, communications in the country etc.? What

communications problems have there been with the head office?

6. How do your achievements compare with those of other firms in the sector?

References

Baldwin, R. (1994a) *Pan-European Trade Arrangement Beyond the Year 2000.* London: CEPR.

Baldwin, R. (1994b) *Towards an Integrated Europe.* London: CEPR.

Barr, N. (1994) *Labour Markets and Social Policy in Central and Eastern Europe.* Washington, DC: World Bank.

Belka, M., Estrin, S., Schaffer, M. and Singh, I.J. (1994) 'Enterprise adjustment in Poland: Evidence from a survey of 200 firms', London School of Economics, Centre for Economic Performance Working Paper 658.

Blanchard, O., Dornbusch, R., Layard, R., Krugman, P. and Summers, L. (1990) *Reform in Eastern Europe.* Cambridge, Mass: MIT Press.

Bos, D. (1990) *Privatisation: A Theoretical Treatment.* Oxford: Clarendon Press.

Boycko, M., Schleifer, A. and Vishny, R. (1995) *Privatising Russia.* Cambridge, Mass: MIT Press.

Caves, R.E. (1982) *Multinational Enterprise and Economic Analysis.* Cambridge: Cambridge University Press.

de Melo, M., Denizer, C. and Gelb, A. (1995) 'From plan to market: patterns of transition', Washington, DC: World Bank, mimeo.

Dunning, J.H. (1980) 'The location of foreign direct investment activity: country characteristics and experience effects', *Journal of International Business Studies,* Vol. 11, pp. 9–22.

Dunning, J.H. and Rojec, M. (1993) 'Foreign privatisation in central and eastern Europe', CEEPN Technical Paper Series No. 2, Central and Eastern Europe Privatisation Network, Ljubljana.

Duvvuri, S., Gyenis, A., Kanz, M. and Szakal, S. (1995) *Direktinvestitionen in Ungarn, Eine Umfrage zu Motiven, Erfahrungen und Zukunftsperspektiven deutscher Investoren in Ungarn,* 2nd edn, edited by Deutsch-Ungarische Industrie- und Handelskammer. Bielefeld: Bertelsmann.

Earle, J.S. and Estrin, S. (1995) 'Employee ownership in transition', in Grey, C., Frydman, R. and Rapazynski, A. (eds) *Corporate Governance in Transition.* London: Central University Press, pp. 111–15.

Ellman, M. (1989) *Socialist Planning,* 2nd edn. Cambridge: Cambridge University Press.

Estrin, S. (1994) *Privatisation in Central and Eastern Europe.* London: Longman.

Estrin, S. (1995) 'Issues in transition from plan to market', London Business School Discussion Paper, November.

Estrin, S. (1996) 'Privatisation in central and eastern Europe', CERT Discussion Paper No. 95/6, Heriot-Watt University, Department of Economics.

Estrin, S. and Cave, M. (1993) *Competition Policy in Central and Eastern Europe*. London: Frances Pinter.

Estrin, S., Brada, J., Gelb, A. and Singh, I. (eds) (1994) *Restructuring and Privatisation in Central and Eastern Europe: Case Studies of Firms in Transition*. London: M.E. Sharpe.

Estrin, S., Hughes, K. and Todd, S. (1996) 'Foreign direct investment into central Europe: the evidence', London Business School Working Paper.

European Bank for Reconstruction and Development (1994) *Transition Report*. London: EBRD.

European Bank for Reconstruction and Development (1995) *Transition Report*. London: EBRD.

Faini, R. and Portes, R. (eds) (1995) *European Union Trade with Eastern Europe: Adjustments and Opportunities*. London: Centre for Economic Policy Research.

Gatling, R. (1993) 'Foreign investment in eastern Europe: corporate strategies and experience', Research Report written in association with Creditanstalt Bankverein. London: Economist Intelligence Unit.

Grabbe, H. and Hughes, K. (1997) 'Eastward enlargement of the EU', RIIA Special paper. London: Royal Institute of International Affairs.

Gregory, P. and Stuart, P. (1988) *Soviet Economic Structure and Development*. New York: Harper and Row.

Hamar, J. (1995) 'Industrial policy and efficiency in the Hungarian manufacturing industry', Discussion Paper No. 31, Kopint-Datorg, Budapest, September.

Hare, P. and Hughes, G. (1992) 'Microeconomics of transition in eastern Europe', *Oxford Review of Economic Policy*, Vol. 8, pp. 82–104.

Hayek, F.A. (1944) *The Road to Serfdom*. London: Routledge and Kegan Paul.

Hoesch, D. and Lehmann, H. (1994) 'Ostöffnung und Reformpolitik in den ostmittel-europäischen Staaten: Auswirkungen auf die Wirtschaft Bayerns', *Ifo Schnelldienst* No. 30/94, pp. 14–23.

Holmes, C. (1993) 'Global strategies in the transition', *Economics of Transition*, Vol. 1, pp. 471–88.

Hughes, K. (1996) 'European enlargement, competitiveness and integration', in Devine, P., Katsoulacos, I. and Sugden, R. (eds) *Competitiveness, Subsidiary and Objectives: Issues for European Industrial Strategy*. London: Routledge, pp. 104–20.

Inota, A. (1994) 'Central and Eastern Europe', in Henning, R.C., Hochreiter, E. and Hufbauer, G. (eds) *Reviving the European Union*, Washington, DC: Institute for International Economics.

Kogut, B. (1996), 'Direct investment, experimentation and corporate governance in transition economies', in Frydman, R., Gray, C.W. and Rapazynski, A. (eds) *Corporate Governance in Central Europe and Russia*, Vol. 1. London and Budapest: Central European University Press, pp. 293–332.

Lakatos, B. and Papanek, G. (1995) 'Motivations for establishing enterprises with foreign participants in Hungary', in *Joint Ventures in Transformation Countries in the Context of Overall Investment Strategies of their Partners*, ACE Research project. Barcelona: Grup d'Analisi de las Transicio Economica, pp. 99–143.

Lane, S.J. (1994a) 'The contribution of business starts and entrepreneurship to the transition in Hungary', Discussion Paper No. 94–24, Boston University School of Management, April.

Lane, S.J. (1994b) 'The pattern of foreign direct investment and joint ventures in Hungary', *Communist Economies and Economic Transformation*, Vol. 6, No. 3, pp. 341–65.

Lane, S.J. (1995) 'Does ownership matter? The performance of firms during the transition in Hungary', Working Paper No. 95-09, Boston University School of Management, March.

Marton, K. (1993) 'Foreign direct investment in Hungary', *Transnational Corporations*, Vol. 2, pp. 111–34.

McMillan, C.H. (1993) 'The role of foreign direct investment in the transition from planned to market economies', *Transnational Corporations*, Vol. 2, pp. 97–119.

Meyer, K.E. (1995) 'Foreign direct investment in the early years of economic transition, a survey', *Economics of Transition*, Vol. 3, pp. 301–20.

Meyer, K.E. (1996) 'Direct foreign investment into central and eastern Europe', PhD thesis, London Business School.

Mollening, J., Radl, R. and Zimmerman, J. (1994) *Deutsche Direkt Investitioner in der Tschechischen Republik: Motive, Erfahrungen, Perspektiven, Ergebnisse einer Umfrage*, German–Czech Chamber of Commerce. Bielefeld: Bertelsmann.

Mutinelli, M. (1994) 'Italian industrial foreign direct investment in central and eastern Europe', Conference Paper, 20th EIBA conference, Warsaw, 11–13 December.

Nachum, L. (1995) 'Do multinational enterprises affect the evolution of market structure in central European countries? Empirical evidence for Hungary', Discussion Paper No. 310, Department of Economics, University of Reading, May.

National Economic Research Associates (1991) 'Foreign direct investment to the countries of central and eastern Europe', mimeo.

Naujoks, P. and Schmidt, K.D. (1994) 'Outward processing in central and east European transition countries: issues and results from German statistics', Kiel Working Paper No. 631, Kiel Institute of World Economics.

Organization for Economic Cooperation and Development (1995) 'Assessing investment opportunities in economies in transition', study prepared by Arthur Anderson. Paris: OECD.

Papanek, G. (1995) 'A comparison of basic data on the performance of enterprises with and without foreign equity capital participation, I', in *Joint Ventures in Transformation Countries in the Context of Overall Investment Strategies of their Partners*, ACE Research project. Barcelona: Grup d'Analisi de las Transicio Economica, pp. 269–88.

Portes, R. (1994) 'Transformation traps', *Economic Journal*, Vol. 104, pp. 1178–89.

Rojec, M. and Jermakowicz, W. (1995) 'Management versus state in foreign privatisation in central European countries in transition', in Schiatterelli, R. (ed.) *New Challenges for European and International Business*, Proceedings of the 21st EIBA Conference, Urbino, Vol. 1, pp. 353–80.

Rojec, M. and Svetlicic, M. (1993) 'Foreign direct investment in Slovenia', *Transnational Corporations*, Vol. 2, pp. 135–51. (Also in *Communist Economies and Economic Transformation*, Vol. 5, No. 1, pp. 103–14.)

Savary, J. (1992) 'The international strategies of French firms and eastern Europe: the case of Poland', *MOCT/MOST*, No. 3, pp. 69–95.

Svetlicic, M. (1994) 'Foreign direct investment and the transformation of central European economies', mimeo, University of Reading and University of Ljubljana.

Szanyi, M. (1995) 'Experiences with foreign direct investment in Hungary', *Russian and East European Finance and Trade*, Vol. 31, No. 3, pp. 6–30.

Wang, Z.Q. (1993) 'Foreign direct investment in Hungary: a survey of experience and prospects', *Communist Economies and Economic Transformation*, Vol. 5, No. 2, pp. 245–53.

Winters, L.A. (1995) 'Policy institutions in central and eastern Europe: objectives and outcomes', in Winters, L.A. (ed.) *Foundations of an Open Economy*. London: CEPR, pp. 1–16.

World Bank (1996) *World Development Report on Transitional Economies*. Washington, DC: World Bank.

Index